Nice Work If You Can Get It

Nice Work If You Can Get It

Life and Labor in Precarious Times

Andrew Ross

NEW YORK UNIVERSITY PRESS
New York and London

NYU SERIES IN SOCIAL AND CULTURAL ANALYSIS
General Editor: Andrew Ross

Nice Work If You Can Get It: Life and Labor in Precarious Times
Andrew Ross

NEW YORK UNIVERSITY PRESS
New York and London
www.nyupress.org

© 2009 by New York University
All rights reserved

Library of Congress Cataloging-in-Publication Data
Ross, Andrew, 1956-
Nice work if you can get it : life and labor in precarious times / Andrew Ross.
p.   cm. — (NYU series in social and cultural analysis)
Includes bibliographical references and index.
ISBN-13: 978–0–8147–7629–2 (cl : alk. paper)
ISBN-10: 0–8147–7629–9 (cl : alk. paper)
ISBN-13: 978–0–8147–7635–3 (e-book : alk. paper)
ISBN-10: 0–8147–7635–3 (e-book : alk. paper)
1. Employment in foreign countries. 2. Alien labor. 3. Globalization. I. Title.
HF5382.55.R67   2009
331.6'2—dc22   2008045880

New York University Press books are printed on acid-free paper, and their binding materials
are chosen for strength and durability. We strive to use environmentally responsible suppliers
and materials to the greatest extent possible in publishing our books.

Manufactured in the United States of America
10 9 8 7 6 5 4 3 2 1

Contents

Acknowledgments

BECAUSE THIS IS the first title in the NYU Series in Social and Cultural Analysis, I'd like to acknowledge the contributions of my faculty colleagues and staff in the Department of Social and Cultural Analysis (SCA). Four years ago, we were given a rare opportunity—to launch a new and genuinely transdisciplinary department within the milieu of a research university. So far, the experience has been bracing and productive, to say the least. We salute NYU Press, and Editor in Chief Eric Zinner in particular, for seeing that the creation of the department was also an opportunity to do something unique at the press. The result was to dedicate a series for publishing work generated from SCA. I'm proud that this book is the first fruit of that collaboration.

For their valuable comments on the entire manuscript, my gratitude goes to Neil Brenner, Toby Miller, Dana Polan, and the anonymous reviewers.

Others who contributed ideas, suggestions, or who served as models to follow include Angela McRobbie, Rosalind Gill, Andy Pratt, Juan Flores, Teddy Cruz, Kristin Ross, Adam Green, Toby Miller, Devon Pena, Katie Quan, Liza Featherstone, Michael Keane, Wang Xiaoming, George Yudice, Dimitris Papadopoulos, Jeff Ballinger, Ned Rossiter, Geert Lovink, Sukhdev Sandhu, Paul Smith, Chris Newfield, and Cary Nelson.

Thanks to the guest editors or staff editors of four journals where some of the material in these chapters first appeared: Ursula Huws, Siva Vaidhyanathan, Marita Sturken, Sam Binkley, Jo Littler, Richard Kim, and Bill Saunders. Each helped to shape the material in new, and more clear, directions. I'm also grateful to Danny Walkowitz, Harvey Molotch, Sophie Watson, and Frank Mort, whose New York–London seminar prompted my comparative research on the Olympics.

Thanks to Michael Palm, Leigh Dodson, and Katie Haskell for research assistance.

Among the many luxuries I enjoy from her companionship, Maggie Gray's eye for detail and for justice has improved every page of the book.

Some of the material in chapter 1 appeared in *Work Organization, Labour, and Globalization*; chapter 4 in *The Nation* and *Cultural Studies*; chapter 5 in *Harvard Design Magazine*; an earlier version of chapter 6 in *American Quarterly*; and chapter 7 in Monika Krause, Michael Palm, Mary Nolan, and Andrew Ross, eds., *The University against Itself: The NYU Strike and the Future of the Academic Workplace* (Philadelphia: Temple University Press, 2008).

Introduction

THE NEED TO make a living has always set people in motion—off the land, into the towns and cities, over the seas. Most have been fleeing oppressive forms of work—chattel slavery, serfdom, indenture, guild dependence, patriarchal servitude, routine wage labor—in search of a more free and humane life. Employers have had little choice but to follow them or try to restrict their mobility to select population centers in hopes of capturing their labor (Moulier Boutang 1998, 2001). In the modern era, mass migration to cities and manufacturing zones was and still is a monumental geographical process, disrupting or reinventing ways of life and fabricating the vast new urban spaces where one half of the world's population currently ekes out a livelihood. Yet these patterns of flight, capture, and escape have ensured that no destination would remain fixed for too long.

Nor has the restless and voracious spirit of capital delivered much in the way of stability. Industrial employers in the United States, for example, began to move from urban to greenfield locations as early as the 1920s, primarily to escape the threat of concentrated union power (Gordon 1978). Their opportunistic moves helped stimulate the mass suburbanization of the 1940s and 1950s (postwar employers did not "follow" the newly suburbanizing masses, as is often assumed), just as they prefigured the flight of manufacturers in the mid-1970s to the U.S. South and then, later, to the global South. As a result, the mass of African Americans (just to cite one highly visible population) who sought relief from Jim Crow in northern cities in the 1920s saw their children and grandchildren abandoned only fifty years later to joblessness and society's neglect.

The last three decades of deregulation and privatization have reshaped the geography of livelihoods for almost everyone in the industrialized world, and for a large slice of the population in developing countries. On the landscape of work, there is less and less terra firma (Beck 2000; Castel 2002; Bowe, Bowe, and Streeter 2000; Sennett 1998). Today's livelihoods are pursued on economic ground that shifts rapidly underfoot, and many of our old assumptions about how people can make

1

a living are outdated pieties. No one, not even those in the traditional professions, can any longer expect a fixed pattern of employment in the course of their lifetime, and they are under more and more pressure to anticipate, and prepare for, a future in which they still will be able to compete in a changing marketplace. The rise in the percentage of contingent employment, both in low-end service sectors and in high-wage occupations, has been steady and shows no sign of leveling off. It has been accompanied by an explosion of atypical work arrangements far removed from the world of social welfare systems, union contracts, and long-term tenure with a single employer.

It is no surprise, then, to hear laments for the bygone world of relatively stable "standard employment" in the core industries and service sectors that characterized the Fordist era in industrialized nations (in which workers were promised incremental wage hikes, expanded benefits, and job security in return for increased productivity and industrial peace). In the rosiest remembrances of that world, chronic insecurity was a parenthetical experience—either the unavoidable burden of those who relied on seasonal employment, or the lot of part-time female workers in the secondary labor market whose waged income was regarded as a supplement to the male "family wage." Yet, however sentimentalized, and however unequally shared its benefits really were, that was no mythical landscape, and there are good reasons why the lived experience of it as a lost utopia still resides within the living memory.

For youth entering the labor market today, stories about those decades of stable employment are tall tales indulged by the elderly, not unlike the lore of Great Depression hardship that baby boomers endured from their parents. In retrospect, the Keynesian era of state-backed securities—whether in the capitalist democracies, the socialist bloc, or the postcolonial, developmental states—was a brief interregnum, or, more likely, an armed truce. It took many decades of struggle to establish that governments and employers had any responsibilities toward securing the livelihoods of citizens. In most countries, even the most affluent, the concession of elected governments to provide poor relief, basic welfare, and social security was a hard-won prospect. Persuading employers to offer benefits, pensions, and assurances of job security was a more bitter fight by far. The consensus that resulted in the postwar era was a massive accomplishment, but it was also a tenuous arrangement, a matter of convenience at worst, cloaked in the thin dress of morality. With the exception of the most solidly built social democracies in Western Europe, Canada, and the vestigial "lifetime employment" corporate culture of Japan, its erosion in recent decades has been rapid, impeded only by the residual ideologies of equality and the populations moved to action by such ideologies. In developing countries, especially authoritarian states where the rule of law can be rewritten with impunity, the impact has been most visible. In less than a decade, the mainland Chinese were weaned from the "iron rice bowl," which guaranteed cradle-to-grave security of livelihoods, and transformed into the most footloose pool of migrant labor in the world (Solinger 1999; Zhang 2001; Pun 2005; Lin 2006; Yan 2008).

If the Keynesian era of standard employment was a brief exception to the more general, historically enduring rule of contingency, the more precarious circumstances we find ourselves in today are seldom experienced as a reversion to some pre-Fordist status quo ante. In most of the industrialized world, the family-based customs and cultural norms that bound and regulated preindustrial life have been rent asunder and are no longer strong enough to cushion the rough justice of market conditions. Variants of so-called Asian capitalism, which rest on a strong, pastoral state and a Confucian understanding of kinship, have not been able to tame the wild, antisocial impact of marketization. Perhaps the most visible countertendency lies in cultures that have been reshaped by resurgent Islamist philosophies, many of which are driven by a reactive mentality. Latin America is the only region where, for the time being, the tide of liberalization is being turned by new social forces that are both secular and democratic. Yet even when these regional forces act in the name of indigenous populations, they are attuned to the shifting wavelengths of the global economy and its fickle map of opportunities and pitfalls. Most nation-states, if their resources were put to equitable use, have the means to guarantee a basic income to their populations regardless of the circumstances of their employment. But they can no longer insulate their people from the transnational traffic of information, iconography, and money. Nor is it so easy to justify any vision of justice that is not internationalist, as it once was for advocates of "socialism in one country." As for those who advocate non-market control over the local provision of livelihoods, they are likely to be labeled as protectionists, one of the most potent fighting words in the lexicon of neoliberalism, the all-pervading philosophy of deregulation and privatization.

What I describe in these pages as the new geography of livelihoods is, in large part, the outcome of economic liberalization in the last two decades. NAFTA, European integration, and WTO-driven deregulation have engendered a frenetic, global traffic in jobs, capital, goods, services, and people. The rapid influx of investment into new regional markets has pushed hundreds of millions of uprooted people into the migrations streams that now crisscross the world. But though the new global economy of supply and demand is crafted to cater to investors and speculators, it is not a winner-takes-all game for them. While mass mobility facilitates the ready availability of workers, often in straitened circumstances, the flighty nature of migrant labor is a source of frustration to the state's strictures of population management and to capital-owners' desire to control labor supply. The evasion tactics adopted by transnational migrants in their running battle with agents of repressive border policies, unfair labor regulation, detention camps, and deportation lie on the front lines of neoliberal conflict, both a consequence of discipline and a fugitive response to it (Mezzadra 2001; Bacon 2008).

So, too, the escape of capital to cheaper locations in other parts of the world is never a clean getaway. Transferring dirty, or dangerous, industrial operations to less regulated regions is increasingly a corporate liability when toxic substances taint the brand by showing up back home via the intercontinental trade in material goods and food produce. The bargaining power of labor gets relocated, as well, and, sooner or later, asserts itself in a variety of ways (Silver 2003). The mercurial rise of worker protests in the world economy's labor-intensive Chinese centers of accumulation is a case in point (Lee 2007). The chronic "shortage" of unskilled workers—migrants in their millions who fail to show up, en masse, in Guangdong's sweated factories each year—is further evidence of the unorganized form that such "refusals of work" can take (Ross 2006a). The more recent response on the part of the Chinese government—new labor legislation (from January 2008) that guarantees the right to sign contracts with no fixed termination dates for employees after ten years of service—is evidence that regulators can be made accountable if a coalition of advocates connects effectively with public concern about the march of precarity (intermittent employment and radical uncertainty about the future) into every stratum of the workforce.

The same dual-sided equation applies to the corporate push for flexibility in labor markets. Capital-owners have won lavish returns from low-end casualization—subcontracting, outsourcing, and other modes of flexploitation—and increasingly expect the same in higher-skill sectors of the economy. As a result, we have seen the steady advance of contingency into the lower and middle levels of the professional and high-wage service industries. In these sectors, managers and consultants have zealously promoted the condition of "free agency" as an existential test of character for youthful entrants into the workforce (Pink 2001). In return for giving up the tedium of stable employment in a large, hierarchical organization, would-be free agents are buzzed by the thrill of proving themselves by finding out if they have what it takes to prevail in the heady swim of self-employment. Once they are in this game, some of the players thrive, but most subsist, neither as employers nor traditional employees, in a limbo of uncertainty, juggling their options, massaging their contacts, managing their overcommitted time, and developing coping strategies for handling the uncertainty of never knowing where their next project, or source of income, is coming from (Reidl, Schiffbanker, and Eichmann 2006; Ehrenstein 2006; Vishmidt and Gilligan 2003; McRobbie 2004, 2007; kpD 2005).

But it is also important to remember that the demand for flexibility originated not on the managerial side, but from the laboring ranks themselves as part of the broadly manifested "revolt against work" in the early 1970s (Zerzan 1974; Tronti 1980; Garson 1975). Alienation on the job arising from boring, repetitive, or otherwise ungratifying tasks produced widespread discontent in white-collar as well as blue-collar workplaces (Bell 1956; Terkel 1974). The outcomes were pervasive sabotage, chronic absenteeism, and wildcat strikes, and they were interpreted by corporate and government managers as a system-wide protest against the factory-centered conditions of Fordist industrialization (U.S. Department of Health 1973). One of the most salient elements of this revolt against work was a visceral protest against the long-term tedium of organizational employment. Many workers concluded that the conformist discipline of this kind of stability had not produced meaningful experiential outcomes, only classic (Marxist) alienation on the job. "Jobs for life" was not a recipe for liberation, nor should it be. No less could incremental gratification through consumer materialism be considered a long-term source of fulfillment, even if it were sustainable as a way of life. The programs of flexible work, offered and imposed by corporate managers in the intervening decades, are not only a response to, but also a perversion of, the original vision of an existence freed from work-life alienation (Boltanski and Chiapello 2006).

So when we posit alternatives today, we cannot speak of security if it entails a guaranteed slot in a sclerotic organizational hierarchy, where employee participation is clearly tokenistic, and where the division of labor functions as a fixed and formal regime of discipline. The appeal of self-employment, so pervasive in the high-skill, value-adding sectors of brain work known as the creative and knowledge industries, has proved a powerful draw, but it should not be associated or identified exclusively with the neoliberal ethos of the self-directed entrepreneur. The market evangelism of neoliberalism has produced so many converts in no small part because it exploits the credo that individuals have power over their economic destinies. Yet this belief is not the exclusive property of market fundamentalists, nor should it be regarded as such. It can be espoused by individuals in more democratic kinds of work environment—ones that are just and vibrant but are also protected from market overexposure. Nor does the appetite for self-direction necessarily lead to selfish neglect for the welfare of others. Autonomy is not the opposite of solidarity. On the contrary, solidarity, if it is to be authentic, has to be learned—it cannot be enforced—and this can only occur when we are free enough to choose it as an outcome of efforts and ideas that we share with others.

Though they occupy opposite ends of the labor market hierarchy, workers in low-end services, both formal and informal, and members of the "creative class," who are temping in high-end knowledge sectors, appear to share certain experiential conditions. These include the radical uncertainty of their futures, the temporary or intermittent nature of their work contracts, and their isolation from any protective framework of social insurance. These common conditions have prompted some theoretical commentators associated with post-*operaismo* (the Italian school of socialist thought that advocates workers' autonomy) to envisage the formation of a multi-class *precariat*, somehow linked by shared concerns about the insecurity of all aspects of their lives (Foti 2004; Neilson and Rossiter 2005; Papadopoulos, Stephenson, and Tsianos 2008). The youthful cast of this formation is often evoked by the slogan of "the precarious generation," and the activist networks generated on its behalf are driven by a spontaneous, though far from dogmatic, belief that the precariat may be the post-Fordist successor to the proletariat (Raunig 2004, 2007). Even if this concept is theoretically plausible, does it make sense to imagine cross-class coalitions of the precarious capable of developing a unity of consciousness and action on an international scale?

Critics of this concept of the precariat dismiss as naive the assumption that a highly trained aristocracy of labor, intermittently employed in high-end sectors, will find common cause, simply on the basis of insecurity, with the less skilled casually employed in low-end jobs. Yet we cannot afford to reject out of hand any evidence of, or potential for, this kind of fellow feeling. In some of my own research, for example, in IT and other technology-driven firms, I found it common for employees to refer to their workplaces as "high-tech sweatshops," especially when they are pressured by long hours, deadline speedups, and divisions of labor that reduce employee autonomy (Ross 2002, 2004). Such throwaway comments are often simply expressions of the most cynical side of office humor. They can also imply that sweatshops are somehow appropriate for the unskilled, but only for that class of worker. Yet I have found that they also contain real elements of self-recognition and identification with the plight of those toiling in workplaces customarily associated with sweatshop labor.

Historical instances of this kind of complicated identification abound. "Wage slavery," for example, once resonated as a slogan, in the 1840s, for skilled artisans opposed to factory deskilling and to employers' efforts to make them compete with Southern chattel labor. The slogan also played a role in abolitionist sentiment and action, though it was increasingly displaced by the explicitly racist shibboleth of "white slavery" (Roediger 1991). However fraught as a catchword for the free labor movement of the time, the continuity—between plantation and factory conditions—established by the slogan had a moral power that helped to establish some measure of cross-class and transracial solidarity. Today, I would argue that this moral power has been claimed for the "global sweatshop." Activists in the anti-sweatshop movement who sought to harness that power have had a similar kind of impact in building associational sentiment across lines of race and class. They have pieced together an agile, international coalition to confront the power of large corporations, and they have had some success in pushing labor rights on to the table of the reluctant policymakers who shape global trade agreements (Esbenshade 2004; Bender and Greenwald 2003; Ross 2004; Bonacich and Appelbaum 2000; Ross, Robert 2006). The student wing of the movement succeeded in orienting student consciousness toward labor causes, arguably for the first time since the 1930s, and some of that impetus has carried over into cross-class campaigns for a living wage for service workers on campus and in campus towns (Featherstone 2002).

While the anti-sweatshop movement helped revive public sympathy for the predicament of workers in labor-intensive jobs, it has also revived a moral language for those in value-added trades who are more and more inclined to see their own occupational sectors following a similar path, offshore and down-market. Now that offshore outsourcing has climbed into white-collar sectors and is taking its toll on the whole gamut of professions, the plight of garment workers, onshore and offshore, can no longer be viewed as a remote example of job degradation, unlikely to affect the highly skilled. Creative workers—the talent pool at the heart of Richard Florida's formula for New Economy development—are only the latest to be told that, come what may, there will always be a domestic, onshore need for their occupational skills, which cannot be replicated elsewhere. While this may be true of the most irreducibly artisanal, it has not offered all that much protection for creatives in the knowledge industries. In those sectors, the industrialization of creativity has been proceeding for some time now, as managers seek out project templates that will impose a reliable rhythm (and an offshore capability) on the delivery of intangibles like ideas, concepts, models, formulae, and renderings (Ross 2002).

Though they tend to share the mentality of elites, independently minded brainworkers are often the easiest to alienate, even radicalize. One conspicuous example is the case of the academic professional. Once an impregnable stronghold of occupational security, higher education in the United States is now awash with contingency; almost two-thirds of its teaching workforce have been casualized, leaving a minority in the tenure stream to exercise the academic freedoms that are the signature of the profession in a society that still regards itself as a leader of the free world. For the largely younger ranks of adjuncts and graduate teachers, the experience of deprofessionalization has triggered an embryonic labor movement that may yet transform the workplace, regardless of whether it can arouse larger numbers of the securely tenured from their apathy (Krause et al. 2008; Bousquet 2008; Berry 2005; Downs and Manion 2004; Johnson, Kavanagh, and Mattson 2003; Nelson 1997). The concomitant demystification of academe and its genteel cult of disinterestedness has cleared the way for a more accurate assessment of its work life—an advance in consciousness that will bear more fruit as higher education moves further along the road of industrial restructuring.

In addition, the erosion of job security and standard employment arrangements have helped forge a new perspective on the conditions of those who never enjoyed such advantages in the first place, whether because of their gender, racial background, or regional location. After all, the breadwinner of the Fordist family wage breathed a different air from those employed in the secondary labor markets of the era, and often did so at the cost of the latter. Employers conceded to workers' gains in core sectors only because they profited so handsomely from the degraded income and status of female pink-collar workers, while the whole system of "standard employment" rested on the sprawling foundation of unwaged labor in the home. Justice for one was not justice for all, and the trade union leadership of that era, notwithstanding its affirmation of an alternative understanding of how the economy works, can rightly be faulted for its complicity with this multitiered arrangement. Today, the casualized features of this secondary labor market are familiar to more and more of us, whether in high-wage or discounted occupational sectors. For that reason alone, such circumstances make it more difficult to ignore the principle of common justice. But, rather than invoke it to vindicate casualization, that principle of justice needs to be reinterpreted as a labor-friendly code for protecting everyone's right to choose their own balance of freedom and security in employment. A guaranteed income, or social wage, unattached to employment, may be the ideal vehicle for delivering such protections, though building the political will for that goal lies along a long and hard road.

Today's labor movement has slowly but surely begun to move beyond the siege mentality of protecting the hard-won privileges of the core sectors. Recent examples include the efforts to organize immigrants and contingent service workers, the push to internationalize campaigns against multinational employers, and the flourishing of alternatives to work site–bound unions for highly mobile workers whose needs are not met by traditional locals (Fine 2007; Bronfenbrenner 2007; Gordon 2005; Waldinger et al. 1998). More imaginative efforts are still required to understand and respond to the needs of employees in the nonunion knowledge industries, especially those who may prefer nonstandard or freelance employment. Organizers will have to approach precarity as an experiential norm for people, not as an unlucky, temporary circumstance that can be remedied simply by acquiring a union card. If the labor movement is to be a resurgent force on the new landscape of irregular work, then the most precarious may have to be accorded moral, and ultimately organizational, leadership within cross-class coalitions.

Last but not least, organized labor has a role to play in helping to build more sustainable livelihoods—ones that will not be left to waste when the global economy shifts on its axis, as it is wont to do these days. These are not simply jobs that will stay put; they are jobs that have to be justified according to environmentalist criteria. It is altogether hypocritical to participate—just for the sake of employment—in the wasteful, hazardous, or worthless forms of production that make our growth-driven consumer societies so destructive to land and life. If the long-overdue promise of allying labor with ecology advocates—teamsters and turtles—is to be realized, then "green jobs," or "jobs for the future" in politicians' parlance, will have to be at the center of any economic development strategy (Brecher, Costello, and Smith 2006). Ultimately, this impulse is what distinguishes mere job creation from the making of "livelihoods" in the broader sense of sustaining planetary life.

In this book, which is a far from comprehensive survey, I have selected case studies of recent tendencies that have not yet been adequately documented. They involve employees, managers, activists, policymakers, trade unionists, designers, scholars, and educators in a range of fields and industries. Each case study argues in its own way for shifting our mentality about the practical meaning of security, flexibility, and autonomy. The book divides into three sections.

The first section begins with a comparative analysis (in the United Kingdom, the European Union, and the United States) of creative industries policymaking, increasingly a favored development strategy for cities and national economies, both in the developed and developing world. As managers struggle to retain a competitive edge in the global economy, they look more and more toward creative workers to generate value for a city, region, and nation. Once marginal on the landscape of production, it is artists, designers, and other creatives who are becoming the new model workers—self-directed, entrepreneurial, accustomed to precarious, nonstandard employment, and attuned to producing career hits. All of these features are endemic to a jackpot economy, where intellectual property is the glittering prize for the lucky few. More to the point, the proven ability of "creative clusters" and mega-events to boost land value is a key factor in the state's attention to this sector of cognitive labor. At the same time, there is an understanding both that jobs in this sector cannot be transferred elsewhere, and that they are models for work gratification on a genuinely humane basis. Chapter 2 considers the efforts of developing countries to institute similar policies and examines the case of China, where many cities incorporated creative industries policy into their most recent five-year plans. Desperate to prove that "Created in China" can coexist with, or even supersede, "Made in China," PRC legislators have turned to promoting cultural production in ways that are markedly different from the political orientation of the Cultural Revolution.

Intensified rivalry among regions for trade and investment is a prominent feature of the new geography of work, and it is more and more institutionalized in the competition to host mega-events—none more monumental than the Olympics. The third chapter compares the respective bids of London and New York for the 2012 Olympics, assessing how different levels of government interact to promote place-based development strategies in a winner-takes-all environment where public monies can efficiently be turned over to private hands.

The next section is devoted to environmentally driven propositions about the conditions of low-end precarious workers—the migrants and sweatshop employees whom Sabine Hess has called "the ground staff of globalization" (2005). The first chapter in this section considers what the anti-sweatshop movement can and should learn from the anti-consumerist movement, and vice versa. Transnational labor activism has scored some moderate successes, but in general it has been inattentive to ecological factors in the life cycle of products, often promoting job retention and job enrichment at the cost of a systematic vision of sustainable development. By that same token, anti-consumerists have been oblivious to the livelihood concerns of those employed in the product life cycle. The second chapter considers the residential needs of highly mobile workers and asks why architects, while adept at espousing ecologically minded values and practices, have not been designing for new immigrant populations. There, I argue that green design, currently executed on a trickle-down principle, might better be advanced from the bottom-up, employing sustainable self-build practices that immigrants often carry with them. In centers of sprawl like the United States, this would be an especially useful form of "knowledge transfer" from the global South.

The last section of the book focuses on the instruments and institutions endemic to the still-emerging mode of production known as knowledge capitalism. The first chapter in the section analyzes the rush to secure intellectual property rights in knowledge and creative industries that are key export markets. Analyzing the battle between "public domain" liberals and privatizing corporations, the chapter dissects the combination of interests represented in the antimonopolist coalition, and argues on behalf of the mass of employees in the copyright-based industries who do not come close to qualifying for the authorial rights championed by the coalition.

The second chapter (and last in the book) analyzes the impact of globalization on higher education, and, in particular, the stampede, on the part of Anglophone universities, to set up programs and campuses off-shore, especially in emerging markets for education services (whose over-all global market is an estimated two trillion dollars). While the obvious model is the global firm, operating on an international fiscal basis, the global university will likely take a different shape. Here, I try to predict the impact of this offshore economy on the teaching profession in general, and on features of its work life in particular. Though higher education em-ployment is still regarded as a somewhat anachronistic work environment, hosting the "last good job in America," as Stanley Aronowitz has put it (2001), the reality is quite at odds with the public image. The combina-tion of work-force casualization—at a rate unequaled in any other pro-fession—with the emergent expansion of offshore higher education may prove to be one of the most illustrative examples of the new geography of work.

Creative Workers and Rent-Seeking

1

The Mercurial Career of Creative Industries Policymaking in the United Kingdom, the European Union, and the United States

TRADE DEREGULATION HAS brought down barriers to the movement of capital and jobs, but it has not freed up movement of people in pursuit of a better livelihood. The upshot is that work is allowed to circulate around the globe with impunity, but workers themselves are not—in fact, many are criminalized if they cross borders (Bacon 2008). The higher up the skills curve, the less strictly this rule applies, if only because it has not proven so easy to separate skills from employees. Nonetheless, corporate strategies loosely known as "knowledge transfer" have been devised to migrate brainpower from the heads of well-paid employees to a cheaper labor pool offshore. Increasingly sophisticated work-flow technologies can now slice up the contents of a job into work tasks, assign them to different parts of the globe, and reassemble the results into a meaningful whole. Most recently, trade liberalization, in India and China in particular, has enabled large amounts of skilled, professional work to be performed in discount offshore locations. As more and more countries strive to enter the upper reaches of industry and services, the competition to attract high-tech or knowledge-rich investment has intensified, and so these skill-intensive sectors are now seen as key to the game of catch-up. In response, new trade policies are being rolled out in the global North to keep wealthy nations ahead of the game.

Most readers will be familiar with how this contest is played out in the technology industries. First Japan, then Korea, Taiwan, Singapore, and, most recently, China, have all taken their place, whether by invitation or by self-propulsion, in the hierarchy of global production chains for advanced technology. In the meantime, the United States has strained to preserve its traditional dominance in innovation and top-end design, in large part by manipulating property law, tax codes, patent procedures, export controls, and immigration regulations. Brainpower is now organized on an international basis, with engineers and their knowledge circulating between Silicon Valley and East Asian nodes: Hsinchu, Penang, Singapore, and Shanghai (Saxenian 2006). Managers at each of the Asian locations have to wheel and deal to leverage technology transfers that will maintain their position in the chain, while all are trying to steal the fire from the United States.

Software follows a similar pattern, but its cultural character and easy replicability feeds into an economy where intellectual property (IP) and other legal efforts to retain traditional monopoly rents play an ever-growing role in capital wealth creation. In such an economy, the competition to capture value mutates more rapidly. During the dot-com years of the late 1990s, the adolescent surge of Internet-based operations appeared to offer a different model of valuation and innovation from the customary patterns in the technology industries. Internet-based development was rooted in content, ideas, and humanistic creativity, as opposed to purely technical invention. This shift in focus, toward skills that had hitherto been quite marginal to the productive economy, promised to open up untapped sources of financial value. For a while, talk about unleashing creativity was all the rage in managerial circles, giving rise to the folie de grandeur known as the New Economy.

The hothouse environment of these years proved to be a heady incubator for the fledgling efforts at creative industries (CI) policymaking. The fiscal windfall promised by the burgeoning new media sector prompted government and corporate managers to imagine that the traditional and emergent creative professions could also be brought into the same orbit of financialization as IT start-ups. The result was a new composite "creative economy"; and because the self-directed work mentality of artists, designers, writers, and performers was so perfectly adapted to the freelancing profile favored by advocates of liberalization, this new arrangement occupied a key evolutionary niche on the business landscape. Cultural work was nominated as the new face of neoliberal entrepreneurship, and its practitioners were cited as the hit-making models for the IP jackpot economy. Arguably more important, the visible presence of creative lifestyles in select city neighborhoods, now designated as cultural districts, helped to boost property value in these precincts and adjacent others in accord with well-documented, and by now formulaic, cycles of gentrification (Smith 1996; Ley 1996).

After the dot-com boom faded, and as offshore outsourcing began to take its toll on technology jobs, the creative sector held out the promise that its skill-intensive jobs would not be transferred elsewhere. Unlike high-end manufacturing industries, which require expensive technical infrastructures and customarily lavish tax incentives, creative occupations do not entail costly institutional supports and they can endow a city or a region with a kind of unique distinction that helps attract investment. The combination of low levels of public investment with the potential for high-reward outcomes was guaranteed to win the attention of managers on the lookout for a turnaround strategy for their faltering urban or regional economies. Accustomed to seeing corporate investors come and go, they seized on this rare opportunity to capitalize on a place-based formula for redevelopment. Governments, both local and national, were quick to provide support with policies aimed at stimulating the entrepreneurial energies of activities now loosely grouped under the rubric of "creative industries" (CI). Under the new policies, which were adopted or emulated in countries around the world, urban and regional hubs would be groomed as centers for unleashing the latent creativity of individuals and communities, and the image of the nation would be irradiated with the wonder stuff of innovation.

It was far from clear whether these policies could support a productive economy with an engine of sustainable jobs at its core. Much of the evidence so far suggests that the primary impact is on rising land value and rent accumulations, which are parasitic side effects, to say the least, rather than transmissions of the ideas originated by creative workers (Harvey 2001). For those who want to see sustainable job creation, the rise of CI policymaking presents a conundrum. The guiding consensus is that culture-based enterprise can be promoted as a driver of economic development for cities, regions, and nations that want to catch up, or else be left out of the knowledge society. At the very least, then, the policy spotlight ought to present some new, long-term opportunities for creative workers accustomed to eking a makeshift living out of art, expression, design, or performance. So far, however, the kind of development embraced by policymakers seems guaranteed merely to elevate this traditionally unstable work profile into an inspirational model for youth looking to make an adventure out of their entry into the contingent labor force. If the creative industries become the ones to follow, all kinds of jobs, in short, may well look more and more like musicians' gigs: nice work if you can get it.

The relevant shift in CI nomenclature—from the rusting coinage of "cultural industries" to the newly minted "creative industries"—is usually credited to the United Kingdom's incoming pro-business New Labour administration of 1997. Prime Minister Tony Blair's zealous modernizers renamed the Department of National Heritage as the Department of Culture, Media, and Sport (DCMS), and promoted, as its policy bailiwick, an entrepreneurial model of self-organized innovation in the arts and knowledge sectors of the economy. In this chapter, I will summarize how this policy paradigm has fared in the years since the establishment of the DCMS. Focusing on its career in the United Kingdom, Continental Europe, and the United States, I will describe some of the reasons for its enthusiastic reception, assess its model of job creation from a qualitative standpoint, and analyze the politicized reaction to its implementation.

Not surprisingly for a policy-intensive paradigm, statistics generated about CI have been legion. By contrast, there has been precious little attention to the quality of work life with which creative livelihoods are associated. Job gratification, for creatives, has always come at a heavy sacrificial cost—longer hours in pursuit of the satisfying finish, price discounts in return for aesthetic recognition, self-exploitation in response to the gift of autonomy, and dispensability in exchange for flexibility. Yet there is nary a shred of attention to these downsides in the statements and reports of CI policymakers, save a passing concern that the "instrumentalizing" of culture might bring undue harm to the nobility of aesthetics, as evinced by Tessa Jowell, Blair's second DCMS minister (2004). No doubt, it is commonly assumed that creative jobs, by their nature, are not deficient in gratification. If anything, their packaging of mental challenges and sensuous self-immersion is associated with a surfeit of pleasure and satisfaction. Proponents of this line of thinking may well concede that the life of creatives, in the past, has often been one of misery, frustration, and deprivation, but the given wisdom is that those pitfalls were primarily the result of economic neglect and social marginalization. In a milieu where creativity is celebrated on all sides, such drawbacks, it is assumed, will evaporate.

Yet the ethnographic evidence on knowledge and CI workplaces shows that sacrificial labor, market overexposure, and self-exploitation are still chronic on-the-job characteristics (Ross 2002; Gill 2002, 2007; Reidl, Schiffbanker, and Eichmann 2006; Huws 2003; Ehrenstein 2006; Perrons 2003). If policymakers were to undertake official surveys of the quality of work life, they would find the old formula for creative work very much alive and well in its newly marketized environment. In this respect, arguably the most instrumentally valuable aspect of the creative work traditions is the carryover of coping strategies, developed over centuries, to help practitioners endure a feast-or-famine economy in return for the promise of success and acclaim. The combination of this coping mentality with a production ethos of aesthetic perfectibility is a godsend for managers looking for employees capable of self-discipline under the most extreme job pressure. It is no surprise then that the "artist" has been seen as the new model worker for high-risk/high-reward employment (Menger 2002; McRobbie 2004).

It would be a mistake, however, to see the CI sector as simply a marketized uptake of these longstanding traditions of painstaking endeavor and abiding forbearance. The precariousness of work in these fields also reflects the infiltration of models of nonstandard employment from low-wage service sectors. The contingent conditions braved by low-skill workers and migrants are more and more normative at all occupational levels, whereas before, in the Keynesian era, they were characteristic of a secondary labor market, occupied primarily by women working on a part-time, contractual basis (Beck 2000). A broad spectrum of employees—brainworkers, adjunct teachers, temps, low-end service workers, migrants—are now existentially subject to these uncertain circumstances. But what are the prospects, if any, for these different class fractions to make common cause on the basis of this shared insecurity? And even if they did so, what would they be striving for?

The Concept Rollout

The antecedent concept of "cultural industries," as David Hesmondhalgh has argued, was initially developed in response to the overly reductive analysis of the "culture industry" by the Frankfurt School (despite their sophisticated blend of neo-Marxist critical theory, social research, and philosophy) (Hesmondhalgh 2007; Adorno and Horkheimer 1972). In the United Kingdom, policies to support cultural industries at grassroots levels were formulated by the Greater London Council (GLC), during Ken Livingstone's term of office, before it was abolished by Margaret Thatcher in 1986. The term *creative industries* was initially introduced in Australia by Paul Keating's government in the early 1990s, but its definitive expression, in the founding documents of Blair's DCMS, bore all the breathless hallmarks of New Economy thinking: technological enthusiasm, the cult of youth, branding and monetization fever, and ceaseless organizational change (DCMS 1998). Regardless, the paradigm survived the New

Economy burnout and was further endowed by statistical and fiscal backing from the Treasury and the Department of Trade and Industry.

While this renewed interest stemmed, in large part, from militantly optimistic estimates of the export trade potential of British creativity, few could have predicted that the CI model would itself become such a successful export. In the space of a few years, it had been adopted as a viable development strategy by the governments of countries as politically and demographically disparate as Russia, Brazil, Canada, and China, to name just a few of the largest. As the global competition for talent heats up, it has been relatively easy to persuade bureaucrats that human capital and IP are the keys to winning a permanent seat in the knowledge-based economy. But those same officials are ever tormented by the task of finding the right kind of industrial strategy to deliver the goods. On the face of it, carefully packaged CI policies appear to fit the bill.

It may be too early to predict the ultimate fate of the CI policy paradigm. But skeptics have already prepared the way for its demise: it will not generate jobs; it is a recipe for magnifying patterns of class polarization; its function as a cover for the corporate IP grab will become all too apparent; its urban development blueprint will price out the very creatives on whose labor it depends; its reliance on self-promoting rhetoric runs far in advance of its proven impact; its cookie-cutter approach to economic development does violence to regional specificity; and its adoption of an instrumental value of creativity will cheapen the true worth of artistic creation (Hesmondhalgh and Pratt 2005). Still others are inclined simply to see the new policy rubric as "old wine in new bottles"—a glib production of spin-happy New Labourites, hot for naked marketization but mindful of the need for socially acceptable dress. For those who take a longer, more orthodox Marxist view, the turn toward CI is surely a further symptom of an accumulation regime at the end of its effective rule, spent as a productive force, awash in financial speculation, and obsessed with imagery, rhetoric, and display (Arrighi 1994, 2005).

Scholars and activists with ties to the labor movement can ill afford to be quite so cynical or high-minded in their response to these developments. Industrial restructuring over the last three decades has not been kind to the cause of secure or sustainable livelihoods, and indeed liberalization has often been aimed directly at destroying the power of trade unions. In OECD (Organisation for Economic Co-operation and Development) countries, the traditional cultural industries (in entertainment, broadcasting, and the arts) have been a significant union stronghold with a long and fruitful history of mutual support among craft-based locals. While capital-owners in these industries have succeeded in offshoring production wherever possible, the power of organized labor has held on in core sectors, especially those dependent on a localized supply of skills and resources that cannot be readily duplicated offshore. In some cases, the migration of an industry to new regions has even helped to generate a pioneer union presence. To cite one example, when Walt Disney created Disney World in Central Florida in the 1960s, he had little option but to bring along the unions from California, instantly making his company not only the largest union employer in Florida but also a wage regulator for the state's tourism and hospitality industry.

Certainly, new patterns of investment, rapid technological change, and global production have all taken their toll on employees' capacity to engage in collective bargaining. But fair labor at union rates and conditions remains an institutional feature of the commercial cultural industries (film, radio, television, theater, journalism, and musical and other performing arts) as they were classically constituted from the 1930s. By contrast, the noncommercial arts have long been a domain of insecurity, underpayment, and disposability, interrupted only by those few who can break through into a lucrative circuit of fame. CI mappings, as pioneered by the DCMS, include the traditionally unionized commercial sectors, but the entrepreneurial paradigm touted by the policymakers defiantly points away from the fair standards commonly associated with a union job. The preferred labor profile is more typical of the eponymous struggling artist, whose long-abiding vulnerability to occupational neglect is now magically transformed, under the new order of creativity, into a model of enterprising, risk-tolerant pluck. So, too, the quirky, nonconformist qualities once cultivated by artists as a guarantee of quasi-autonomy from market dictates are now celebrated as the key for creative souls with portfolio careers to integrate into the "global value-chains" central to the new topography of creative markets.

Even more challenging, from the perspective of organized cultural labor, are the rapid flourishing of activities tied to self-publication or amateur content promotion. The most admired artifacts on the new information landscape are Web 2.0 sites like YouTube, Flickr, Twitter, Friendster, Second Life, Facebook, and MySpace, which, along with the exponentially expanding blogosphere, attest to the rise of amateurism as a serious source of public expression. Hailed as a refreshing break from the filtering of editorial gatekeepers, these social networking sites are also sources of free

or cut-price content—a clear threat to the livelihoods of professional creatives whose prices are driven down by, or who simply cannot compete
with, the commercial mining of these burgeoning, discount alternatives.
The physical construction of the World Wide Web was itself a mammoth
enterprise of free or under-compensated labor (Terranova 2000); its adoption as a commercial delivery model (based on the principle of "disinter-
mediation," or cutting out the middle men) has taken its toll on jobs and
small businesses in the brick-and-mortar world of sales, distribution, and
retail; and its use for unauthorized file sharing has been legally opposed
by all the entertainment unions as a threat to their industries' workforce.
In many other respects, the rapid flowering of Internet amateurism has
hastened on the process by which the burden of productive waged labor is
increasingly transferred to users or consumers—outsourced, as it were, to
what Italian autonomists like Mario Tronti and Raniero Panzieri described
as the "social factory" at large (Tronti 1966; Panzieri 1973).

Nor is the Web-enabled "liberation" of individual creators an easy escape from corporate capture. Self-generated Internet buzz has been hailed
as a viable avenue for artists looking to market their work independently
of the entertainment majors. The most well-known examples include the
musical careers of Sandi Thom, Arctic Monkeys, Lily Allen, and Gorillaz;
films like *The Blair Witch Project* and *Snakes on a Plane*; and a variety of
Chinese Internet celebrities, including brazen bloggers (Muzi Mei, Sister
Hibiscus, Zhuying Qingtong), lip-syncing bands (Hou She Boys), and
more exotic, provincial commodities like the Sichuanese mountain girl
known as Tianxian MM. Arguably, the long-term beneficiaries of all these
innovations are the corporate majors, for whom the profitable co-option
of amateur strategies has long been a studied preoccupation: as in "cool
hunting," the adoption of "indie" aesthetics and attitudes, the manufacture
of microbrews, and the tactic of viral marketing among college students.
In traditional media sectors, the related discount practice of reality-based
programming is by now an indispensable principle of profit. Nothing
has more radically undermined union efforts to preserve the integrity of
pay scales for talent in the media industries than the use, in television
and radio, of amateurs on reality (and talk) shows of every genre and
description.

Wherever unions side with corporate employers—in the IP clampdown against file sharing, for example—there is every justification for
lamenting the conservative character and outcome of business unionism.
But in nonunionized industries like IT and software design, the labor

implications of nonproprietary activities waged against the big corporate powers are equally fraught. For example, the cooperative labor ethos of the FLOSS (Free/Libre/Open Source Software) networks of engineers and programmers has been lauded as a noble model of mutual aid in the service of the public good (Stallman, Lessig, and Gay 2002; Weber 2004). But FLOSS, as I will argue at length in chapter 4, has been much less useful as a model for sustainable employment. Indeed high-tech multinationals, seduced by the prospect of utilizing unpaid, expert labor, have increasingly adopted open source software like Linux, reinforcing concerns that the ethical principle of free software for the people equals free labor for corporations.

Like corporations in pursuit of nonproprietary public goods, national economic managers are keen to discover fresh and inexpensive sources of value—hidden in off-the-chart places or unexploited cross-industry connections—that can be readily quantified as GNP. The biggest returns are in high tech, of course, and so it is not surprising that the CI bandwagon is being driven by the much-lionized experience of lucrative fields like software design. Indeed, the original inclusion of this sector in the DCMS map of the creative industries helps explain why governments were so willing, initially, to promote CI policies.[1] Wherever convenient, IT statistics can be used to embellish metrics in technology and cultural fields alike.

But what if the newfound interest of states and corporations were a genuine opportunity for creative labor? After all, the demand for creative, meaningful work in factories and offices was a rallying cry of the 1970s "revolt against work" that eroded the foundations of industrial Fordism. Ever since then, calls to humanize the workplace by introducing mentally challenging tasks and employee innovation have been pushed as an alternative to the humdrum routines of standard industrial employment (Fairfield 1974). However co-opted by management fads, the underlying desire for stimulating work in decent circumstances persists as a goal of nearly any employee. Could some of those hopes be realized through the elevation of creativity to a keystone of a genuinely progressive industrial policy, one that is rooted in public health rather than private profit?

If that is to happen, then critics of the new policy paradigm have an obligation to look for emerging profiles of qualitatively good work that might stand the test of time in an economic environment where the ground now shifts underneath workers with disturbing regularity. At the very least, and from a purely pragmatic perspective, as long as policymakers are open to information and ideas that they can turn into a rising index, then they are likely to be attentive to such qualitative input. But the higher goal must be not simply to generate GDP but to build livelihoods worth writing home about, and to fully realize the loose rhetoric about the creativity of ordinary people.

A Very UnBritish Coup

At the dawn of the postwar Labour government, its policy architect, Aneurin Bevan, depicted Britain as "an island of coal surrounded by a sea of fish." It was a memorable image of the nation's natural assets, and it captured his own party's mid-century sharp appetite for nationalizing them. Fifty years later, in the wake of Thatcherite denationalization, film honcho David Putnam offered an update: Britain was to become "an island of creativity surrounded by a sea of understanding" (Ryan 2000: 16). Not a winning phrase, for sure, but Putnam's characterization was an equally faithful reflection of the temper of the New Labour government that he would shortly join as an adviser to the DCMS on science and culture. More than a touch of Hollywood glitz attended the proceedings. From the outside, Tony Blair's "Cool Britannia" looked like a massive PR campaign to persuade the world that the country Napoleon once mocked as a nation of shopkeepers was now a nation of artists and designers, with the future in their enterprising bones. "Creative Britain" was rolled out under the klieg-light scrutiny of the tabloid media and, for several years, resembled one never-ending launch party, with artists and arts grandees playing front-page Eurostar roles ordinarily reserved for sports and movie celebrities.

The real story behind Creative Britain was much more prosaic. By the 1990s, the nation's economy was no longer driven by high-volume manufacturing, fueled by the extractive resources that Bevan had extolled. Like their competitors, Britain's managers were on the lookout for service industries that would add value in a distinctive way. In the bowels of Whitehall, an ambitious civil servant came up with a useful statistic. If you lumped all the economic activities of arts and culture professionals together with those in software to create a sector known as the "creative industries," you would have, on paper at least, a revenue powerhouse that generated £60 billion a year. (In 2000, revised and improved estimates put the figure at £112 billion.) Even more illustrative, the sector appeared to be growing at twice the rate of the general economy. For an incoming government looking to make its mark on the sclerotic post-Thatcher scene, the recent performance and future potential of CI were a godsend. Britain could have its hot new self-image, and Blair's ministers would have the GDP numbers to back it up. Unlike Bevan's coal and fish, or Thatcher's North Sea oil, creativity was a renewable energy resource, mostly untapped: every citizen had some of it, the cost of extraction was minimal, and it would never run out.

As far as cultural policy went, almost every feature of the old dispensation was now subject to a makeover. When the Arts Council was established in 1945, its first chair, the serenely mischievous John Maynard Keynes, described the evolution of its famous "arms-length" funding principle as having "happened in a very English, informal, unostentatious way—half-baked, if you like" (1945: 142). He purports that Britain acquired its arts policy, like its empire, in a fit of absentmindedness. In truth, it was simply falling in line with every other Western social democracy by acknowledging that the market failure of the arts should be counteracted through state subsidies. Keynes's batty boosterism—"Let every part of Merry England be merry in its own way. Death to Hollywood"—was a far cry from the regimen of requirements demanded fifty years later by Chris Smith, the first DCMS minister, who declared ex officio that he did not believe in "grants for grants' sake" or "something for nothing" (1999: 14). Wherever possible, the thirteen industries included in the government's 1998 mapping document (film, television and radio, publishing, music, performing arts, arts and antiques, crafts, video and computer games, architecture, design, fashion, software and computer services, and advertising) had to be treated like any other industry with a core business model. While it was acknowledged that some institutions and individuals would still require public support to produce their work, this would be spoken of as an "investment" with an anticipated return, rather than a "subsidy" offered to some supplicant, grant-dependent entity. Moreover, much of the arts funding would come through a source—the National Lottery— widely viewed as a form of regressive taxation.

To qualify for public funding from Smith's department, artists had to show a demonstrable return on this investment; they had to prove that their work furthered public goods like diversity, access, relevance, civic pride, community innovation, and social inclusion. DCMS policies asked artists to play directly functional roles in society: assisting in the improvement of public health, race relations, urban blight, special education, welfare to work programs, and, of course, economic development (Smith

1998). Politicians began to recount visits to homeless shelters or hospitals where the introduction of some worthy arts program had transformed the lives of residents. Soon, they were speculating on how a savvy application of arts skills could help reduce crime, truancy, teenage pregnancy, poverty, and neighborhood degradation. According to this mentality, the only problem seemed to be how to measure the actual impact so that it could be chalked up as a government success.

Not surprisingly, most working artists, suspicious of their newly designated role as naked instruments of government policy, saw these functions as more appropriate to glorified social workers than to traditional creative practitioners. For those who had never subscribed to arts for arts' sake, and who were committed to the more progressive ethos of service to political ideals, New Labour was demanding that artists be socially conscious in passive and compliant ways. None of this was compatible with a posture of real opposition to the state. In the 1930s in the United States, Harold Rosenberg spearheaded a similar complaint when he declared that the New Deal's WPA programs, offering a government wage in return for socially useful art, heralded the death of the bohemian avant-garde as a radical force (1975).

But to see the policy changes simply as a way of reining in artists' often-rebellious citizenly energies, or of exploiting their conscience, is to miss much of the rationale for the shift in government focus. Nicholas Garnham, for example, has argued that the new policy paradigm was driven, in large part, by innovation fever around IT development, and therefore should be seen primarily as an extension of information society policy as formulated around the impact of computerization (Garnham 2005). The key creatives and the highest economic performers in this scenario were the engineers and technologists whose entrepreneurial efforts as change agents in New Economy start-ups rode the trend of business management away from the stifling, cumbersome domains of the large hierarchical corporation. The IT industry buzz around creativity caught the imagination of British politicians who saw a convenient bridge to other sectors that were potentially rich in IP exploitation. Indeed, by 2003, the figures for software, computer games, and electronic publishing clearly dominated (at 36.5 percent) the revenue statistics for the CI as a whole (Prowse 2006).

With the Creative Industries Task Force lighting the way, every region of Britain soon had its own Cultural Consortium, along with designated creative hubs and cultural quarters. Pushed as an all-purpose panacea, the development formula was even embraced as common sense by left-leaning academics weaned on critical cultural policy studies (Hartley 2004). Most conspicuously, the triumph of the paradigm was achieved in the absence of any substantive data or evidence to support the case for culturally led regeneration (Oakley 2004). After all, what quantitative measures are useful in assessing the impact of cultural activity, in any given community, on reducing crime, binge drinking, adult illiteracy, or sexual intolerance? Common sense observation tells us that these results are much more likely to be offshoots of the gentrificated demographic changes that typically result from cultural quartering.

Despite the lip service paid to supporting independent artistic initiatives, which are liable to evolve in unforeseen shapes and sizes, the preferred framework for business development in this sector remains some version of the New Economy start-up, a micro business or small and medium enterprise (SME) structured to achieve a public listing, or geared, in the short term, to generate a significant chunk of IP by bringing ideas to the market. Thus, in the Creative Economy Programme, the latest DCMS productivity initiative "to make Britain the world's creative hub," the government offers its services as a broker between the creative entrepreneurs and potential investors in the understanding that creators are not always the best placed to exploit their ideas. Though they might win awards, they will remain commercially weak and incapable of breaking through to the market unless they are incubated and groomed for growth or for hitting the jackpot.

While creative work can surely be organized and channeled in this enterprising way, and to patently profitable ends, it has yet to be shown that the nature of the enterprise produces desirable work, never mind good jobs. The productivity statistics that orbit, halo-like, around CI policy do not measure such things, nor has there been any DCMS effort to date that assesses the quality of work life associated with its policies. This omission is all the more remarkable if we consider the high status that governments, historically, have accorded cultural creativity when it comes to maintaining a nation's quality of life in general. Imagine how much less powerful the self-image of the British nation would be without its Shakespeare, Wren, Burns, Hume, Byron, Darwin, Turner, Dickens, Brontës, Woolf, Lennon and McCartney, Bowie, Olivier, Beckham, Kureishi, Rowling, Dench, or Hirst to boast about.

The Creative Economy Programme was launched in the last year of the Blair administration to ensure that his policies carried over into his successor's term. The day before Blair stepped down in the summer of

2007, the Work Foundation (top consultants to the DCMS) released a report that boosted the UK sector as the largest and most productive in the European Union—though it was by no means clear how the productivity of arts practitioners can or should be measured. In the preface, outgoing DCMS minister Tessa Jowell noted that the size of the thirteen creative industries, at 7.3 percent of the economy, was equivalent in volume to financial services, and that it employed 1.8 million people, if those working in related creative occupations were included (2007). In his years as Blair's heir apparent, Gordon Brown dutifully acknowledged that the creative sector was the vital spark of the future national economy, but there was widespread skepticism that the overhyped creative economy would fare so well under a new leader who so prudently promised financial reality over things like breathless celebrations of the value of entertainment.

Europa, Europa

In the interim, CI policy had become an entrenched part of EU treaties, and there were few members without their own national and regional agendas. According to *The Economy of Culture in Europe*, a 2006 EU-commissioned report, the creative sector turned over more than €654 billion and contributed 2.6 percent of EU GDP in 2003, employing at least 5.8 million people, equivalent to 3.1 percent of the total employed population in Europe (KEA European Affairs 2006). While these overall figures lagged behind those of the United Kingdom, the explosive rate of growth was similar and that rising index is what captured headlines. From 1999 to 2003, the growth of the sector's value added was 19.7 percent. Largely on account of such favorable data, CI policymaking was coordinated into the European Union's Lisbon Strategy, adopted in 2000 to address economic development in neglected regions and vaingloriously aimed at making Europe, by 2010, "the most competitive and the most dynamic knowledge-based economy in the world, capable of sustainable economic growth with more and better jobs and greater social cohesion" (European Council 2000).

The Lisbon Strategy was primarily focused on R&D investment in the flagship information and communications technology (ICT) industries of the digital economy. Though the cultural sectors were seen as natural allies and contributors to the creative economy, contention over whether and how their performance and productivity could be assessed shielded them initially from the full attention of regional managers. The statistical tools and data collection techniques developed for the 2006 EU report were touted as the first comprehensive effort to gauge the socio-economic impact of the cultural and creative sectors. Why was this so important? Within the relatively informal culture of arts policy, peer professionals were entrusted with assessing the worth of candidates and their proposals, and the details of grant outcomes were rarely recorded, let alone evaluated. Industrial policy, by contrast, had more direct oversight from career bureaucrats, and it required an evidence base in the form of serviceable data and measurable outcomes, which would then justify investment. Ever since the DCMS map of 1998, the authoritative mapping of cultural sectors that traditionally eluded statistical capture ("evidence-free zones") had been viewed as a bureaucratic triumph and a prerequisite for formal accounting of the process of investment and outcome evaluation. Submitting to these measurements was the "price to be paid," as Sara Selwood put it, "for increased funding and proximity to mainstream politics" (2003).

But there was more to it than that. In complying with these requirements, the arts were not only brought into the orbit of economic assessment, but their practitioners were more and more inducted into the purview of the state as *productive* citizens: too busy or else too responsible to cause trouble. In like fashion, EU policy in this area is aimed at much more than simply the raw economics of culture-driven development. Policymakers have also seen an opportunity to promote and cement the idea of Europe itself and have seized on the potential to mold citizenly identity. From the standpoint of a bureaucracy geared toward binding its constituents to a common purpose, if not a cohesive mentality, culture is still a great divider. The stubborn uniqueness of their local cultures encourages member nations to withhold their own assets from incorporation into the conglomerate. This is especially the case when it comes to affective entities like national customs and national heritage.

In 2007, a new Culture Programme (2007–2013) was initiated by the European Commission, in part, to counteract this parochial outlook and push for a more federal view: "The general objective of the programme shall be to enhance the cultural area common to Europeans through the development of cultural cooperation between the creators, cultural players and cultural institutions of the countries taking part in the programme, with a view to encouraging the emergence of European citizenship" (European Commission 2007). Faced with the challenge of EU integration, the CI model emerged as an expedient vehicle for the making of European citizenship. The manipulation of culture has long proved useful as a top-down tool of citizen formation, but its newfound fiscal value also now promised that native cultural assets—the heritage of the "glories" of European civilization along with its modern updates—could prove serviceable as a core component of a forward-looking economy.

Toward that end, 2008 was declared a European Year of Intercultural Dialogue, and a new series of prizes was announced for the arts, architecture, and heritage. (The public media buzz around prizes, like the Man Booker, Turner, Pulitzer, Oscar, and Pritzker awards, has become a huge promotional element of the creative economy.) Also placed under the auspices of the new program was the competition for the prestigious European Capital of Culture (along with European Culture Months, initiated in 1992). This annual designation (formerly European City of Culture and begun in 1985 with Athens as the first choice) had been one of the earliest efforts to stimulate the impact of culture-led regeneration on the image of cities and regions. These days, in the many cities that compete, the campaign to win the title starts earlier and earlier, and is used to attract attention and investment. Indeed, the campaign, which can endure for several years, more often becomes the primary vehicle for investment and promotion, regardless of whether the bid is successful. It is enough for city managers to claim that they are in the running in order for this development strategy to kick into top gear.

One of the most celebrated, and well-studied examples, was that of Glasgow, which held the title in 1990. Under the funding rubric of the program, this "workers city," which had seen the steepest decline of its industrial base and suffered some of the worst socio-economic urban deprivation in Europe, got a downtown makeover (the grime on buildings was literally scrubbed clean) and an injection of funding that endowed it as an arts mecca open for all sorts of related enterprise (Landry 1990). The laboring classes, now severely underemployed, who had given the city its renowned salty character, were "socially cleansed" out to the urban periphery lest their blunt conduct and customs offend tourists and upper-middle-class arts audiences. The transition from a city famous for its slums and razor-wielding gangs to one that could host genteel culture vultures, if not the glitterati themselves, was a rough one for the populations excluded from the party (McLay 1990; Nesbitt 2008).

Business cartels organized to profit from the focus on iconic city-center investment proved to be the biggest beneficiaries. Like the Victorian mercantile elites who flourished in the "Second City of the Empire," it was the downtown real estate elites who prospered in its newly rebranded life as the "Second City of Shopping." The familiar lopsided footprint of neo-liberalism made itself visible in a system of labor apartheid that displayed an ever-firmer spatial demarcation between the residences, workplaces, and playgrounds of the ascendant professional service classes and those of the low-wage and unemployed populations at the city margins. From the standpoint of arts practitioners themselves, a 2004 study showed that the progressive legacy of 1990 was widely perceived to have been squandered by the data-focused bureaucracy in charge of cultural policy in the intervening years. An obsession with audience numbers and quotas had inhibited the sustainable growth of jobs in the sector (Garcia 2005).

Despite the patterns of uneven development across city neighborhoods, and the low level of sustainable impact on cultural workers' livelihoods, its emulators have lionized the "Glasgow renaissance" as a shining example of culture-driven revitalization. If Glasgow was able to pull it off, the story went, then any city could. Yet by 2006, city boosters who followed the model were locked into what a Demos report (on social inequality in Glasgow) called a "cultural arms race," competing for finite pools of investment resources, cultural workers, audiences, tourist streams, and signature architectural icons (Hassan, Mean, and Tims 2007). A 2004 EU-commissioned report acknowledged that the failure to ensure social inclusion had emerged as a consistent problem associated with the legacy of the European Capitals of Culture program. Attention to cultural inclusion—addressing alternative subcultures and minorities—had been impressive, but there was no mistaking the class polarization that had occurred in most cities that hosted the title (Palmer Rae Associates 2004).

Regardless of whether they were accorded the annual title and undertook a makeover on the scale of Glasgow's, most sizable European cities have adopted the model of the cultural district—the fashioning and promotion of an urban quarter that houses significant institutions and populations in the creative field. Examples include the creation of museum quarters in cities like Vienna and Rotterdam; or the arts-based conversion of disused industrial sites like the Cable Factory in Helsinki, the Veemarktkwartier in Tilburg, Westergasfabriek in Amsterdam, Manchester's Custard Factory, and the Manufactura textile factory complex in Lodz; or the marketing of districts like Barcelona's Poble Nou, Hoxton/Spitalfields in London, Temple Bar in Dublin, the Ticinese Quarter in Milan, and the Northern Quarter in Manchester. Creative clusters are perceived to be especially important to medium-sized cities, which suffer a brain drain to the larger urban centers. Signs of cultural activity are expediently promoted as soft location factors for recruiting investor interest. Small quantities of high-octane cosmopolitan fuel fed into engines of local boosterism are perceived to go a long way. Citizenly concerns about the social harm of uneven development can be mitigated when a broad cross section of middle-class residents are profiting from rising housing prices. As long as the booming property market held up, belief in the expedient use of cultural policy as a catalyst for revitalization could be sustained. The single biggest proven factor in attracting investment in the CI model is rent extraction from the perceived boost in land value.

In a few instances, it is possible to argue that the results have been relatively benign. In Helsinki, for example, unemployment skyrocketed to 18 percent after a sharp recession in the early 1990s, but the city was able to mold its cultural policy around a strong ICT sector and used its timely 2000 selection as European Capital of Culture (its advertising slogan was "Culture Does You Good") to build on this mix without sacrificing its social commitments to the general population (Castells and Himanen 2002; Kelly and Landry 1994; Landry 1998, 2000; Florida 2005). As a result, Helsinki began the new millennium with a cosmopolitan profile as the rapidly growing hub of a small nation that had long subsisted on the periphery of Europe but was now widely renowned for innovation. It was an ascendant city, with most of its Nordic welfare state and social-inclusion policies intact, and gentrification was relatively contained to the most obvious, eligible neighborhoods, like the liberal, bohemian district of Kallio.

But in many other instances, the CI formula, as it is applied, is little more than thin camouflage for gentrification. In Amsterdam, for example, urban planners have used the conventional branding of a "Creative Knowledge City" as a rubric to convert large sectors of social housing into luxury residences for prized beneficiaries of the creative economy. At the same time, neighborhoods are actively encouraged to compete for the attention of these much sought-after talents. Unlike the urban renewal schemes of the postwar period, undertaken in the spirit, at least, of addressing poverty, the new top-down effort on the part of the national government to mix class by transplanting middle-class housing into poor neighborhoods has resulted in the removal of poverty from sight (Oudenampsen 2006, 2007). In more ways than one, this new geography has been ushered in through "creative destruction," to use the phrase most associated with Joseph Schumpeter, the anti-Keynesian economist who is lionized both by neoliberal CI policymakers and the framers of the Lisbon Strategy (1942).

As the European Union's programs for the economization of culture pick up pace, driven by the urgency of meeting the Lisbon Strategy goals, Schumpeter's ideas about the creative entrepreneur are increasingly dominant over other, more socialized models, though it is a much tougher contest than Tony Blair's government faced. Compared to the United Kingdom, most Western European policymakers, influenced by UNESCO traditions, are inclined to pay more lip service to the concept of culture as a public good, which is quite at odds with its capacity to be marketized. The defiant French custom of protectionism—whereby cultural goods are protected from market forces and considered exempt from free trade agreements—holds some sway in this respect, while most Western European states have maintained intact their high levels of state subsidies for the arts. Envy of the United Kingdom's economic growth profile has been tempered to some degree by skepticism about the Anglo-Saxon model of marketization as it has been developed under neoliberalism. But as the "jobs and growth" components of the Lisbon Strategy increasingly take precedence over its initial social and ecological aspirations, the focus on grooming for market competitiveness has become an unstoppable force (Minichbauer 2006). As a result, self-organizing entrepreneurs, committed to incubating small start-ups and responsible for their own exploitation, are more and more cited and admired as the Schumpeterian heroes of national development. So, too, some of the earlier concerns of policymakers about social security, job quality, and sustainable income have given way to more naked recognition of the economic gains to be generated from a sector with such an apparently high growth record.

There is an ever-widening gap between the wild, but organic, profiles of creativity forged by Europe's rich avant-garde traditions—nurtured by radical politics and bohemian rents—and the flat world (suits-but-no-ties) of CI policymaking—where self-styled consultants broker the conversation between government bureaucrats, arts entrepreneurs, and investors. In the last decade, many forms of homegrown resistance have sprung up from within that gap to question and combat the march of neoliberalism. Prominent among them are the social movement groupings loosely organized around the agitprop slogan of precarity. First adopted by antiglobalization demonstrators at the Genoa G7 countersummit of 2001, subsequently precarity became a mobilizing concept for grassroots protests against the European Union's policy drift toward liberalization (Foti 2004; Raunig 2004).

The activism of the anti-precarity groups resulted in "a long season of protests, actions, and discussions, including events such as EuroMay-Day 2004 (Milan and Barcelona), 2005 (in seventeen European cities), Precarity Ping Pong (London, October 2004), the International Meeting of the Precariat (Berlin, January 2005), and Precair Forum (Amsterdam, February 2005)" (Neilson and Rossiter 2005). Organized groups like the Chainworkers in Italy and Les Intermittents in France captured headlines with their inventive actions, and feminists like the Colectivo Precarias a la Deriva in Spain have been effective in underlining the highly gendered dimension of the landscape of precarity (Colectivo Precarias a la Deriva 2004; Fantone 2007). In France, government plans to introduce labor policies that discriminated against youth (making it easier to fire those under twenty-six years old) generated massive student resistance and occupations of universities in 2006, and again, in the fall of 2007, when efforts to marketize the university system were introduced. In 2006, the reappropriated May Day was marked by mass rallies of immigrants in the United States. This event has been claimed as part of the precarity movement, as have a broad spectrum of labor protests and organizing efforts on the part of low-wage temporary workers in various parts of the global economy. As one typically combative declaration put it: "MayDay! MayDay! We are the precarious. We are hireable on demand, available on call, exploitable at will and fireable at whim. We have become skillful jugglers of jobs and contortionists of flexibility. But beware! We are agitating with a common strategy to share our flexfights" (*Greenpepper* 2004).[2]

As derived from the Latin verb *precor*, the literal meaning of precarity is to be forced to beg and pray to keep one's job. It is most often used as shorthand for the condition of social and economic insecurity associated with post-Fordist employment and neoliberal governance, which not only gives employers leeway to hire and fire workers at will, but also glorifies part-time contingent work as "free agency," liberated from the stifling constraints of contractual regulations. Low-wage immigrant service workers and high-tech consultants alike might share these conditions, and this commonality has inspired activists who see the opportunity for cross-class solidarity. Theorists of Italian post-*operaismo* (Lazzarato 1996; Hardt and Negri 2000; Virno 2004) who see the cognitive workforce of "immaterial labor" as harboring a potential source of power are often invoked to lend heft to the political consciousness of anti-precarity activists.

Unlike in older models of the primacy of the proletariat, and despite the fact that precarity affects migrants and low-waged women in vastly disproportionate numbers (Parrenas 2001; Ehrenreich and Hochschild 2002), the vanguard of the precariat is perceived to lie with the high-wage brainworkers, whose conscientious core consists of creative workers for whom irregular employment has long been a customary way of life. The most politicized of their ranks see themselves on the front line of capitalist accumulation, whether in the copyfight over intellectual property or against the industrialization of bohemian cultural activity. While the acceleration of offshore capitalist investment has boosted the rate of primitive accumulation in labor-intensive sectors, accumulation in the more advanced onshore sectors of the service economy is based, in part, on the CI policy of incorporating arts, crafts, and other creative practices into profit centers. Many of those involved in the struggle over this newfound attention to creative sectors have predicted, with good reason, that the future shape of skilled livelihoods is being hammered out on the anvil of CI policymaking. The voice of resistance is most plainly exemplified in the slogan "No Culture Without Social Rights," adopted by Les Intermittents, the French organization of part-time theater and audiovisual workers who have loosely coordinated their actions with the Chainworkers in Italy, Kanak Attak and Preclab in Germany, and Precarias a la Deriva in Spain.

The Great American Bootstrap

In the case of the United Kingdom and the European Union, CI policymaking has seen the state take a more active role, elbowing aside the old arm's-length tradition of arts policy, but only to ensure that reliance on state assistance will recede as rapidly as possible. Government action, in the CI model, is aimed at stimulating and liberating the latent, or untutored, entrepreneurial energies that lie in reserve in every pocket of cultural activity: a hand-up, in other words, rather than a hand-out.

The American case history is complicated, from the outset, by the selective lip service paid to the First Amendment. As Toby Miller and George Yudice have argued, the widely accepted claim that the United States does not dabble in cultural policy because it strives to maintain a strict constitutional separation between the state and cultural expression is more than a little disingenuous. The state, for example, has long nurtured the entertainment industries—especially Hollywood—through tax credits, a range of other subsidies, and lavish trade promotion (Miller and Yudice 2003). These myriad forms of market protection have been extended, more recently, to the U.S.-based media Goliaths—General Electric, Disney, Time Warner, Viacom, Liberty Media, and News Corporation—whose conglomerate operations and properties dominate almost every sector of cultural expression in the United States. Their ability to secure government-granted monopoly franchises brings untold wealth and power (McChesney 2004). Who could maintain that this long-established reliance on government largesse does not amount to cultural policy in all but name?

Nor is the practice limited to domestic operations. Though the United States took the best part of two centuries to become a net IP exporter, its strong-arm overseas efforts to enforce the IP rights of Hollywood and other content exporters through international agreements such as TRIPS (Trade Related Intellectual Property Rights), along with those brokered by the WTO, have been a driving preoccupation of U.S. trade policy since the 1960s. Indeed, from the perspective of many developing countries, IP protection ranks with the projection of preemptive military force as the dual face of U.S. power abroad. In the case of the conflict in Iraq, for example, State Department plans to privatize that country's economy gave undue prominence to the sanctity of IP rights.

While the state's market protections for these industries are not necessarily content specific, cultural content has long been an active component of U.S. foreign policy. This was especially the case during the era of the Good Neighbor policy in Latin America, when Nelson Rockefeller headed up the Office of the Coordinator of Inter-American Affairs (Yudice 2004). It would be impossible, moreover, to ignore the explicit use of targeted cultural policy in the Cold War in the broad range of activities sponsored by CIA fronts like the Congress for Cultural Freedom (Saunders 2000). While more formally abstract, the profile of free artistic expression promoted by government agencies like the USIA (U.S. Information Agency) to highlight the virtues of living in the free world was no less ideological (Von Eschen 2004). With the end of the Cold War, the propaganda value of the autonomous artist evaporated overnight; the spectacle of American artists strenuously exercising their freedoms was no longer serviceable. In 1997, the same year as the New Labour turnaround, the National Endowment for the Arts's policy document *American Canvas* laid out a remarkably similar template for applicants to follow, applying their work to socially useful ends, "from youth programs and crime prevention to job training and race relations" (Larson 1997). Just as in the British case, the artist was reconceived as the model citizen-worker—a self-motivated entrepreneur able to work in a highly flexible manner with a wide range of clients, partners, and sponsors.

While American fine arts policy, strictly speaking, has been mired in the moralism of the Culture Wars, the commercial cultural industries have been consumed with the gold rush to secure ownership of IP rights in every domain of expression. For the most part, they have enjoyed a first-mover advantage in global markets, and so there has been little need, if any, for the change in nomenclature—from culture industries to creative industries—that New Labour initiated. Nor is there much pressure on in-stitutional authorities to view creativity as a national development strat-egy for catching up. Instead, in the United States, the creative industries are more routinely, and bluntly, referred to as copyright or IP industries, and the emphasis is on business strategies to guarantee that they hold on to their lead.

Rhetoric used by Ronald Reagan in his 1966 California gubernatorial campaign has been cited as an American origin for the current neoliberal turn toward CI policies (Holmes 2008; Reagan 1966). Reagan's proposi-tion that California's native talent could generate a "Creative Society" was explicitly intended as a corrective to the federal government programs launched by the Johnson administration under the rubric of the Great So-ciety. The libertarian strain of this innovation rhetoric, often termed the Californian Ideology, has helped to bolster development policy and secure government patronage for the state's dominant regional industries, cen-tered in Hollywood and Silicon Valley. In the rest of the nation, and more recently, the most visible expression of the turn to creativity has been in urban policymaking.

Urban renovation anchored by sites of cultural consumption was pio-neered in the 1970s by the Rouse Company in the form of "festival mar-ketplaces" (Baltimore's Harborplace, Boston's Faneuil Hall, New York's South Street Seaport) while the arty retrofit of vacant industrial buildings after the SoHo (New York) model has more and more been incorporated into the real estate industrial cycle (Zukin 1989, 1994). The creative clus-ter was widely adopted in the 1990s as a development strategy for cities that had lost their industrial job and tax base (Landry 2000). This often involved public investments in museums or heritage centers, in hopes of attracting a steady tourist stream, if not the kind of destination pay dirt eventually achieved by the Bilbao Guggenheim. In the United States, this strategy dovetailed with the fiscally disastrous policy of building down-town stadiums, mostly at taxpayer expense, for major league sports teams

(Rosentraub 1997). In the world of interurban competition, managers of second- and third-tier cities were persuaded that they had no alternative but to enter into this beggar-thy-neighbor game of attracting prestige (Cagan and deMause 1998). Unlike the sports teams, the museums and heritage centers were not nomadic franchises of a monopoly cartel, but they were often a harder sell in provincial cities.

Richard Florida's 2002 book, *The Rise of the Creative Class*, gave city managers a new rationale for upgrading their competitive status. Urban fortunes, he argued, depend on the ability to attract and retain the creative talents whose capacity to innovate is increasingly vital to economic development. Because these cherished souls are highly mobile, they are choosy about their live/work locations, and the cities they tend to patronize are rich in the kind of amenities that make them feel comfortable. Tolerance of ethnic and sexual diversity, for example, rates high on Florida's indexes of livability. Though Florida estimated the creative class in the U.S. to be thirty-eight million strong (lawyers and financiers are lumped along with artists, entertainers, and architects), its demographic was unevenly distributed and heavily skewed toward liberal enclaves in the blue states (Florida 2002). Aspiring cities in pursuit of better regional leverage in the creative economy would need to become eligible suitors by submitting to a makeover, somewhat along the lines of television's *Queer Eye for the Straight Guy*.

Civic leaders rushed to embrace Florida's vision, express ordering a creative city strategy from his private consultancy group. Announcing that Detroit, Dearborn, and Grand Rapids would soon be "so cool you'll have to wear shades," Michigan governor Jennifer Granholm commanded her state's mayors to adopt hipsterization strategies that were part of a new Cool Cities commission (Michigan 2004). A hundred signatories from almost fifty cities gathered in Tennessee in May 2003 to draft the Memphis Manifesto, a blueprint for turnaround communities willing to compete for creative talent (Creative 100: 2003). In 2004, the U.S. Conference of Mayors passed a resolution on the role that CI could play in revitalization. Jobs in these sectors, it was agreed, were unlikely to be outsourced to other countries and could prove more sustainable than the high-tech employment that cities had spent so much money trying to attract in the previous decade. Aside from the domestic impact, the mayors also acknowledged the potential for global export: overseas sales of creative product was estimated at thirty billion dollars (U.S. Conference of Mayors 2004).

The zeal for jumping onto the creativity bandwagon was also inspired by some supporting data. A 2004 mapping of the country's creative industries by the nonprofit Americans for the Arts showed almost three million people working for 548,000 arts-centric businesses (2.2 percent and 4.3 percent, respectively, of U.S. employment and businesses). One in twenty-four U.S. businesses were estimated to be arts-centric—and they belonged to the fastest growing sector of the economy (Americans for the Arts 2004). The World Bank reported that more than half the consumer spending was on CI outputs in G7 countries, and that creative industries account for 7 percent of world GDP (Nabeshima and Yusuf 2003). The export data encouraged the view that the competition for creative talent was being waged on a global scale. In 2005, Florida published his alarmist sequel, *The Flight of the Creative Class*, warning that the Bush administration's domestic and foreign policies were driving the best and the brightest overseas (Florida 2005). City officials in Europe and East Asia responded by rolling out the red carpet for Florida's consultancy. In tune with the hapless efforts of midwestern mayors to attract gay college graduates, the government of Singapore relaxed the city-state's prescriptions against homosexuality (*Economist* 2004), furthering its ham-fisted effort to sex up a culture long associated with a rigid observance of the morally censorious side of "Asian values" (Tan 2003). Today, it is more likely to be known as the gay, rather than the creative, capital of Asia.

The solutions being prescribed for strivers hoping to move up in the creativity rankings are easy to satirize: Jamie Peck has described them as "another variant of the Papua New Guinean cargo cults, in which airstrips were laid out in the jungle in the forlorn hope of luring a passing aircraft to earth" (2005: 752). Nonetheless, the cures are advertised as low-cost, and almost pain-free, often consisting of little more than image regeneration around public amenities, such as the creation of bike paths, the makeover of some center-city ex-industrial warehouses, or the stimulation of hip entertainment and consumption zones. Compared to the lavish tax exemptions and infrastructural outlays used to attract large corporations, creativity initiatives are soft budget items, requiring minimal government intervention with little risk of long-term commitments from the public purse. Moreover, traditional chamber of commerce businesses can rest easy that no significant public resources will be diverted away from serving their interests. As Peck observes, "For the average mayor, there are few downsides to making the city safe for the creative class—a creativity strategy can quite easily be bolted on to business-as-usual urban-development policies. The reality is that city leaders from San Diego to Baltimore, from Toronto to Albuquerque, are embracing creativity strategies not as *alternatives* to extant market-, consumption- and property-led development strategies, but as low-cost, feel-good *complements* to them" (2005: 763).

Left-wing critics of these development strategies have pointed out that cities high in the creativity rankings also top out on indexes of class polarization and social inequality; that the gentrification of creative neighborhoods drives out those most likely to innovate; and that Potemkin cultural zones too obviously staged for consumption scare away the precious recruits (Marcuse 2003; Maliszewski 2004; Peck 2005). Moreover, those unlucky enough to be designated as uncreative have little to look forward to but trickle-down leavings since they will almost certainly be performing the low-wage service jobs that support their lifestyling superiors. Right-wingers have been even harder on the Florida cult, seeing nothing but a policy to elevate liberal havens as models of growth (Malanga 2004; Kotkin and Siegel 2004; Kotkin 2005). In fact, they argue, Republican cities that don't rate as particularly creative—low-tax, business-friendly suburban cities, like Phoenix, Houston, or Orlando—are the ones with the best performance on job and population growth.

If the creative city is a liberal plot, it is a far cry from the liberal city of the postwar economy, which relied on federal block grants to oversee the basic welfare of its citizens. With budgets cut to the bone, and the citizenry increasingly cut off from institutional protections, U.S. urban policymakers have all but embraced the accepted neoliberal wisdom that self-sufficient entrepreneurial activity is the best, if not the most just, stimulant to growth. The individual career portfolio of the young, freelancing creative is a perfect candidate for this profile of self-reliant productivity. Whether the policies will generate employment remains to be seen. They cannot do worse than their stadium-based predecessors. Surveys over the last three decades have shown that the presence of professional sports teams or their facilities failed to register any significant impact on employment or city revenue (Noll and Zimbalist 1997). Indeed, Allen Sanderson, a University of Chicago economist, famously estimated that if the public money expended on a typical stadium project were dropped out of a helicopter over the city in question, it would probably create eight to ten times as many jobs (Noll and Zimbalist 1997: 37).

But, unlike the helicopter drop, the creative jobs in question will not be scattered over a wide area. They have a tendency to cluster, and those zones become socially exclusive in short order. If the creative-cities campaigns do result in more jobs, and if they prove to be economic accelerators, they will almost certainly intensify the polarization of city life between affluent cores and low-income margins. Any significant spoils will be captured in the zones of growth, and by a minority of creative workers at that, because most of the profit—in a winner-takes-all IP-driven economy—is extracted by intermediaries in the value chain and not by those who are the original innovators. In this context, Florida's nostrum, that creativity is everyone's natural asset to exploit, is difficult to distinguish from any other warmed-over version of American bootstrap ideology. From the individual creative's standpoint, it appeals to the ideology of the self-reliant, small producer—the mainstay of the nineteenth-century work ethic—who is promised just rewards for his or her artisanal toil. The recipe on offer to city managers is more like a get-rich-quick scheme—high rates of return from minimal investments with little risk involved.

Most of the urban neighborhoods considered eligible for a creative makeover were downtowns still struggling with the legacy of disinvestment; others were classic artist-pioneer quarters, for which SoHo's much-lionized rehabilitation is still the gold standard worldwide. The biggest risks were in inner-city areas ravaged by poverty and underdevelopment, but, of course, they also promised the biggest rewards from rent accumulations. As part of the assistance it offered to the rollout of neoliberalism in cities, the Clinton administration, in 1994, established a series of Empowerment Zones (EZ) and Enterprise Communities in distressed communities around the country. Public funds and tax incentives were made available as catalysts for revitalization through private investment. Quickly labeled a "third way antipoverty program," the EZ initiatives were intended to replace publicly financed community development in the inner cities with incentives for private enterprise. The most conspicuous was in New York City, where the EZ was targeted for the Upper Manhattan neighborhoods of Harlem, East Harlem, Washington Heights, and Inwood. These neighborhoods comprised "a city within the city" that was poor in resources and employment but rich in cultural assets, having led the world in setting popular trends in music, fashion, and lifestyle for decades. The city and the state each matched the federal commitment of one hundred million dollars to create a three-hundred-million-dollar pool of funds, all targeted at existing or start-up businesses, but especially solicitous of non-local investment.

Harlem, in particular (and to the detriment of the other districts, like East Harlem—see Davila 2004), was considered eligible for repositioning as an arts tourism mecca because of its high international recognition as the capital of black culture and its array of cultural icons—the Apollo Theater, the Studio Museum, Sylvia's restaurant, the Boys Choir of Harlem, the Dance Theater of Harlem, Harlem School of the Arts, the National Black Theater, and the Schomburg Center for Research in Black Culture. The neighborhood already occupied a place in the global imagination. Its assets just needed to be exploited to highlight the potential for investment in this newly labeled cultural district. Accordingly, in 1998, the Upper Manhattan EZ established its own Cultural Investment Fund, aimed at supporting the more prominent museums or performing arts institutions and at stimulating heritage tourism. While these grants helped to stabilize the larger, more efficiently and professionally run organizations (such as Museo El Barrio in East Harlem), they bypassed the edgier, more experimental outfits and did little to stimulate the kind of grassroots initiatives that lend cohesion to a community's social life (but which do not generate revenue or audience data).

No less significant, as an aesthetic pull for mobile, moneyed professionals pushed out of Manhattan's other real estate markets, was Harlem's attractive, but rundown, housing stock of brownstones built for affluent dwellers in the nineteenth century. As the EZ grants flowed in (along with ex-president Clinton, who established his offices on 125th Street), housing prices leaped up. "Harlem is the last great frontier of Manhattan real estate," declared Barbara Corcoran, manager of the city's leading real estate brokerage ("Corcoran Group" 2000). Sotheby's International set up shop and, within a decade of the launching of the Upper Manhattan EZ, was advertising, and briskly selling, multimillion-dollar properties. National retail chains, gourmet groceries, and corporate developers steadily moved in (Maurrasse 2006). More and more residents questioned who exactly was being empowered by the Empowerment Zone (Taylor 2002; Pitman Hughes 2000). Gentrification was now a fact, and those who were not part of the creativity or property bandwagon were further marginalized, further cut off from social services, and further alienated from the street life that had been the soulful core of Harlem. Overall, the strategic nature of the EZ funding had put communities literally in the position of selling their culture and heritage—and potentially losing control over the destiny of the neighborhood.

The outcome was a familiar footprint. The use of the arts as a tool for place-based development and marketing had helped price the poor, and arguably the most authentically creative, out of the neighborhood. With the gentrification of Upper Manhattan, the island was no longer affordable for the traditional creative soul, thriving on low rents, peer stimulation, and institutional access. More than any other large urban center, Manhattan was well on its way to maximizing its creative economy, but it could no longer offer residential haven to those traditionally associated with artistic expression, let alone to any functioning member of the once-famous American middle class.

Good Jobs, Bad Jobs

The conditions for the emergence of CI policy differs from nation to nation, as do the resources available in any country, region, or city to fit the policy requirements. At the very least, the quicksilver international adoption of the concept can be taken as evidence of the ready globalization of ideas about governance and citizenship. But there are other, more tangible reasons for its mercurial career: its core relationship with the exploitation of IP; its connection, in urban development, with property revaluation; its potential for drawing marginal cultural labor into the formal, high-value economy; and the opportunity to link dynamic IT sectors with the prestige of the arts. Most mundane of all, the creative policy requisites are generally cheap to implement, involving relatively small investments on infrastructure and programs, and even smaller outlays on human capital, because the latter rely mostly on stimulating the already proven self-entre-preneurial instincts of creative workers, or on mining the latent reserves of ordinary people's creativity. The returns on these slight investments, if they are realized, promise to be substantial, even though they are more likely to be reaped from collateral, or parasitical, impacts like rising land value. In sum, it is fair to observe that all the above-mentioned attributes are familiar features of capital formation, whose managers and investors are ever on the lookout for fresh sources of value, labor, and markets.

While the rage for CI policy has sparked no end of skepticism, and even contempt, from radically minded artists and artist groups (Wallinger and Warnock 2000), the larger cultural organizations have gone along with it in general, seeing the potential for greater economic leverage, more direct access to patronage, and an expanded range of partners and clients. To the degree that the policy returns are envisaged as a high-stakes lottery—with hot tickets in the hands of those quickest to market—there are indeed likely to be some handsome winners, reinforcing the residual

Romantic concept that creativity resides in select geniuses (albeit a genius for business). The "single, big hit," as Angela McRobbie has pointed out, is the breakthrough project that lifts prospects above the exhausting micro world of multitasking and social networking and into the attention economy of key global circuits (McRobbie 2007). Yet, for most of the players, the lottery climate of sharpened risk will only accentuate the precarious nature of creative work—its endemic cycles of feast and famine—and generally reinforce the income polarization that is by now a familiar hallmark of neoliberal policymaking.

So, too, the rhetoric about taking creativity seriously has won admirers in unlikely places. For one thing, it feeds into longstanding demands for humanizing the workplace. Who would pass up the promise of inventive, mentally stimulating alternatives to the repetitive routines of assembly lines, data entry pools, and cubicle farms? A self-managed work life free from rigid supervision and conformity, where independent initiative was prized above all? For those who value this kind of flexibility, sympathetic, qualitative assessments of work life are desperately needed.

Indeed, policymakers would do us all a favor if they put aside the productivity statistics and solicited some hard analysis about what it takes to make a good creative job as opposed to generating opportunities for finding occasional "nice work."

To do so, we must first acknowledge the taint acquired by the concept of quality of work life because of its association with managerial responses, in the course of the 1970s, to the broad manifestations of the "revolt against work" earlier in the decade. In the first of a long series of management innovations designed to stimulate a jaded workforce, employers like GM introduced quality of work life (QWL) programs to inject some participation into decision-making and deliver more personal fulfillment to employees. These efforts to make work more feel-good, meaningful, and flexible also marked the onset of a long decline in job security as managers stripped away layers of protection and accountability (Fraser 2002). Just as the corporate workplace became more inclusive, free, or self-actualizing for employees, it became less just and equal in its provision of guarantees. This rule applied to production workers, reorganized into teams exercising a degree of decision-making around their modules; white-collar employees, encouraged to be self-directing in their work applications; and the ever-growing army of temps and freelancers. In most cases, the managerial program to sell liberation from drudgery was accompanied by the introduction of risk, uncertainty, and nonstandard work arrangements. As far as corporate conduct went, it is fair to say that one hand gave while the other took.

This two-handed tendency reached its apotheosis in the New Economy profile of the free agent, when the youthful (and youth-minded) were urged to break out of the cage of organizational work and go it alone as self-fashioning operatives, outside the HR umbrella of benefits, pensions, and steady merit increases (Pink 2001). By this time, large corporations were being scorned by management gurus for their bureaucratic stagnancy, just as their work rules, hierarchies, and rituals were condemned for stifling initiative and creativity. The small, entrepreneurial start-up was hailed as a superior species, likely to adapt more quickly and evolve further in a volatile business environment (Henwood 2003). These were the roots of the much-hyped face-off between the Old Economy and New Economy in the 1990s. The former was seen as risk averse, coddling employees with a sheltering raft of benefits and securities, and smothering their sense of individual purpose and potential. The latter was risk-tolerant and tested employees with an endurance course of challenges and edgy feats, rewarding their mettle and initiative with jackpot-style wealth.

The legacy of this face-off is clearly visible in the breathless business rhetoric applied to the creative economy, often portrayed as the rule-defying guarantor of the next bonanza. Temporarily homeless in the wake of the dot-com bust, corporate lip service to the powers of creativity quickly found a new haven. Because the creative industries are, in part, a construction of the state's making—policymakers routinely lump together a motley range of professions under that rubric—this rhetoric has also become the language of government, at federal, regional, and city levels. In place of exhortations to think outside the box addressed to systems analysts, sales agents, project managers, and other corporate echelons, politicians and policymakers now proclaim that the future of wealth generation might lie in the hands of bona fide creative practitioners.

As before, however, the condition of entry into the new high-stakes lottery is to leave your safety gear at the door; only the most spunky, agile, and dauntless will prevail. This narrative is little more than an updated version of social Darwinism, but when phrased seductively, it is sufficiently appealing to those who are up for the game. The unpredictable tempo of effort required of the players is far removed from the gospel of steady, hard work and thrifty gain glorified in the nineteenth-century work ethic (Rodgers 1978). It is more like the survivor challenge of an action video game, where skills, sense of timing, and general alertness to the main chance enables the protagonist to fend off threats and claim the prize. Neoliberalism has succeeded wherever its advocates have preached the existential charge of this kind of work ethic and the virtues of being liberated from the fetters of company rules, managerial surveillance, and formal regularity.

The low-wage equivalent is a different kind of limbo. For one thing, the rungs on the ladder of social mobility have almost all been knocked out, so there is little chance of upward advancement for those in the vast majority of low-end service jobs. While there are no prizes to be won, the prospect of being trapped in a dead-end job further lubricates the labor markets in employment sectors already characterized by churning. High rates of turnover, stagnant wage levels, and chronic disloyalty are characteristic features of a formal service economy where intermittent work is more and more the norm. Casualization, driven home by market deregulation and neoliberal labor reform, has placed an ever-growing portion of the work force on temporary and/or part-time contracts. In the informal economy, migrant workers occupy more and more of the vital positions; without their contingent labor, the whole machinery of services would grind to a halt. While their rights and work conditions are degraded by off-the-books employment, their freedom of movement is also prized. Migrancy is what guarantees their remittances, their transnational options, and their ability to evade state scrutiny and capitalist discipline.

To insist, today, on the quality of work life is certainly to call attention to these precarious conditions, both in high-end and low-income occupational sectors. But the ingredients of that demand require careful consideration. It would be a mistake, for example, to simply hark back to the diet of security enjoyed by a significant slice of white collars and core manufacturing workers in the Fordist era. It should be remembered that the revolt against work was, in part, a protest against organized labor's championship of members' security at all costs (Zerzan 1974). Because the labor chieftains of the era so obviously disciplined the workforce, delivering strike-free productivity in return for a steady regimen of wage and benefit increases, dissident workers had to resort to independent action to call attention to the inhumanity of an industrial work process that treated them like cogs in a machine.

So, too, it would be misguided to dismiss the hunger for free agency as a mere product of market ideology; the flexibility it delivers is a response to an authentic demand for a life not dictated by the cruel grind of excessively managed work. Autonomy is a critical goal, and while its attainment is more approachable for the self-employed, there is no reason why it cannot be nurtured inside organizations where the work process has been genuinely humanized. In either case, the ability of individuals to take pleasure in freely applying their skills depends on a just social environment that supports and rewards all the players and does not stigmatize those who fail to land the most glittering prizes.

Contrary to market dogma, basic cultural freedoms can only be secured through regulation. Media deregulation, to take one example, has resulted in a drastic reduction in the range and quality of available public opinion. (Conversely, the power of the dominant culture industry corporations depends on the lavish support of several government agencies.) Regulation of creative work need not stifle innovation (another marketeer myth); rather, it just formalizes its conditions of possibility, outlawing the kind of hypercompetitive environment where most of the players turn into losers, along with all those declared unfit for the contest, for reasons of age, attitude, or unreadiness. Consequently, it is harmful to perpetuate the belief that innovation is solely the product of preternaturally endowed individuals. All creative work is the result of shared knowledge and labor; originality springs forth not from the forehead of geniuses but from ideas pooled by communities of peers and fellow travelers. Aesthetic champions are good at what they do, but we cannot promote the assumption that they alone should be beneficiaries of a winner-takes-all culture of creativity centered on the acquisition of intellectual property.

Among the other resident dogmas of the creative life is the longstanding equation with suffering—as expressed in the stereotype of the struggling artist—but there is no natural connection there. Personal sacrifice is not a precondition of creativity, though widespread acceptance, or internalization, of this credo is surely one of the reasons why employees in the creative sectors tolerate long hours, discounted compensation, and extreme life pressure in return for their shot at a gratifying work product. Few things are more damaging to the quality of work life than this belief that physical and psychic hardship is the living proof of valuable mental innovation. When compared to the ravages of heavy industrial labor, this may appear to be a lesser threat to public health, but its lionization in cutting-edge sectors like high-tech design has accelerated its spread to an alarming range of workplaces and occupations.

In place of this debilitating ethos, we need to see creative work as a basic human right, or entitlement, of the workforce. Of course, to speak of rights and entitlements is also to speak of obligations on the part of the state and employers. Yet most governments and firms have been with-drawing from their obligations for over two decades now through a combination of (a) welfare provision reforms and weakened labor regulation on the part of the state and (b) subcontracting, offshore outsourcing, and benefit offloading on the part of corporations. The latest retreat has been in the privatization of and/or reduced state payments to pension plans, even to the most securely employed. As a result, the ever-aging retiree population in advanced economies will soon be joining the ranks of their precarious brethren in the developing world (Blackburn 2007a, 2007b).

In contrast to the neoliberal drift in Anglophone countries, some of the European social democracies have created new forms of welfare to protect workers in flexible labor markets. Termed *flexicurity*, the policy was pioneered in Denmark and the Netherlands in the 1990s and was subsequently adopted in other Nordic countries (Wilthagen, Tros, and van Lieshout 2004; Jørgensen and Madsen 2007). On the one hand, flexicurity acknowledges the advantages of flexibility for employers and so it deregulates the labor market, making it easier to hire and fire. On the other hand, it increases the pay and welfare entitlements of flex workers over time and it strengthens welfare provisions for those who are temporarily unemployed in flexible labor markets. The overall emphasis is on employment security—as opposed to job security—and, in its strongest versions, flexicurity preserves and extends core labor rights to all workers, regardless of contractual status. The successes of these strategies in reducing unemployment, sustaining growth, and reinforcing the state's obligations to protect and secure the most vulnerable members of the workforce have encouraged European legislators to take them up as a goal for the European Union as a whole (European Expert Group 2007; Cazes and Nespova 2007). No such entitlements apply to migrants, however, and as their numbers swell, the low end of the workforce is more and more awash with unregulated forms of flexploitation.

In the informal sector, where the perils of low-wage contingency are most acute, considerations of the quality of work life have to start with the demand for dignity and respect, and end with full recognition of equal rights and status. As for creativity, it does not take much for employers to enhance and reward workers' inherent impulse to extract meaning and pleasure from their idiosyncratic completion of the most routine tasks. Workers are ingenious about accomplishing such tasks—flipping burgers, performing checkout, cleaning apartments—with flair and individual panache (Kelley 1994). Moreover, a good deal of creativity on the job is devoted to employee resistance, in the form of slowdowns, sabotage, pilfering, and other petty acts that enable workers to win back from their employer some control over their time and effort. These everyday skirmishes give meaning to workplace routines and help sustain self-esteem.

In addition, the heated debate about immigration shows how a society's scrutiny of work connects to larger considerations of its quality of life. Advocates for immigrant rights argue that a host society owes a standard of life to all those who contribute their labor, and that this obligation should extend to family members, young and old, who may not be employed. Labor, in this paradigm, is a pathway to quality of life in general, as envisaged through the basic provisions available to regularized citizen-residents: access to public education and other services, social housing, labor and civil rights, living wages, social security, and, above all, amnesty for the undocumented. So, too, the moral clarity of this claim is buttressed by knowledge, on the part of workers and recipients of the services alike, about the essential utility of the jobs in question. Unlike vast slices of the economy that are devoted to producing unnecessary, and environmentally unsustainable, goods and services, immigrant-dominated sectors like agriculture, food processing and preparation, construction, trucking, textiles, and cleaning and janitorial services are rightly considered indispensable. In this respect, they satisfy some of the requirements of "useful toil" set by William Morris, the nineteenth-century British patron saint of quality work. In many others, however, they fall into the category of "prison-torment," which he reserved for burdensome toil that should be done only intermittently, for short periods of work time, and by a greater variety of individuals from different classes (1886).

The Cross-Class Challenge

Anti-precarity groups in Europe have made formative efforts to link student movements, service-worker struggles, immigrant rights, and proto-militancy in the new media sectors. The goal has clearly been to build a cross-class alliance—drawn from sectors of the service class, the creative class, and the knowledge class—that students and trade unions would come to support (Foti 2006; Mabrouki 2004). On the face of it, an alliance of farmworkers, domestics, Web designers, and adjunct teachers, just to cite some representative occupations, is an unlikely prospect. It is easier to imagine on paper, as a theoretically plausible construct, than as a flesh-

and-blood coalition in broad agreement on strategies and goals. For one thing, there is a sizeable imbalance in the social capital enjoyed by this range of constituents. Those in occupations with the most cachet would almost inevitably expect to be front and center; over time, they would surely sideline the others (Vishmidt 2005; Mitropoulos 2005; Shukaitis 2007).

So, too, many members of this putative coalition would like nothing more than to have the security of full-time work, with benefits thrown in. Others surely prefer the intermittent life and take part-time employment so that they can finance other interests, like acting, writing, travel, or recreation. Even among low-end service workers, there are reasons to favor flexibility over being locked into dead-end jobs. In this respect, precarity is unevenly experienced across this spectrum of employees, because contingent work arrangements are imposed on some and self-elected by others. In and of itself, precarity cannot be thought of as a common target, but rather as a zone of contestation among competing versions of flexibility in labor markets. Ideally, workers should be free to choose their own level of flexibility in a socially regulated environment where the consequences of such choices are protected against unwanted risk and degradation. Of course, the chances of realizing that ideal are much greater in regions where employment protection is still a matter for active governance, like the European Union. In countries with no tradition of social democracy, like the United States, the prospects are dimmer.

So, too, there appears to be a gulf between the highly individualizing ethos of creative and knowledge workers and the tolerance, even enthusiasm, for traditional, collective action on the part of service workers. Immigrant organizing in campaigns like the Service Employees International Union's Justice for Janitors has played a large, ongoing role in renovating the trade union movement in cities like Los Angeles (Milkman 2006) and may yet transform the U.S. labor movement as a whole. On May Day 2006, the mass mobilizations against repressive anti-immigrant legislation in a host of U.S. cities were a tribute to the power of collective protest and organization. These developments prove that "organizing the unorganizable" was not only feasible, but that the results far exceeded expectations and have given fresh hope to trade unions in decline (Milkman and Voss 2004). Indeed, the unions that are growing are the ones for whom immigrants are the backbone of organizing drives (Bacon 2007).

By that same token, creative and cognitive workers are often assumed to be incapable of organizing on account of their self-directed mentality.

Yet wherever they have turned to union-based action, they have been surprised to find how quickly a common sense of purpose emerges. Recent North American examples include the IT workers in the WashTech union (an affiliate of the Communication Workers of America), who have become a lobbying force on a range of industrial legislation; the adjuncts and graduate teachers who jumpstarted the academic labor movement by organizing at the margins of the profession; and even the most recent Hollywood writers strike, whose internal resolve was buoyed by prominent support from other industry professionals. In each case, employees were organizing in the teeth of industrial cultures that promote an individualist professional ethos, and each discovered that a little solidarity can go a long way. Not long after the writers strike was resolved, actors joined janitors and longshoremen in a twenty-eight-mile march, billed as "Hollywood to the Docks," as part of an LA campaign for good jobs.

Cross-class coalitions are not easy to envisage, let alone build, but there are instructive precedents (Rose 2000). One salient international example was the Popular Front of the 1930s. In the American version, the ecumenical spirit of the CIO challenged the craft exclusiveness of the AFL trade unions through its advocacy of organizing the unskilled alongside the skilled (Denning 1998). Creative-sector unions from the fields of entertainment, journalism, and the arts made common cause with proletarian interests and reached out to the unemployed, displaced, and destitute. The Popular Front was an antifascist formation, officially promoted by the Comintern and its fellow travelers from 1935, but it would not have been popular if the foundation for its cross-class relationships had not been laid in the years before. That the liberal version, at least—often termed the New Deal coalition—endured for several decades is a testament to the strength of these alliances.

The backdrop for the Popular Front was, of course, the Great Depression, whose widespread propagation of precarity was the result of a *collapse* of capitalist control. By contrast, today's precarity is, in large part, an *exercise* of capitalist control. Postindustrial capitalism thrives on actively disorganizing employment and socio-economic life in general so that it can profit from vulnerability, instability, and desperation. Some thinkers allied with the Italian autonomist school see this disorganization as an advantage, because it harbors the potential for pushing creative labor outside the orbit of disciplining institutions such as the state or the trade unions. One of the slogans that captures this tendency is the "self-organizing precariat." It speaks not only to the oppositional side of the free agent mentality lionized by liberation capitalists, but also to the longstanding traditions of grassroots democracy in worker movements.

In some respects, this autonomous tendency may be interpreted as a clear rejection of the path taken by New Left advocates who pursued the "long march through the institutions" from the early 1970s onward, with the goal of reforming the culture of power from the inside. But today's institutional boundaries are no longer demarcated so cleanly. The centrifugal impact of deregulation has shifted some of the balance of power toward *outlying* locations: renegade centers of accumulation in the economy (hedge funds, or start-ups gone global like Google, eBay, and Starbucks); civil society and outside-the-Beltway organizations in politics and welfare delivery (evangelical churches, human rights NGOs, corporate social responsibility divisions); and, in the sphere of ideology, the myriad "alternative" sites of cultural and informational activity that populate the busy landscape of attention. So, too, work has been increasingly distributed from sites of production to the realm of consumption and social networking. The outside is no longer extraneous, marginal, or peripheral to the real decision-making centers. Increasingly it is where the action is located and where attention to building resistance and solidarity might be best directed. The recent focusing of policymakers' interest in a heretofore-fringe sector like creative labor can quite rightly be seen as part of that story.

2

China's Next Cultural Revolution?

NEWLY INDUSTRIALIZED COUNTRIES in the global South have not been slow to try out the creative industries policy model. Some of the more advanced ones are fast losing their manufacturing-sector jobs to mainland China and Southeast Asia, and they need higher-skill services to add value to their economies. But such is the heady economic growth of the PRC itself that its Chinese Communist Party (CCP) policymakers are already competing in the creativity stakes, hoping to drive the national economy toward the most prized IP fruit at the top of the value chain by maximizing its monopoly on the extensive Chinese language market, both at home and overseas. In the surest sign that the PRC had joined the ranks of such nations, CI policy was introduced into the eleventh five-year plans of several cities in the course of 2006: Beijing, Shanghai, Chongqing, Nanjing, Shentzen, Qingdao, and Tianjin. In the space of only a few years of hothouse consideration, the party bureaucracy had accepted, albeit cautiously, the CI concept and had fashioned policies to support its development (Zhang 2007).

In his keynote speech to the CCP's seventeenth National Congress in the fall of 2007, Chinese president Hu Jintao referred to the industrial policy, noting that "culture has become a more and more important source of national cohesion and creativity and a factor of growing significance in the competition in overall national strength" (Hu 2007). Shortly thereafter, the UN's Committee for Trade and Development (UNCTAD) released the results of a survey on the creative economy undertaken by a high-level panel commissioned by the secretary general. By 2005, data showed that the international trade in creative goods and services had ballooned to $445 billion, with an annual growth rate of 8.7 percent over the previous five years. China, to the surprise of many, had ascended to the top of the list of exporters; its 2005 exports were estimated at $61.4 billion, more than twice the volume of second-placed Italy, at $28 billion, and if Hong Kong's numbers were added, the total would be $89.1 billion. In ten years, the PRC's creative exports had jumped 233 percent from their 1995 level at $18.4 billion (UNCTAD 2008). While these numbers were impressive (and were duly trumpeted by the national press), the lion's share reflected the impact of offshore outsourcing. For example, these estimates would include a fashion product by a French designer that happened to be made in China. UNCTAD had declined the challenge of figuring out how to quantify export products whose design was of domestic origin solely. In China's case those numbers would be much smaller, reflecting the more sober reality of its longstanding cultural trade deficit.

The British Council (an unabashed leader in the CI policy export field, and an influential presence in that sector in China) defines a state in transition like China as "one which has moved beyond the development stage but is still unable to protect intellectual property rights in creative goods and services." To say the least, leading IP exporters like the United Kingdom have a vested interest in seeing Chinese authorities enforce IP rights protection in that nation's transition to a mature market economy. The British Council is more ambivalent about the prospect of aiding the transition from a labor-intensive "Made in China" economy to an innovation-based "Created in China" economy with firm domestic control over patents and IP rights. Nonetheless, this is the direction of the PRC's breakneck growth, and it is fully backed by a powerful, centralized state authority firmly committed to a policy of techno-nationalism that has its origins, well before the reform era, in Mao's nation-building decades.

Up until recently, this nationalist drive has been fully apparent in high-tech sectors. National innovation campaigns in the 1990s saw the establishment of a wave of science and technology parks: companies, with large-scale capitalization, financed both by the state and private overseas investors, were offered generous aid and tax protection to locate there; and foreign expertise and industrial knowledge was closely courted. Now that party officials have given the green light to the softer creative domains, it remains to be seen whether the smaller, free-spirited enterprises that are the crucible of idea innovation will flourish in the same settings, or indeed whether they will be allowed to operate with the kind of independent verve associated with liberal polities that have a more fully developed civil society. Innovation in technology is one thing, but the spirit of cultural invention is a different beast entirely in a country where tight control is exercised over expressive content in general. Indeed, after the slow but sure liberalization of the Jiang era, the first several years of Hu Jintao's leadership saw an incremental clampdown on the range of open expression permitted in the PRC's public sphere. For many party bureaucrats, unleashing such unpredictable energies is tantamount to opening Pandora's box.

As long as the creative sector behaves like other industries, then Beijing's rulers have nothing to worry about. They can be groomed and promoted, in tried-and-true fashion, to absorb foreign investment and foreign ideas, to exploit low production costs, and to incubate national champions in the domestic market and the export field. Because of the gargantuan Chinese language market and because national and regional economic managers are experienced in overseeing a broad spread of industrial operations, from low-level assembly chains to skill-intensive R&D, it is likely that the creative sector will be offered the same treatment as the high-tech sector. It may well achieve similar records of growth on the basis of a cheap labor supply and business-friendly state incentives. If those are the outcomes, they may well affect livelihoods everywhere, further destabilizing the already precarious world of creative jobs. We have seen this in the case of manufacturing and white-collar services. Is there any reason to think that creative occupations will be different?

The answer to that question is not entirely resolved. The gingerly approach of China's leadership cadres to CI policy reflects a complex understanding of the political role of culture and creative expression. In the PRC, arguably more than in any other country where CI policy has been developed, the debate among elites about this area of development draws on conflicting experiences and histories of the post-1949 period. The Cultural Revolution is officially remembered as a period when too much primacy was given to culture and the economy was put in the passenger's seat. Consequently, in the reform era, the watchful officials who oversee all media content have been accustomed to subordinate cultural policy to the goals of developing a market economy. Most of China's leadership cadre since the philosophically colorful rule of Mao have been sober engineers, sworn to uphold the techno-nationalist project. The pro-democracy movement that precipitated the Tiananmen Square crackdown in 1989 was understood to have been fomented by the explosion of "culture fever" (*wenhua re*) in the mid-1980s, when the status of the intelligentsia was fully rehabilitated, the spectrum of publication outlets broadened, and a new openness in the range of expression appeared. These consequences served to remind nervous party elites of the volatile power that could be unleashed by shifts in cultural policy. As a result, the more conservative tendency since Tiananmen has been to restrict, and thereby relegate, policy about culture to the traditional domain of heritage arts and crafts.

Notwithstanding the impact of the Tiananmen crackdown, market fever had already encroached on cultural domains, and official calls for reform were sure to follow. Beginning in the 1990s, and in tandem with the push for managerial efficiency and accountability, the state-owned media, publishing, and other information institutions were encouraged to reform themselves along lines similar to manufacturing industries. The managers of select media organs were told to prepare themselves for the withdrawal of state subsidies. Ultimately, all but the most vital propaganda organs would have to "stand on their own feet." In 2001, the fourth session of the ninth National People's Congress ratified the concept of cultural industries (*wenhua chanye*) almost a decade after the term began to appear in internal party documents (Keane 2007). Since then, the ongoing partial commercialization of state-owned media and the Internet sector has been a politically fraught endeavor, with the government playing a highly visible game of cat and mouse with commentators who push the envelope of permissible expression in regional newspapers or on the Web.

Compared to the Internet's porous universe of information and opinion, the prospect of stable project teams of entrepreneurial individuals chasing the dragon of commercial success is a source of comfort to party officials. After all, the individual appetite for self-expression is widely tolerated as long as it avoids politically sensitive topics. Indeed, if this appetite can be steered into well-regulated industrial channels, then government elites can well imagine that they will have contained an otherwise volatile source of public dissidence. This *utilitarian* view differs sharply from the post-Liberation CCP view of culture as a *pedagogical* tool, and even more so from the induction of culture into a revolutionary political program of the kind that flourished in late Maoism.

But political expediency is not the primary reason for climbing aboard the creativity bandwagon. The adoption of CI policy could not have arrived at a more relevant time for the Asian giant's economic development. China's march forward cannot be sustained unless the nation proves that it can generate its own intellectual property by jumpstarting homegrown innovation rather than imitating or adapting foreign inventions. Speaking at a national conference on innovation in January 2006, Premier Wen Jiabao declared that "independent innovation" (*zizhu chuangxin*) would be at the core of the country's development strategy over the next fifteen years. Nothing less than the honor of the nation was at stake.

Boosters are never slow to mention China's historical achievements in the field of invention: the roll call includes gunpowder, writing, paper, printing, the magnetic compass, the abacus, the crossbow, cast iron, the pendulum, the seismometer, mines, differential gear, rockets, and textile-spinning technology (Needham 1986). In the reform era, the government can point to fledgling industrial design achievements in hard technology such as automobiles, white goods, and semiconductors, while global firms in a whole range of advanced industries have rushed to set up offshore R&D centers, employing local talent, in Shanghai and Beijing's free trade zones. It is highly likely that officials will continue to incubate design-based enterprises in the high-skill manufacturing of hardware and soft-ware while channeling knowledge transfers from the global corporations into the path of native start-ups.

But these initiatives are all in catch-up industries, where foreign pro-ducers are more and more accustomed to using China as a cheap offshore base, as evidenced in the 2005 UNCTAD export figures. While this off-shoring model pertains to old media sectors like television and film, where Korean, Japanese, and Taiwanese product is shot and assembled cheaply on the mainland, new media presents a cleaner slate. China's designers are expected to enjoy a running start in sectors like video gaming, advanced computer graphics, and multimedia communications—fields directly rel-evant to consumer electronics and digital media. Online gaming (officially recognized as a competitive sport by the state's sports agency) and mobile media (in a country with several hundred million cell phone users) are already proven as dynamic sectors, and government backing in these areas is readily available.

Moreover, the potential for promoting cultural nationalism, and lim-iting foreign content, through the use of Chinese theming is bottomless. The utility of this formula was on full view in the historical pageant of the opening ceremonies at the Beijing Olympic Games in 2008. Producers of multimedia genres can draw on a reservoir of several centuries of myth and legend as well as courtly and folk narratives that are well-known ele-ments of the national patrimony. The popular hunger for costume histori-cal drama, in the PRC and in East Asian countries generally, more or less guarantees a vast market to monopolize, while the successes of Chinese film epics in the West may prove substantial enough in the long term to work their way into the DNA of Hollywood. Indeed, Disney is only the first of the entertainment majors to recognize the potential of selling Chi-nese-themed product back to the China market. *The Secret of the Magic Gourd*, its first venture into localized Chinese content, and its first non-Hollywood film ever, was released in the PRC in May 2007. The company plans to develop a series of Chinese Disney characters to build on the impact of *Magic Gourd*, which was based on a famous Chinese children's story.

Regardless of whether foreign producers succeed, efforts like Disney's highlight the vast commercial appeal of Chinese theming. The economic significance of the cultural heritage is now also being fully realized in China's tourism industry, where sites from the feudal past are marketed as spiritual anchors of the national culture. This emphasis has a marked political dimension and is largely the legacy of the Deng and Jiang eras, when "socialist spiritual civilization" was promoted to offset the drive toward moneymaking; this was also done to distinguish the new cultural policies from those of the Maoist era, when such monuments to the feudal past were neglected or destroyed. Restoring the people's access to China's rich traditions was endowed with a nationalist stamp that had equally been applied, albeit with more zeal, to the Cultural Revolution's anti-feudalist goal of creating modern traditions. The development of such tourist sites, along with the investments in costume drama theming, fulfills a number of government needs: growth in GDP, foreign exchange earnings, and domestic consumerism, but also a mode of citizen formation steeped in neo-Confucian sentiment.

Traditional stories and myths, reworked as safe commentary on contemporary politics, are a relatively stable commodity, easy to drop into an industrial product cycle and serve up for consumer demand. If intellectual property rights (IPR) regulation can ever be properly implemented, then this heritage domain of CI policy may have a sustainable future in the public and private sector, offering dependable employment. But what about the more idiosyncratic and unpredictable initiatives characteristic of the Western creative paradigm of originality? Can China's policymakers afford to accommodate, let alone stimulate, offbeat expression that is altogether out of step with Beijing-approved content?

Pathways to Precarity

The evidence so far suggests that the PRC's foreboding bureaucracy is more likely to be an obstacle in the path of independent creative producers, who depend on permits from a range of different industry regulators (the Ministry of Culture; State Administration of Industry and Commerce; the State Administration of Radio, Film, and Television; the Ministry of

Information Industry; and the General Administration of Press and Publication), each with its own prescriptions for a cultural field or genre (Cunningham, Keane, and Ryan 2005). This licensing system, which doubles as a mechanism of content surveillance, is particularly fraught for new (or cross-) media production, which customarily straddles several of these traditional industries. The more high-tech, the more chance producers have of qualifying under the rubric of the Ministry of Science and Technology, whose top-level mandate to back innovation generates the most fast-track results (Claydon Gescher Associates 2004). Even so, the focus there is on getting big companies publicly listed.

This macroeconomic policy of "securing the big and letting go the small," as Jing Wang observes, is a "vision contrary to that of the creative industries," and so the preferred PRC policy has been to push the SME creativity initiatives in Hong Kong with the mainland export market in mind (Wang 2004). Hong Kong's economy had long drawn on the pool of creative talent that fled from Shanghai after Liberation, and it had been earmarked by Beijing for concentrating on the kind of high-value services under whose rubric CI policy would fall. So it was there, where the influence of the UK model would also be strongest, that the first CI mapping survey was completed in 2003. While similar mapping efforts followed in the mainland, PRC statistics are notoriously elastic, no more so than in a sector like CI where hard data is difficult to come by. The most reliable has been the *Blue Book of China's Cultural Industries*, an annual report issued by the Chinese Academy of Social Sciences since 2002.

It took two decades of liberalization to wean China's state-owned enterprises off the state subsidy system of nonperforming bank loans. Many of the new CI micro-businesses postdate the era of state ownership and are being developed with a minimal number of public purse strings attached in the full expectation that they will become self-sufficient in the short term. If their start-ups fail to reach the threshold for market entry, or if they cannot secure the necessary licenses, these small creative producers will take their chances in the unauthorized gray economy where precarity and uncertainty are a way of life. No doubt, this underground economy is where the more interesting, unpredictable energies will thrive, but it is also a crucible for the worst kind of exploitation. As for the new entrants who successfully navigate the ministerial agencies, government support is short term and highly conditional not only on the commercialization of product but also on finding private investors or sponsors as soon as possible. The resulting imposition of entrepreneurial enterprise often results in unorthodox forms of investment that flaunt legality and transparency, exposing producers to chronic risk.

Though it is the world's most unionized economy (the national labor federation claims as many as 150 million members), China's trade unions are ineffective (mostly providing social services) and have only a weak foothold in the commercialized sectors where the new creativity initiatives are being launched. Mainland enforcement of labor laws and standards is notoriously feeble, and the labor markets that have formed in the most dynamic sectors of the economy are the most volatile and unstable, prone to high turnover and a chronic workplace culture of disloyalty, both on the part of employers and employees. Job-hopping has become a national pastime in a country where, only yesterday, livelihoods were guaranteed by an "iron rice bowl," and fewer and fewer workers, whether skilled or unskilled, expect their current employer to be around for very long. Moreover, it is in the high-skill sectors, where contracts include no stipulations on maximum working hours, that seventy-hour workweeks are increasingly an expectation on the job (Ross 2006a). The new focus on creative industries is being developed in the heart of this superheated, flexible work environment, where pressures from market exposure and project deadline crunches combine to inject extra anxiety into the perennially immature labor markets that plague cultural production.

Unlike "British creativity," for example, which is a recognizable global commodity with a proven historical track record, the Chinese counterpart must be labored into being in a media environment where content is still largely a state monopoly, and it must do so in the teeth of longstanding Orientalist stereotypes about the static and derivative nature of Chinese society. How creative can Chinese people be in the PRC? The anxiety of national elites about native constraints on dynamic thinking has tended to focus on perceived deficiencies in an education system heavily imbued with the Confucian ethos of learning through copying. Traditional learning in the form of repetitive drills and rote memorization is deemed conducive to an obedient citizenry and a disciplined workforce capable of following orders or replicating other cultures, but it is recognized as inadequate for stimulating original acts of creativity. Efforts to reform the system will not take effective hold until the retirement of at least one generation of teachers trained in the traditional mode, and even then they are likely to focus on select fields at elite schools. This is a far cry from the Blairites' easy populist truism that "everybody is creative." For sure, there are Chinese equivalents of the working-class characters in the film *The Full Monty* (a feel-good allegory of New Labour's CI policy), laid off and down on their luck but tapping into their latent creativity to stage their own entrepreneurial comeback. Yet they are unlikely to be lionized as "model workers" (a Maoist-era tradition now being extended to CI employees) unless they produce some credible IP. Nor is a one-party government obliged to sell the creativity paradigm to socially marginal and underemployed populations, as is the case in a democratic polity like the United Kingdom.

To ensure the market capture of IP, most of the CI activity is being placed in designated locations, mostly in industrial spaces vacated by factories that have been moved out of the cities to improve air quality. In this respect, CI policy managers are following the international CI script of establishing creative clusters. But clustering was also the model used for the science and technology parks established in the 1980s and 1990s, and to some degree it is continuous with the large-scale industrial compounds created during the era of collectivization. More important, it is a location decision that allows officials to keep a close eye on the often-maverick activities of creative workers.

The first, and most significant, of these creative clusters was established, organically, by artists who in the late 1990s took up residence in Factory 987 compound (a disused arm of the Cold War military-industrial complex) in Dashanzi, an outlying neighborhood of Beijing's Chaoyang district. Dashanzi has since flourished as a cultural district in its own right, though its proximity to the Olympic zone put its continued existence in peril. Thanks to determined resistance by its resident artists, the zone was saved from redevelopment, but by the time the 2008 Olympics opened, it was transitioning rapidly into one of the city's top upmarket tourist and lifestyle destinations. Creative industry compounds in other cities have been more consciously engineered with state funding: Tianzifang, Tonglefang, Bridge 8, Media Industry Park, M50, and Fashion Industry Park in Shanghai; Loft 49 and Tangshang 433 in Hanghzhou; and the Tank Loft in Chongqing.

By 2005, centers and institutes had been established in Shanghai (the Shanghai Creative Industry Center and, at Jiaotong University, the Cultural Industries Research and Innovation Centre) and Beijing (the State Cultural Industries Innovation and Development Research Institute). In 2006, the government approved the construction of creative industry zones in select cities with proven talent pools. These included a constellation of creative districts in Beijing; dozens of centers in Shanghai developed under the auspices of the Creative Industries Association; the

"Window of the World" zone in Nanjing; "Creation 100" in Qingdao; and further-flung outposts in technology-driven urban economies like Xian and Chengdu (Sun 2006). Investors who set up in these locations would enjoy the same kind of trade, tax, and operational incentives as in the export-processing and high-tech zones familiar from earlier phases of the reform era. Overseas investors with unrealistic expectations of fast profit will doubtless enter into the same kind of informal agreements as before: conceding technology and knowledge transfers in return for the promise of government, or market, access. In the case of the new CI sectors, however, the proximity to fresh IP will render the transfers ever more sensitive to the foreign owners, and ever more attractive to homegrown entrepreneurs and the officials who back them.

As is the case in the high-tech manufacturing sector, the labor market for industry talent is a tight one. In New York, an estimated 12 percent of workers are from the creative sector, with the figure reaching 14 percent and 15 percent in London and Tokyo, respectively; in Shanghai in 2006, however, it was estimated at only 1 percent (Li 2006). To ease the bottleneck, which accounts for a wage spiral in the region, the government announced a massive training and recruitment scheme in 2004 to produce more than a million additional "gray-collar" employees (incorporating elements of both white- and blue-collar work), a category that includes software engineers, architects, graphic artists, and industrial designers (Xinhua 2004). If Beijing succeeds in training these employees, then the current labor shortage, and the accompanying wage spiral, may come to be short-lived. But the cause of the instability does not lie simply in the lack of supply. Employeees are now as footloose as global corporations and less likely to commit to employers beyond the short term. In stunning contrast to their parents, Chinese youth who are entering the urban labor markets have been weaned in a socio-economic environment where loyalty to anything other than the family is either an anachronism or a liability. Having witnessed the shredding of securities in all aspects of their lives, Chinese of a certain age have truly seen all that was solid melt into air, and their children have been raised to believe that they must be authors of their own lives. In China, this descent into precarious circumstances has occurred within a generation and on a much more momentous scale than anywhere else.

The advent of the CI sector as a tentative object of state attention comes at a moment well before the maturing of the requisite labor market. Will this sector produce its own version of the exploitation endemic to the low-wage, labor-intensive sweatshops of South China's export-processing and assembly zones? Will the same ominous combo of demographic pressure, sky-high turnover, lax regulation, and cut-rate bidding emerge in the micro-businesses and SMEs of the creative economy? If so, then China's pivotal position in the global economy means that its creative sector, like its other industries, could set norms that will affect wages and working conditions in other parts of the world. The "China price," so feared by domestic manufacturers in OECD countries, may well come to be associated with "Created in China" just as it has been the overseas hallmark of "Made in China."

Foreign producers of digital products and services already use China's cheap labor pool for offshore operations that include rendering, animation, and modeling, along with a host of other CAD applications. This kind of contracting extends from video game producers to architectural and software firms, where the quality of the work being outsourced to mainland China is leaping up the value chain. To cite one remarkable development, Chinese youth are being paid to play online fantasy games to earn virtual currency and create avatars that can be sold to time-starved game players in affluent countries. In 2005, an estimated one hundred thousand of these "gold farmers" were toiling in China's online gaming factories, bedding down in overcrowded dormitories in remote provinces far from the CI hothouses of Shanghai and Beijing (Dibbell 2007; Barboza 2005). In this new virtual economy, where online currency and play has real exchange value, the geographical location of work has almost ceased to matter. There is no doubt, however, that offshore operations like this affect working conditions elsewhere, where managers drive down wages by threatening to transfer jobs to China. But the downward wage pressure on employees is not just being felt onshore. For most young Chinese, the pristine opportunity to work at a creative craft under their own initiative is likely to come at the cost of a high-stress work life dictated by chronic uncertainty, where self-direction morphs into self-exploitation, and voluntary mobility is a fast path to disposability.

Policymakers in China have paid even less attention to these work-life hazards than their Western counterparts have. When set beside the volume and severity of fatalities that occur daily in unsafe coal mines, the barbarism of slave labor in brick kilns, or the cruelty of sweatshop conditions in South China's export-processing factories, the problems faced by skilled gray-collar employees barely register on official state consciousness. Labor regulation tends to be governed by the three chief priorities of

Beijing's rulers—to stave off popular insurgencies, maintain GDP growth numbers, and consolidate party power. On the face of it, any labor fallout from the development of culture and creativity initiatives is not going to rate highly. Yet no one in Beijing can afford to ignore the momentous role that cultural policy played in the upheavals of the late Maoist era, or in the "culture fever" period that preceded, and, in part, fomented, the 1989 crisis in Tiananmen Square. For those currently in power, the lessons of the Cultural Revolution and Tiananmen are a reminder of the very real impact of cultural politics, and this is one of the reasons why officials have approached CI policy with so much caution.

Indeed, Michael Keane has shown how the debates that preceded official recognition of CI were contentious and multisided (2007). The concept ultimately adopted into official state nomenclature—"cultural creative industries" (*wenhua chuangyi chanye*)—was a hybrid term, carefully chosen as a compromise to reflect the distinctive development gloss—known as "Chinese characteristics"—that PRC policy puts on all paradigms that have originated elsewhere.

To understand the backdrop to this debate and the future of employment in this sector, a lengthy excursion through the Maoist era is necessary. Communist Party managers expeditiously manipulate the iconography of Mao, and evocations of the cultural policies of that era are carefully kept at bay. Because of this attention, these paradigms are no more dead in their own way than the postwar era of state cultural subsidies in the West that predated neoliberalism. Just as significant has been the influence overseas of cultural politics derived, however indirectly, from Mao's cultural policies. Prior to China's emergence as an exporter of most of the clothes in Western closets, its export of Maoism was working its way into *our* mental wardrobe. Until recently, Western intellectuals were more likely than their counterparts in Shanghai to be using Mao's cultural legacy. Understanding how that came to be will help account for the prehistory of the rise of the CI paradigm in the West, while adding depth to the understanding of its reception in the PRC.

The Turn to Culture

No one would reasonably dispute that Maoism was received in the West in a highly idealized version. Indeed, what we think of as Maoism was often far removed from how the Chinese themselves experienced the

Chairman's shifting body of doctrine, at least insofar as it came to be embodied in state-driven campaigns like collectivization, the Great Leap Forward, or the Cultural Revolution. Sometimes it is indeed more important to grasp the conditions of reception than the cogency of the doctrine itself. In the 1950s and 1960s, there was no shortage of reasons or opportunities for politicized Western youth to imagine the "Wind from the East" as a dynamic force that would help sweep away the structural rot of capitalist societies if only it were harnessed in the right way. In some respects, the dynamism they attributed to the New China was merely the inverse of Marx's concept of the "Asiatic mode of production"—a vision of static, and unproductive, feudalism stretching from Russia's eastern shore to the Arabian Sea. For its Western adept, China's "awakening" by Mao was as vibrant as the slumber of Marx's Asiatic mode of production had been profound. They were two sides of the same Orientalist coin.

Even so, the novelty of Mao's appeal to Western imaginations would soon fade for those who actually tried to follow, but were understandably bamboozled by, each new spasmodic cycle of revolt and reaction—each new factionalist crosscurrent—generated as the Cultural Revolution progressed in the late 1960s.[1] It was much easier to condense this appeal into a media-friendly image packaged for youthful consumption. In *The Dreamers*, filmmaker Bernardo Bertolucci's bittersweet 2003 paean to the events of May 1968, a protagonist speaks of Mao as a kind of genius director who was using China as a stage set for producing an epic film. Bertolucci leaves the viewers to decide whether this is a crushing self-comment on the speaker's naivety or a heady sample of the climate of the era.

Either way, his retrospective mood is broadly shared. Today, it is routinely accepted that the infatuation of Western youth with Third World icons like Mao, Che Guevara, and Ho Chi Minh was a period fancy, in tune with the first generational rush of rock star adulation. On the other hand, in the early 1990s, Rey Chow, the U.S.-based film scholar, suggested provocatively that the spirit of the Cultural Revolution was alive and well in American cultural criticism, of all places. Having grown up in Hong Kong in the 1960s, when mainland corpses occasionally washed up at the mouth of the Pearl River, she found it baffling to encounter, among U.S. academics, mental habits that she associated with the Red Guards and their patrons. Among these habits were a knee-jerk skepticism about all things Western, an instinct for moralistic prosecution, and a belief that only victims can speak truth (Chow 1993). On reflection, I think that Chow may have been right—she was writing at the height of the so-called Culture Wars—though not necessarily for the reasons she cited; it is worth examining this proposition further because it will help in understanding the historical backdrop to the emergence of CI policymaking.

A brief review of the Chinese historical context will be helpful. Mao's gradual Sinification of Marxism, summarily reflected in his break with Moscow in the early 1960s, was saluted in many parts of the world as a fresh opportunity to redeem communist ideals from the bureaucratic torpor that they had suffered under Stalinism. Mao's appetite for peasant populism and his zeal for continuous revolution from below was perceived as a stark departure from the fixed Soviet reliance on urban industrialization as directed by technical elites. This tendency struck a chord with Westerners who were turning against their own overprocessed societies, grimly administered by military-minded technocrats. So, too, Mao's focus on self-reliance, equitable regional development, and his promotion of "organic experts" arising from the ingenuity of peasant life were directly in sync with the efforts of decolonizing countries to break free not only from the old colonial powers, but also from the clientelist system maintained by Washington and Moscow. While Maoist politics enjoyed their most sustained run of influence in the Third World left, his alternative model of socialist development, pursued in the two decades before the Cultural Revolution, spoke directly to dissidents in the industrialized West who were themselves looking for alternatives to the Strangelovian death struggle of the Cold War.

In the West, this image of Mao as the anti-Soviet was increasingly preferred, largely because it was uncomplicated by his own lifelong tendency to embrace contradictions. Contrary to his foreign image as a committed pastoralist, Mao never ceased to encourage the kind of Stakhanovite productivity that came with rapid industrialization ("We must walk on two legs," he exhorted). If he neglected the treaty port cities, like Shanghai, where foreign powers enjoyed extraterritorial privileges, it was to promote urbanization elsewhere so that cities in the interior could share the benefits. So, too, his often-messianic beliefs in the revolutionary potential of the "blank" rural masses coexisted with an unyielding Leninist faith in the centralism of party leadership (Schram 2002: 395–498). Ironically, it was precisely the moment in which he appeared to depart from this faith—the confrontation with the party that generated the Cultural Revolution—that rewarded him with iconic status overseas.

If the deviation from the Soviet economic model won him foreign admirers, it was Mao's turn to culture just a few years later that really lit the prairie fires among his overseas admirers. The victory against feudalism and imperialism in 1949 and the nationalization of capitalist assets in the 1950s had transformed the economic infrastructure of China. But economic change was not enough, Mao insisted. The remnants of the old system of beliefs lived on in many sectors of society—dispossessed landlords and capitalists, petty property-owning peasants, expropriated compradores, gangsters, tenured bureaucrats, teachers, and other professionals held over from the rotten republican state. Most threatening of all, in Mao's view, were the "party people in authority, taking the capitalist road," many of whom held high policy office in government, industry, and other state institutions. In sum, the vast majority of Chinese were still inclined to shape the world according to the ideology and training of their prerevolutionary upbringing. Consequently, he concluded that the decisive battle over the direction of the Chinese revolution would be fought in the realm of ideas among those who were in a position to exert influence over the next generation.

In theory, their influence could be combated in many ways. Mao chose a particularly dramatic path—Bombard the Headquarters!—that would mobilize youthful passions. Real progress, he proclaimed, could only come about through open criticism and replacement of those whose positions in the party, educational system, and other cultural institutions still allowed them to mold the minds of youth in prerevolutionary ways. In his own fashion, and for his own purposes, Mao was declaring war on the policymakers. It is astonishing, in retrospect, to consider the enthusiasm with which students—many of them adolescent girls in middle schools—initially interpreted Mao's directive. In a culture where teachers are venerated to the point of blind obedience, the prospect of questioning their authority, never mind subjecting them to physical abuse (as happened in some instances), was a stunning violation of custom. By comparison, the radicalism of Western youth during this period was more conventional (though it took on many surprising, improvisatory forms), because it was able to draw heavily on traditions of bohemian dissent.

Even so, the example of the Cultural Revolution helped give Western students an additional rationale (I am not suggesting that it was the only one) for turning their attention toward authorities and curricula within their own schools and universities. Bombarding the headquarters and politicizing the curriculum became a rite of passage on college campuses. The net result was to inspire serial waves of reform and revisionism that are still being played out today in higher education and, as their influence filters out, in the realm of public mores itself. So, too, the theoretical implications of Mao's cultural turn appeared to complement the rising influence of Western Marxism, most visible perhaps through the teachings of the Frankfurt School. While it was undertaken for quite different purposes, Mao's critique of Soviet-style economism resonated with Western thinkers who had long questioned the determinism espoused by reflectionist theories of orthodox Marxism. Mao's new assertions about the importance of culture seemed to be on the same wavelength as those who had moved beyond the rigidity of Marx's base-superstructure relationship to develop more complex analyses of power and resistance. For reasons quite removed from the Chinese context, the institutions of culture and media—Ideological State Apparatuses, as Louis Althusser famously termed them—became targets of contention and conflict.

For Mao, it could be said that the turn to culture was entirely strategic. Up until the mid-1960s, cultural policy has been pedagogic in nature—"serving the people" meant that they had to be instructed in socialist ideals, and so all cultural products were directed to that end. In the new policy paradigm, culture was a weapon to turn against party elites who had become capitalist roaders. This shift in tendency, which launched the Cultural Revolution, was deemed necessary to defend the achievements that had been built out of the CCP takeover of state power. Immediate results were expected, after which the monumental effort to build a new kind of social personality, with new customs, habits, and daily instincts, could then be launched. In the West, the turn to culture was shaped by quite different circumstances. It came as a call to arms against the institutions that functioned to ensure consent for established authorities in society and the state. Mao's campaign was set in motion by a charismatic patriarch who had transcended state power to the degree that he could call for attacks on its citadels and bureaucratic elites. The eruption of dissent among Western youth was shaped by those who stood, at best, to take over the reins of policy and power but had no interest in accepting the job as it was defined at the time. The vast difference between these two circumstances helps, in part, to explain the subsequent divergent career of cultural politics in China and the West.

Aside from the general assault on holders of authority, many of Mao's precepts proved wildly popular in the West. Liberals born into white-skin privilege, for example, took up the practice of self-criticism, and it rapidly spread to other kinds of privilege related to class, gender, and sexuality. It became almost obligatory for speakers on certain political topics to publicly acknowledge, or apologize for, any such privilege that might have shaped their opinions. In time, self-criticism also became an important confessional ritual within the culture of popular therapy and self-help, demonstrating how effectively its resident spirit has passed into the mainstream. So, too, the Cultural Revolution's initial focus on youth action resonated with the generational politics of the so-called baby boomers. For youth especially it became "right to rebel," a rule that has proved quite resilient, even though it is probably more important, these days, in consumer branding than almost anywhere else, again displaying a considerable influence on the mainstream. Consciousness-raising, pioneered in China's rural communes during the "speaking bitterness" campaigns, had enormous influence in second-wave feminist circles, whence it spread to other social movements.[2] It is now taken for granted as a method for boosting esteem among members of socially disadvantaged groups.

Arguably, these and other Maoist principles have had a much longer, and more successful, career run in the West than in China itself. Nor was their influence confined to social movements or educational reforms. In the course of the 1990s, bucking hierarchies, questioning authority, and speaking freely became customary features of corporate culture in the knowledge and technology industries. The phenomenon of the "corporate revolutionary," touted as the ultimate "change agent" by New Economy ideologues, was a recognizable, if transfigured or co-opted, version of the instincts and energies awakened by the Cultural Revolution. As a side effect of the 1980s shareholder revolution, respect for managerial authority was steadily eroded in large firms, and layer on layer of middle management was eliminated. In place of the inflexible, vertically organized corporation there arose the ideal of the flat, decentralized organization, nimble enough to shift direction, to re-invent or re-brand itself to respond to market demands and openings. The entrepreneurial DNA of this reconditioned corporate entity was the same wonder stuff that policymakers would eventually come to see as the resident genius of the creative economy.

From Cultural Revolution to the Culture Wars

With the exception of some sectarian groups who strove to understand and defend each of the doctrinal twists and turns in Maoist policy, Western interpreters were more inclined to approach Mao's thought as a user-friendly code that they could program for their own uses. Nor was the reception of Maoism in the West very unified. In the United Kingdom, for example, where I grew up, Trotskyism was far more influential among the student and worker political vanguards. In France, the country where the broad left was most transformed by Maoism, the character of Mao- ist organizations like Vive la Révolution and Gauche Prolétarienne was most typically antiauthoritarian, antihierarchical, and, perhaps, most de- tached from events in China themselves. There, especially in Gauche Pro- létarienne, the legacies of Rousseau, Proudhon, and Sorel fundamentally shaped the context in which Maoist thought was taken up (Fields 1988; Ross, Kristin 2002).

By contrast, the American Maoist groups like the Progressive Labor Party, Revolutionary Communist Party, and the Communist Party (ML) were quite moralistic and hierarchical. Basically Leninist in their organiza- tion, their disputes tended to reflect, or refract, ongoing factional struggles in China. Where the French Maoists were more true to anarchist and lib- ertarian traditions, and thus open to cultural radicalism, their U.S. coun- terparts were often at odds with the embryonic social and cultural move- ments of the time, such as the counterculture, the women's movement, gay liberation, and race-based nationalism. Indeed, the American Maoists tended to emulate what they saw as the cultural conservatism of the pro- letariat, and so they dressed, behaved, and proselytized accordingly. Much more innovative in their interpretation of Maoism were minority nation- alist groups like the Black Panthers and their ranking cognates in Asian American, Latino, and Native American communities. Heavily under the sway of the thesis of "internal colonialism," which saw Black, Brown, and Red America as underdeveloped colonies, analogous to Third World na- tions, they had their own selective uses for the Maoist principles of self- reliance, "serving the people," culture building, and confrontational action (Kelley 2002; Jones 1998; Wei 1993).

In the United States, the strong impulse of these nationalist groups toward decentralization and community-based organization meant that neo-Maoist ideas about how to serve the people filtered out into society and became indigenized in the process, rather than remaining the exclu- sive preserve of elite intellectuals or vanguard politicos. This diffusion of ideas was much more far-reaching than the impact of the middle-class ac- tivists who went into industry as would-be factory organizers, and who were as frustrated in their efforts as many of the educated urban youth in China who were assigned to factories or sent down to the countryside. As in China, one of the ostensible goals of this direction (undertaken by

Progressive Labor faction of the SDS) was to challenge the divide between mental and manual labor. But in the U.S. case, even the theory ran aground as a result of rapid changes in the economy. From the mid-1970s, manufacturing would be hollowed out amid a long season of economic restructuring that brought immaterial labor to the fore. As a result, the traditional identities of manual workers were eroded and therefore too unstable to assert as strong vehicles for progressive politics. It was not until the 1990s, and the dissolution of the "iron rice bowl," that a similar phenomenon occurred in China where, in any case, workerism had a much more powerful hold on state policy.

In the area of education, there was a different story to tell. Largely because the Cultural Revolution disrupted the education of a whole generation, Mao acquired the reputation of being *against* education, just as he is now remembered as being against intellectuals. Both views are inexact. When colleges were reopened after the first two years of the Cultural Revolution, they were subject to a ferment of institutional reform, affecting everything from governance of schools and universities to the preparation of textbooks and curricula. For the first time, they enrolled workers and peasants. In general, these changes were guided by Mao's elevation of praxis over abstraction—a priority that put him in the company of John Dewey (whose work he knew) and Paolo Freire. While little was achieved in the West that approached the record of the worker universities, the reform of secondary and tertiary education was greatly inspired by efforts to make curricula, teaching methods, and access to learning less mandarin in nature—that is, more comprehensible, practical, and accountable to socially denied communities.

More consequential yet was the entry of a generation of activists into the teaching ranks. In contrast to the cadres who went into the factories, there is the more enduring example of student protesters who made a career choice to take "the long march through the institutions" by entering the superstructural professions—mostly in education, law, and the arts—most important to the framing of national cultures. It was in the humanistic sectors of these professions (and often in their most elite locations) that neo-Maoist impulses ran their course over the next three decades, long outliving the fervor of the Cultural Revolution. Widespread in these circles was the influence of French intellectuals like Jean-Paul Sartre, Louis Althusser, Roland Barthes, and Michel Foucault, each of whom had experienced transformative encounters with Maoism. The impact of their ideas was especially pronounced among Anglo-American cultural critics, many of whom absorbed Gallicized Maoist slogans and precepts as if they were holy writ—an incredible phenomenon in retrospect.

Over the same period of time, the neo-Maoism that had filtered into community life (as I described earlier) emerged in the form of demands and claims for cultural recognition on behalf of a broad spectrum of causes and identities—ethnic, racial, feminist, and lesbian and gay. Arguably, it was in these separate but cognate movements that a hundred flowers bloomed most freely. While these demands' impact on legislation was measured, often taking decades to work its way through courts, it was more immediately felt in education reform. Again, it was cultural critics, along with historians and value-oriented social scientists, who were in the forefront of pushing these claims in their efforts to revise both standard and advanced textbooks. The result was a far-reaching overhaul of the semiofficial canons that formed the core of the national culture. New schools of queer criticism, eco-criticism, and postcolonial criticism sprang up to join those that had already substantially altered the elite white, male profile of the history books. Textbooks had to be rewritten, time after time, in order to do justice to each new paradigm of identity. The process is far from exhausted and, in some unforeseen respects, has come to reflect the spirit (though hardly the letter) of Mao's idea of an "uninterrupted revolution." As with most of the Western examples I have cited here, their Maoist pedigree was only one of several genealogical influences, but I would argue that its significance has been consistently overlooked. In the self-conviction of their champions that these superstructural reforms were radical, even revolutionary, in character, it is difficult not to detect the traces of a neo-Maoist ardor.

In like fashion, some critics saw the implementation of these reformist efforts as a destructive exercise redolent of the dark side of the Great Proletarian Cultural Revolution. The resulting backlash came from sectors of the left as well as the right. Beginning in the late 1980s, American neoconservatives launched the so-called Culture Wars, which consumed a hefty portion of national political attention through the mid-1990s (Hunter 1992; Messer-Davidow 1993; Graff 1992; Newfield and Strickland 1995). In forcing a debate about the moral character of the nation, the Culture Wars offered a model for conservatives in other countries to emulate. This hullabaloo took the initial form of controversy about which literary texts were being taught in schools and universities. It quickly spread, however, to almost every corner of social and cultural life, fueling media-saturated debates about the politics of affirmative action, sexual harassment, gay and lesbian rights, and all forms of workplace discrimination. In doing so, the conflict moved from the realm of cultural politics, played out in educational institutions, to the broader arena of what I have called cultural justice, where citizenly rights to recognition involved state action (Ross 1998).

Because some of the revisionist ideas made for sensational press copy, crude caricatures of the reformers circulated widely in the media. So, too, some voices on the left registered their own opposition to what conservatives, in a strategic coup, had renamed "political correctness" (Gitlin 1995; Tomasky 1996; Rorty 1999; Sleeper 1997). Most of these voices belonged to white males of the New Left generation, and so the roots of their reaction were widely attributed to a sense of resentment at being dispossessed or displaced from traditionally entitled roles as left champions (Lott 2006; Kelley 1998; Duggan 2003). Their genre of nostalgia differed from that of the conservative cultural warriors, but they often shared the tendency to castigate youth for their shortsighted political passions. In some anecdotal accounts, revisionist students were indeed characterized as latter-day Red Guards, pulsing with self-righteous zeal as they hounded hapless teachers for committing the politically incorrect sin du jour.

But if you could get beyond all the finger-pointing and lazy misrepresentations, the Culture Wars posed a weighty question to consider for those on the left. Did all this fierce appetite for cultural reform siphon off energies that might otherwise have been devoted to social and economic justice? Or was it a necessary fellow traveler? Those who saw it as a costly distraction argued that politics of the superstructural sort was not sufficiently rooted in economic soil to change the lives of working people. Besides, they surmised, culture divides people more than it unites them. On the other side, advocates insisted that social and cultural identity is a condition of equal access to income, health, education, free association, housing, and employment. According to this view, many people feel this right to cultural recognition almost as strongly as they seek the benefits of a social wage, and so it must be seen as a necessary supplement to the basic human rights pertaining to freedom of speech, assembly, and conscience.

No matter which side you came down on (and, even as a pragmatic matter, it seems to me impossible and, at the very least, a waste of time to try to separate these different strands of politics), the whole debate had a Maoist flavor. Under different circumstances, Chinese critics of the Cultural Revolution made similar arguments ("You can't eat culture") while its defenders insisted that their revolution should not be reduced to *economism*—the code word to describe politics waged exclusively on behalf of wage hikes or increased material benefits.[3]

Making Common Sense

Over time, it has become customary to view the strategic use of the Culture Wars by conservatives as an example of how the left's tactics had been appropriated by the other side (Bérubé 1994; Grossberg 1992). In this scenario, it was the right-wing cultural warriors who were the real Maoists because they were political utilitarians, canny enough to exploit cultural issues for their own political ends, as the Republican Party did with considerable success from the early 1990s onward. Had not Mao, after all, used culture to launch a rectification campaign (which subsequently got out hand) aimed at repossessing the commanding heights of the CCP?

However persuasive, the sophistry of this analysis depends on the belief that Mao's attitude to culture was entirely instrumental—in other words, that it was simply a useful vehicle for a power play and not an authentic effort to deepen the revolution. For those fixated on the desecration of cultural artifacts or the persecution of cultural workers that marred the Cultural Revolution, the late Mao's position on culture was no different from that of prominent Nazis like Hermann Göring. But the "culture" in the Cultural Revolution was not primarily about books, artists, or ancient temples. On the face of it, Maoist cultural policy had more to do with the transformation of subjectivity and the reeducation of citizens. If the endeavor to forge a new kind of mental and social personality was to succeed, the "bourgeois within" would have to be supplanted. Mao's antecedents, in this regard, were thinkers like Gramsci himself, who had analyzed the goal of socialism to create "a new type of man." Che Guevara, among Mao's contemporaries, had a similar vision of the "new socialist man." If the Mao-inspired path of cultural politics in the West was influenced at all by this epic aspiration, it has had a more restricted environment in which to do its work, and the methods adopted along the way have been more discrete and syncretic by far. Yet the spirit of the overall project of personal transformation has not only been retained, but it has also been extended into areas beyond that of exorcizing the bourgeois— such as expunging the patriarch, exposing the heteronormative, and abolishing white privilege.

With the exception of those propelled by utopian strains of Christian fundamentalism (perhaps the purest form of identity politics), the culture warriors on the right had no comparable designs; they were driven, first and foremost, by reaction and bigotry. The same cannot be said of the proponents of neoliberalism, who had to inculcate the general population with the fiercely competitive ethos of enterprise culture (Comaroff and Comaroff 2001; Harvey 2005). Here was a challenge worthy of Gramsci, Mao, and Guevara. Neoliberal Man had to be ushered into being in an environment where, for most people, Margaret Thatcher's axiom that "there is no such thing as society" was a largely alien concept. Even for the so-called children of Thatcher (and Reagan and Deng), the reeducation of their sentiments was an arduous campaign that had to be waged in day in, day out, until neoliberal instincts like self-optimization were regarded as common sense. In a market civilization like the United States, the neoliberal outlook was always an easier sell, but in the United Kingdom, it took the best part of two decades to establish entrepreneurialism as a default outlook on daily life, and in many European social democracies, this mentality is still castigated as an "Anglo-Saxon" belief system.

For reasons that have been described in these pages, CI policy was, in part, an outgrowth of that campaign. Insofar as its exponents view individuals as contestants in a game, competing with their mental assets for the prize of IP value, the policies are a faithful expression of the neoliberal outlook. Just as important, however, the expedient view of culture as a resource to be maximized promised a way out of the Culture Wars, a path beyond the messy political brawl about who gets to shape the national culture. In the successor CI paradigm of creativity, whoever contributes the most GDP wins—an ethos not unlike Deng Xiaoping's pragmatic dictum that "it doesn't matter whether cat is black or white so long as it catches the mouse." Last but not least, CI policy seemed to rise above the fractious face-off between economism and culturalism. Culture was now seen as something you could eat, quite literally. No longer simply a "way of life," in the famous definition bestowed by Raymond Williams on the school of cultural studies, culture was a livelihood that could be sustained if you played by the market rules and seized your chances.

Despite Deng's gradualist policy of "crossing the river by groping for stones," the neoliberal shift to marketization has been more much more pronounced in China than in Western countries. Certainly, the Chinese people had become accustomed to heeding the state's shifts in direction, but the outcome of liberalization has been much more uneven, and intentionally so, given the CCP's policy of developing some regions, populations, and sectors well before others. But while CI policy has been introduced in line with market imperatives, officials are far from persuaded that the concept brings with it no baggage from the Culture Wars, whether those fought overseas or in China itself during the Cultural Revolution. That is why the policy, in part, is one of selective quarantine and not wholesale endorsement or exposure. It is one thing for the government to acknowledge, perhaps even hail, the overseas successes of Chinese film or Chinese art (the target of a buying frenzy by international collectors in the last few years), but unlimited domestic consumption of these same products is not encouraged, any more than consumption of foreign films, whose import is still limited annually to twenty in number. Most party cadres would prefer that the CI policy of sending culture to the market be concentrated in the export field, lest the ghosts of the past, buried in a very shallow grave, make an unwelcome return.

3

The Olympic Goose That Lays the Golden Egg

CI POLICYMAKING CANNOT survive without a regular intake of statistics, and so it was only a matter of time before Chinese officialdom's own addiction to issuing numbers came up with the goods. In January 2007, the Beijing Municipal Bureau of Statistics announced that the cultural and creative industries accounted for 10.2 percent of the city's 2005 GDP, while figures for the first eleven months of 2006 showed an 18.7 percent growth over a year earlier, outpacing all other sectors in the municipality's roaring economy. A few months earlier, at the Shanghai International Creative Industry Expo, it was announced that China had become the world's third-largest exporter of creative products and services. The state's media outlets trumpeted both data sets to back claims that the government's newly formulated CI policies were bearing fruit in a sector described as "the huge profit cake of the 21st century" (*People's Daily* 2006a, 2006b).

The accuracy of these numbers, like all PRC statistics, was dubious at best. Regardless, in the countdown to the 2008 Beijing Olympics, data that suggested great leaps forward in CI development would come thick and fast. Readiness for the mother of all mega-events had long been designated as the criterion by which the rest of the world would finally reckon with the results of China's reforms. Indeed, no event would showcase China's creative industry initiative more visibly than the opening and closing ceremonies of the games in August 2008. The justly spectacular History Scroll (covering five thousand years) that formed the centerpiece of the ceremonies was crafted to dramatize the traditional cornerstones of China's claim to be a world power in creativity: calligraphy, martial arts, opera, acrobatics, dance, costumery, and painting, along with prominent technical inventions such as paper and printing.

Notably, the filmmaker Zhang Yimou was entrusted with overall direction of these events. Zhang, a master of the Chinese epic form, and the most internationally visible of the country's filmmakers, had the right credentials for the job. Banned and censored in the early part of his career, he more than anyone else could demonstrate that China's rulers had put aside their distrust of the creative spirit and placed their confidence in a future more palatable to liberal societies. Because not a few commentators had likened the award of the games to Beijing to the Berlin Olympics of 1936, Zhang's participation was inevitably compared with that of "Hitler's filmmaker," Leni Riefenstahl.

The Olympics is a far different beast today than it was in 1960s, let alone the 1930s when Riefenstahl was called to national duty. Before the 1970s, the contest to host the games was primarily symbolic in nature, and hosting was more a matter of national pride than the mammoth economic undertaking it is today. In the past two decades, global mega-events have emerged as the opportunities of choice for city managers to promote and stimulate neoliberal urban development, and so the process of bidding for and hosting the games has become ever more consequential (Roche 2000). The potential for image enhancement, large-scale physical improvement, and high-value job creation proves irresistible for politicians, while investors and speculators see a golden opportunity to pocket vast sums of public money.

Over that same period of time, the pressure to compete with other cities and regions in a flexible global economy has become a prime characteristic of urban policymaking. As a result, the competitive process of Olympic bidding is a showcase for how cities are encouraged to see their future in the world trade in goods and services (Brenner and Theodore 2002; Scott 2001; Leitner and Sheppard 1998). With each round of bidding, the price of entry is raised. These days, winners have to persuade the International Olympic Committee (IOC) that its bestowal of the games will result in an epic contribution to social progress. As for the contests themselves, the games are far removed from being the simple embodiment of the ideal of pure competition—their respective medal tallies are a more accurate reflection of national GDP distributions than anything else.

Beijing's 2008 Olympic bid, which culminated in the IOC Moscow meeting of July 31, 2001, was widely castigated on account of the PRC's record of human rights violations. In addition, there were severe doubts that the games, which are increasingly a showcase for green policymaking, could be staged in a city with such appalling air quality. Yet the 2008 event, it was commonly held, should go to a developing country, and the opportunity to promote China's further integration into the global, capitalist economy was too momentous to pass over. In addition, the Olympic-related development of China's capital city would better the living conditions of the region's vast population, thereby fulfilling the increasingly grandiose humanitarian requirements of the Olympic mission. It did not harm Beijing's bid that the mayor of Toronto, its chief rival, had made an extremely racist comment while on a goodwill trip to win the support of African IOC members: "Why the hell do I want to go to a place like Mombasa? . . . I just see myself in a pot of boiling water with all these natives dancing around me" (Cohen 2001).

The contest was increasingly a lopsided choice between the two entirely different urban entities of Beijing and Toronto (Paris ran a distant third), and so the bidding process was less revealing than it might have been. Nor did Beijing's zealous record of post-bid preparation bear comparison with any previous efforts. In 2005, the IOC had to implore city managers to slow down construction to avoid incurring vast maintenance expenses if the infrastructure were to be completed well before the events. This was the first time that a host city had been asked to delay its venue construction, and it occurred amid an astronomical twenty-billion-dollar urban improvement undertaking. So, too, the ancillary events staged to anticipate the games registered a new high in scale and innovation. Five lavishly funded Olympics Culture Festivals were executed from 2003 to 2007, cementing the importance of the event to CI development in the city.

Last but not least, Beijing far outpaced other host cities in the number of poor residents evicted to make way for venues and supporting infrastructure. A June 2007 report from the Center for Housing Rights and Evictions estimated that as many as 1.5 million residents would be displaced to make way for the games, more than twice the previous record of 720,000, held by Seoul in 1988 (Center for Housing Rights 2007). (These numbers match the official, and more widely publicized, population displacement caused by the building of the Three Gorges Dam.) Notably, however, the Dashanzi cultural cluster in Chaoyang was left largely untouched, thanks in part to the development-friendly appeal of resident artists. Its existence had been threatened in the years following 2001, but its economic success in boosting adjacent property values and generating added cultural cachet to the city's new Central Business District (also in Chaoyang) saved it from the wrecking ball.

If the nonpareil case of Beijing stood on its own, the next contest—to secure the 2012 Olympic Games—cried out for comparative analysis. In the final round, New York was pitted unsuccessfully against London (with Paris, again, a distant third) in a textbook case of interurban rivalry. This time, both cities had a similar wealth of resources to draw on, and each could boast of its preeminent status as an affluent global city of the first rank. The playing field, from the outset, appeared to be more level, and so any comparison promised to offer some useful lessons about how some groups use cities to compete with each other—or, more accurately, how they seek to turn public money over to private hands.

Atlantic Urbanity

It has become commonplace to speak of cities competing against one another, but this is loose talk. It is always more accurate to say that distinct city elites, rather than cities themselves, are the relevant actors in the locational competition for such things as resources, investment, talent, status, or attention. Yet, in the case of London and New York, each metropolis hosts separate and distinct global city functions, and so it is unlikely that their more advanced economic sectors have to compete in the same niches or from anything like the same bases of positional advantage. Furthermore, from the vantage point of the world's most socially and economically denied populations, London and New York are simply complementary poles of the North Atlantic axis that has more or less dominated world trade and geopolitics in the modern period, and most recently according to the "Anglo-Saxon" model of neoliberalism. Why then distinguish between fractions of capital that retain some kind of nominal loyalty to a specific postal code in either city? Their combined power to subordinate vast regions of the globe has been sustained for so long that fraternal cooperation among their financial gentry has arguably been much more consequential than any transatlantic rivalry.[1]

Yet urbanists can hardly rest easy with such an indiscriminating view of the geography of power (even if such an approach offers substantial moral gratification), nor can they afford to throw out curiosity with the bathwater of neoliberalism. There is too much to be learned about urbanism from comparative changes in the scale of place making in these two metropolitan centers. Like it or not, the future of modernity is still being hammered out on the uneven surfaces of their transatlantic anvil, and a profile of that future is as likely to emerge from proof of rivalrous differentiation as from the one-size-fits-all template that critics often want to see as the stock trait of globalization.

That London won and New York lost the 2012 bid is not all that significant from a political perspective. If the contest had occurred immediately after 9/11, Gotham may well have monopolized the sympathy vote. Because another leading contender, Madrid, also represented a nation from the original "coalition of the willing," the globally unpopular war in Iraq was not a likely factor in the coordination of international sentiment around the decision.[2] Who could say that Paris, for long the contest favorite, was being punished for the French government's notable dissent any more than London was being rewarded for Messrs. Blair and Brown's eager prosecution of the Bush administration's war effort? Such conjecture is nourished by, if it is not an inevitable by-product of, the national typologies thrown up by the Olympian model of competing nations, both in the bidding and in the games itself.

Much more significant, at least for the purposes of this book, is what the bids revealed about the cultures of policymaking in London and New York, and *the overlap of governmental will and capital formation* that has shaped these respective cultures. Consider the statements made by their respective mayors after the announcement of the result in June 2005. Ken Livingstone's declaration—"When we began this bidding process, very few people believed that we could win, but London's renaissance has overcome all the obstacles"—spoke to the quasi-ideological drive that lay behind the London bid. It was a drive that began with Livingstone's nemesis, Margaret Thatcher, and was now being consummated, in the monumental regeneration of East London, under a leader, Tony Blair, with whom the mayor had made his peace. By contrast, she argued that Mike Bloomberg's post-bid observation was a blunt but nonchalant assessment of New York City's distance from the regional authority upstate in Albany and the federal authority in Washington: "What we tried to say was, this is New York. We've never tried to be anything other than what we are" (Zinser 2005).

Always ready to supply the ideological edge that Bloomberg abhors, the Manhattan Institute (the right-wing think tank responsible for shaping former mayor Rudy Giuliani's urban policies) weighed in with a diagnostic editorial in its house organ, *City Journal*: "America's dynamic private-sector economy—even in an overtaxed place like New York—is at a natural disadvantage to incubate a successful Olympics bid, by comparison with the economies of the four European cities that competed with Gotham for the games. And that's a good thing." The "top-down, centrally planned economies of Europe," editorialist Nicole Gelinas continued, have produced a citizenry that "meekly submitted to the proposed physical and economic remaking of their communities by their local and national Olympic planners." By contrast, she argued, New Yorkers instinctively favor a private-sector economy in which "economic development starts at the bottom, with private investment at the local level, not at the top, with federal dollars." The elite planning and fiscal packaging of the bid was such an affront to Gothamites that "the IOC found that New York had the lowest level of local public support of the five competitors." Nonetheless, Gelinas's editorial took the occasion to lambast the city's own "cradle-to-grave welfare state." The maintenance of this thoroughly un-American arrangement requires the collection of more "local tax revenues than the four competing European cities combined," and generates, she noted, a municipal debt "which eclipses the city's operating revenues" through its "Olympic-sized government spending—but without the Olympics" (Gelinas 2006).

For the sake of symmetry, consider the following response to the London triumph from one of that city's left-wing publications. Writing in *Red Pepper*, a magazine known for its opposition to New Labour, Oscar Reyes surveyed the aftermath of Athens 2004, "where almost all of the 36 purpose-built Olympic venues now lie empty," and where the chief legacy has been "the destruction of public spaces, a massively increased security apparatus, and a huge public debt." Athens, he noted, like many other venues, underwent an Olympics-led regeneration "that displaces poverty rather than redistributing wealth," and, notwithstanding the mayor's promises of a "lasting and sustainable legacy," London 2012 will blaze a "trail of privatization" unlikely to deliver an alternative outcome. Reyes ran through the list of ills associated with the games: a mammoth debt burden; the widespread displacement of low-income populations; a corresponding displacement of traditional, skilled working-class jobs; the diversion of funding from community to elite sports; expedient flouting of planning laws; offloading of vacant buildings on to corporate investors; and the militarization of public space around the games, beefed up by new anti-terror legislation ("Long after the TV cameras have moved on, the CCTV would still be watching") (Reyes 2005).

The readers of *City Journal* and *Red Pepper* are not likely to agree on much, but the interurban competition to land the Olympics appears to be a common butt of contention on either end of the political spectrum. In the face of such opprobrium, why would anyone want to play host, and what does the heated race to do so tell us about urban policy in these target cities?

Common Ground

The degree to which London and New York have been subject, historically, to the same urban and economic transformations is quite remarkable. Both cities have morphed from being their nation's largest manufacturing centers (with the world's largest concentrations of the garment industry, and with a similar spread of social stratification) into global cities with FIRE (finance, insurance, real estate)—and ICE (information, culture, education)—based cores tied to their respective, and often interlinked, roles in the international economy. In the process, their inner-city populations have been hit hard by waves of deindustrialization, outmigration to suburbs, disinvestment, and the erosion of social provisioning. These blows were followed by select patterns of spatial and economic development, aimed at promoting advanced sectors, and accompanied by rising inequality and class polarization across the metropolitan areas as a whole (Fainstein, Gordon, and Harloe 1992). The geography of this polarization was most evident in the class quartering of high-wage professional service workers and a steady immigrant stream of low-income service workers, often from the same offshore locations where these cities' routine jobs in manufacturing had been shipped.

In both cases, the regeneration of preexisting financial sectors was pivotal to the changes. The City, in London, which historically never had a great impact on the metropolitan economy, was able to build on its preference for, and experience with, overseas investment to seize the prized midway niche (between North America and Asia) for financial traffic. New York's financial sector, at a handy distance from the federal government, was always much more embedded in the city's fabric through its investments and influence on local governance. As a result, its reorientation, after the 1975 fiscal crisis, toward the global economy was arguably more wrenching. The physical monuments to these changes—Battery Park City/World Financial Center/World Trade Center in New York, and the Canary Wharf/Docklands development in London—spoke volumes about the earth-moving powers made available to the most globally oriented fractions of capital. While some of each city's finance houses and producer service firms do compete for business on an interurban basis, the London and New York sectors specialize in different functions—the City in international currency, commodity trading, and insurance, and Wall Street in equity trading and corporate finance—and so they tend to be linked through cross-border networks (Sassen

1991; Abrahamson 2004). Both metropolitan economies are much more dependent on the finance industry than was the case only two decades ago.

Governance structures are another matter; in this area, the differences are more starkly apparent. New York City's municipal authority is notoriously weak and dependent on a Republican-dominated state senate in Albany that routinely underserves the city's needs. As for federal support, Gotham was the fattest beneficiary of the New Deal decades and was therefore the first to be starved when Washington began to close off its grant pipeline in the 1970s. In the post-federal era, when cities have been forced to cultivate private entrepreneurial activity, there is much nostalgia for the spoiling life of the 1930s when all levels of power—Tammany, La Guardia, FDR—were synchronized, like the jackpot signs on a slot machine. Notwithstanding the patterns of class, gender, and racial discrimination built into planner Robert Moses's empire of public works, the memory of a time when such large-scale feats were possible is still an omnipresent feature of the city planner's professional imagination. Indeed, many advocates of the Olympic bid cited this memory, declaring that the games—a likely magnet for federal and state dollars—would be a chance to think and act big in ways that New York had not enjoyed for several decades. A similar sentiment was echoed, though for more self-serving reasons, by signature architects in leading design firms, headquartered in a city where they are seldom given license to ply the most virtuoso aspects of their trade.

To fill the power vacuum left by the federal pullout, government and investor elites have turned to public development corporations and urban development corporations, administered by developer-friendly boards, to push through regeneration schemes of dubious public benefit. The ideology of growth is seldom questioned, especially if it shows a clear path to high-value tax revenue, but large development projects can be blocked by effective community coalitions. Indeed, significant community opposition to the proposed West Side stadium over the Hudson Yards helped to founder the Olympic bid. The worst defeat of the first Bloomberg administration, the stadium was ultimately done in by an Albany power move, underlining, once again, the vulnerability of the city's municipal authority. The lesson was reprised in his second administration when Albany sabotaged the mayor's effort to introduce a congestion pricing plan modeled after London's successful policy of charging autos entering the central city.

Because it is the seat of national administration, London has never en-joyed very much home rule, and its limited autonomy in this sphere is eas-ily subject to countermanding by the party in power, especially when there are sharp ideological differences, as was the case in Thatcher's outright ab-olition of the Greater London Council in the 1980s. While the Southeast generally, and Outer London specifically, was the beneficiary of select re-gional promotion under her administrations, Thatcher squeezed the inner city more directly and more effectively than her American counterparts could do in New York. Subsequently, the promise that New Labour would not fail London became a cornerstone of Blairite policymaking. The ve-hicles for regeneration—urban development corporations—and the end result—surefire gentrification—were not, however, appreciably different from the Thatcherite formula.

By far the biggest shift in the orientation of London's governance has come from the impact of European integration. Economically, the city's institutions compete now in a single market that is more like the size of the continental market in the United States, while interurban competi-tion with counterparts in other European cities has arguably reformatted the geopolitical mentality of the insular British more than that of other member states. The Parisian resolve to edge out London by building the Île-de-France metropolitan region into Europe's dominant global city—the grandest of the "grand projets"—was a subtext of the heat generated by the Olympic bidding. That President Chirac resorted to archaic insults about British food on the eve of the IOC decision, and that France sub-sequently decided not to bid again for several years, is indicative of how sordid and zero-sum the competitive game has become.

This was a far cry, indeed, from the hugely popular *Jeux Sans Fron-tières* television escapades of the 1960s and 1970s (initiated by Charles de Gaulle himself), in which provincial European towns competed against one another in carnivalesque games designed to humble rather than glo-rify the contenders. This early, innocent expression of ecumenical EU spirit has been largely superseded by a territorial imagination dominated by the emergence of the competition state (Brenner 2005). The resulting tendency of national governments to selectively target globally integrated cities and regions for investment rather than promote equity in growth has been mitigated to some degree by supranational EU social welfare initiatives, but it has become an idée fixe nonetheless of national policy-makers that they should groom only the most likely hit makers (Leitner and Sheppard 1999). Indeed, the Olympic bid process highlighted this tendency among the three primary EU contenders, who were convinced they were competing only against one another. The IOC rotates its gift of the games among the world's eligible continental regions, and it was informally understood that 2012 was Europe's year.

The New York Bid

To make Manhattan the center of New York City's Olympic bid was against all political and planning rationality. It also went against the historical grain. There had been no effort to win a world-scale event for the borough of Manhattan since 1892, when the city made a disastrous bid for the World's Fair to commemorate the four-hundredth anniversary of Columbus's voyages. By contrast, the borough of Queens had hosted two culturally important World's Fairs in 1939 and 1964. The earlier event was especially significant for urban planners, not only because of the physical reclamation of Flushing Meadows, but also because the unifying theme— building the City of Tomorrow—was a frank promotion of the freeway-busy world favored by Robert Moses, the architect of both events. Flushing, Queens, was also the site of the city's most serious Olympic bid in 1984, coming in a close second behind Los Angeles.

Even so, support for a bid has been increasingly *de rigeur* for every New York mayor since the 1960s, reflecting the institutionalization of a general culture of global bidding. The campaign to center the 2012 bid in Manhattan was initiated by an investment adviser, Daniel Doctoroff, who became Bloomberg's deputy mayor after his nonprofit organization, NYC2012, secured sizeable donations from many of the city's major corporations. The clout afforded by a City Hall position with power over the city's economic development decisions enabled Doctoroff to line up contributions from every leading sector with a significant interest in the development plans for the Olympic bid—corporations, real estate groups, labor unions, and construction firms, among others. The conflict of interest between his obsession to land the games and his duties as deputy mayor was officially overlooked, and so corporate leaders looking for concessions from City Hall knew they could bring home the goods by talking Olympics with Doctoroff (Robbins 2005). So, too, the infrastructural plan for the Olympic bid offered something to every borough: an equestrian center atop the old Fresh Kills landfill in Staten Island; an aquatics center on the Brooklyn waterfront; a velodrome in the South

Bronx; an Olympic village by the East River in Queens; and a boxing center in Harlem.

With the boroughs bought off, and the corporate kingpins already lined up behind Doctoroff to make a killing, the icing on the cake was supposed to be the Olympic Square complex on the far West Side of Manhattan. It would be the cornerstone for the long-awaited redevelopment of the island's largest remaining chunk of neglected real estate, almost twenty blocks running south from the Javits Convention Center, and four mega-blocks running east to Madison Square Garden. The centerpiece West Side stadium was slated to be built on a platform over the Hudson rail yards as the new home for the NFL's New York Jets, currently sharing the New York Giants' stadium in New Jersey. Financing for the proposed $2.2 billion stadium (the most expensive in the world) included projected public funding of at least $600 million, which at that time promised to be the largest public subsidy offered to any professional sports team. But it was this subsidy from the city and state that proved to be the Achilles' heel of the entire Olympic bid. Despite a gargantuan effort on the part of City Hall to line up political support and popular opinion, approval for state money was denied by the bipartisan agreement of top Albany legislators just one month before the final IOC decision. Without the guarantee for the stadium's financing, the bid was doomed, and the mayor's effort to drum up an alternative—a site in Queens (Queens again!) for a new stadium for MLB's New York Mets—came too late to be seriously considered.

Why did such a routine part of the mega-event solicitation process prove to be its undoing? To answer this question requires a brief foray into the cockamamie world of stadium-based urban policy. The definitive history of stadium politics is itself a venerable one that remains to be written. It ranges from the "bread and circuses" utilization of Roman amphitheaters to the "homeless shelter" of the Louisiana Superdome, from Hitler's adoption of the Nuremberg Stadium to Pinochet's use of the National Stadium in Santiago. The most recent U.S. contribution to that history is especially painful for urbanists to contemplate.

For much of the 1980s and 1990s, American cities, from the most depressed to the most flush, were urged to mortgage their fiscal futures to the construction of stadiums for leading sports franchises. Indeed, it became almost obligatory for image-conscious municipalities to host a major league team as evidence of their status as comeback or renaissance cities. Politicians in second- and third-tier cities like Baltimore, Cleveland,

Indianapolis, Jacksonville, Memphis, Charlotte, and St. Louis were especially vulnerable to the threat of losing face if they did not participate in
the resource-draining competition for sports-franchise prestige. Touted by
urban policy consultants as a viable development strategy based around
sports tourism, the practice of luring away a coveted name, or saving a
struggling home-based franchise, was a surefire recipe for interurban competition with negative-sum, rather than zero-sum, results—even the winners were habitually left with massive public debt burdens (Delaney and
Eckstein 2003). By 1997, half the owners of the nation's 115 major professional sports franchises had succeeded in persuading municipalities to fun-
nel public funding into new or renovated facilities (Cagan and deMause
1998: 29). At a time when funding in the public sphere had slowed to a
trickle, this spectacle of corporate welfare (all the franchises are privately
owned) was especially obscene. In describing the phenomenon, Bob Herbert, the *New York Times* columnist, coined the memorable term *ball pork*
(1998).

Scholars who analyzed the craze for taxpayer-funded stadiums consistently demonstrated that there were no returns to be had on the public
investments. An extensive survey by the Heartland Institute of forty-eight
cities over thirty years showed that "professional sports teams generally
have [had] no significant impact on a metropolitan economy" (Baade
1994) and, in many cases, have generated grievous economic damage.
Rosentraub looked at private-sector payrolls for all U.S. counties with at
least three hundred thousand residents and found that only 0.6 percent
of jobs were associated with professional sports teams (1997). The rosy
job creation forecast by chamber of commerce consultants usually turns
out to be in temporary construction work or in low-wage service-sector
jobs. Nor is there any evidence that the presence of stadiums entice any
businesses to relocate in the vicinity. Where the developments do exhibit
a bounce in economic activity, it is usually revenue displaced from somewhere else in the metro region (Zimbalist 2003).

Despite the overwhelming evidence, and in the face of repeated public testimony at legislative hearings from the scholars (Zimbalist, Noll,
Baade, and Rosentraub) who have undertaken the studies, the stadium
projects continue to win approval, while owners continue to extract tax
abatements and renovation subsidies, habitually fleeing for sweetheart
deals elsewhere, and leaving their erstwhile hosts with white elephants and
decades of debt service. Of course, there are some cultural benefits that
cannot be calculated. The romance of top-class sports and the elevation

of community identity and pride are factors that play into popular support for the projects, but they have increasingly turned sour as stadiums are perceived as being built for elite consumption, top-heavy with luxury box suites for the politicians and corporate lions who approved the deals. All things considered, stadium-based development policy is probably the most egregious example of the iniquities of the "urban growth machine," as it was first defined by Harvey Molotch and elaborated by many in his wake (Molotch 1976; Logan and Molotch 1987; Jonas and Wilson 1999). Wherever the ideology of growth is accepted as common sense, elite coalitions are able to leverage local government powers to harvest profits at the expense of their counterparts in competing cities. Study after study shows that growth costs much more than it adds to the tax base, and yet politicians can no more question growth than they can afford to be seen as laggards in the competition to beggar their neighborly rivals.

In the case of stadium development, the competition is controlled and ordained by the cartel structure of American sports leagues, which limits the number of franchises in any regional market, creating artificial scarcity from which owners profit royally. The MLB, in particular, enjoys an antitrust exemption dating to the 1920s, but the NHL, NBA, and NFL all exercise monopolistic powers in their respective markets and prohibit municipal ownership of teams. Critics of the monopolies generally rest their case on arguments for authentic competition in a genuinely free market—that is, there should be more teams and more leagues, each with their chance to compete. Yet the interurban rivalry over sports franchises is not qualitatively different from similar contests for investment and jobs in which cities squander badly needed public funds. It is simply more visible, though the details are rarely transparent.

Consider the first, and the most emotionally laden, example of a sports owner fleeing town. When Walter O'Malley moved the Brooklyn Dodgers to Los Angeles in 1958, it was a grievous affront to a community for whom the team was a key expression of its urban political culture. Yet the flight of the Dodgers was a harbinger of what would become a familiar pattern of corporate conduct. In the wake of deindustrialization, any firm that could muster a credible threat to leave town was likely to be rewarded with tax abatements and other lavish subsidies. As part of the bidding game, land and cash incentives have depleted the resources available to municipal services. It is a game played by every major firm in New York's finance sector and, to some degree, by owners of its sports teams (two of which, the Giants and Jets, actually did forsake the city for New Jersey).

The most prominent single practitioner has been George Steinbrenner, hardball owner of the MLB's New York Yankees since 1973, who convinced the city to pay top dollar for major renovations of the "House That Ruth Built." His demands on successive mayors have been unrelenting. The mawkish spectacle of Steinbrenner pleading poverty and threatening to move the nation's most successful sports team to New Jersey has been part of the New York way of life for several decades. In 2001, he finally persuaded die-hard Yankees fan Mayor Giuliani to pledge half the cost of a new eight-hundred-million-dollar facility, slotted for the same location as Bloomberg's West Side stadium. Any decision to shower public subsidies on Steinbrenner would be unpopular, and, by that time, the economic rationality of stadium-based urban policy was being questioned nationwide. A month later, the newly elected Bloomberg called a halt to public financing for sports stadiums only to reverse his policy when the Olympic bid needed its centerpiece.

Outrage at the hypocrisy surrounding the reversal, and at the audacity of a mayor trying to play stadium politics in the heart of Manhattan (hitherto immune to the policy disease), unquestionably fed into strong community sentiment against the West Side stadium. When set inside the context of the Olympic bid, what resulted was a clear disjunct between the *regional* and the *global* scale of interurban politics. A policy imbroglio that had a peculiarly local, or subnational, dimension severely damaged a properly global project in the nation's most global city. A dogged community coalition sprang up to combat the plans, and it was assisted by a strange bedfellow, the sports capitalist James Dolan, who owns Madison Square Garden and the NBA's New York Knicks, both threatened by the proximity of the West Side stadium and the projected arrival of the New Jersey Nets in Brooklyn. Dolan warred with Bloomberg through a multimillion-dollar advertising campaign carried by Cablevision, another Dolan family property. The construction unions, cheered by the prospect of jobs, joined forces with Bloomberg and warred with neighborhood activists.[3] The mortal blow was delivered by Sheldon Silver, speaker of the state assembly in Albany and elected representative of Lower Manhattan, whose nominal reason for shelving the state funding for the stadium was that rebuilding the World Trade Center site would be further sidelined by fiscal attention to Olympic construction. Efforts to remedy the disaster of 9/11, which had generated much of the emotional drive behind the Olympic bid, stood to suffer, ironically, from a success in the 2012 contest.

Last but not least, the proposed public financing for the stadium violated what had become the customary American tradition of funding the Olympics through private channels. After the publicly financed 1976 Montreal Games left taxpayers with a billion-dollar debt, no city wanted to bear the fiscal burden of the 1984 event (astonishingly, more than fifty cities entered the competition for 2008). Los Angeles picked up the ball, and its Olympics—profitably staged without a cent of taxpayer funding—proved to be the IOC's wet dream. The American follow-up, in Atlanta in 1996, turned into something much more messy. The city was eventually cut out of all planning and decision-making but was still forced to pony up several hundred million dollars in the course of the games (Ruitheiser 1996: 231). After Atlanta, the IOC decreed that the host city, or national government, had to accept ultimate fiscal responsibility, even if the backing and conception for the events were private affairs (Preuss 2004). The brouhaha over the West Side stadium put a wrench in the works because it came too early in the process. Compromising the bid itself with a public-money debacle upset the preferred American formula, whereby private capital gets a risk-free shot at harvesting profits from development, while the state stands ready to bail the investors out if their business model misses the mark.

The London Bid

European traditions of state intervention made a significant difference to the bids of the other finalists—London, Paris, Madrid, and Moscow. Though each of the bids was planned with a public-private mix (as the games had been in Barcelona, Seoul, Sydney, Athens, and even Beijing), they would all have the full backing of the national state. Indeed, national leaders, including members of the British and Spanish royal families, participated in the bidding process in a way that was conspicuously absent from the New York bid. Jacques Chirac was a visible player, but George W. Bush was nowhere to be seen.

Nor did the Europeans have to contend with the sticky legacy of interurban stadium swindling. While they are increasingly controlled by concentrations of power among the elite clubs, the European soccer leagues do not operate on a regional franchise model. London, for example, has had several teams competing regularly in the Premiership since its inception. Consequently, stadium financing is not a significant feature of interurban competition. Nonetheless, traditional intercity rivalries in the United Kingdom have been affected by the steady marketization of the sport, the corporate reorganization of clubs into publicly listed entities, and the powerful fiscal pull of global media markets. So, too, regional fan rivalries have not been immune to the uneven impact of neoliberal development policy. In the Thatcher and Major years, it became quite common, for example, for London fans to taunt supporters of Liverpool and Manchester teams about the lack of employment prospects in their depressed northern cities. Even so, the abundance of clubs enjoying a loyal, local fan base as well as meritocratic access to open league and cup competition militates against the more corrosive forms of promotional boosterism favored by urban entrepreneurialism. There is no better example of this than the bittersweet inversion of self-esteem loyally touted by the Millwall FC supporters' chant: "No one likes us, we don't care" (Robson 2002).

But that is not to say that stadium politics was an insignificant factor in the London bid. For example, if the timing had been different, it might have made fiscal sense to reconfigure the new national stadium at Wembley as an Olympic centerpiece. Wembley had hosted the 1948 games, and the new facility had lavish, top-level backing as the most expensive stadium ever built, not to mention a physical dimension that allowed for the obligatory Gaul bashing ("twice the size of the Stade de France," according to the brochure of its building authority). Even so, its imperial origins and its later resonance as a landmark of Little Englandism bespoke a kind of nationalism that was at odds with the Blairite push for regional and global leadership. Planned initially as a tower to outdo Eiffel's effort in Paris, it was eventually built as the Empire Stadium, centerpiece of the 1924 British Empire Exhibition, and its use as the imperial show grounds is irredeemably associated with Virginia Woolf's remarkable, meteorologically inspired vision, set forth in her essay "Thunder at Wembley":

> Dust swirls down the avenues, hisses and hurries like erected cobras round the corners. Pagodas are dissolving in dust. Ferro-concrete is fallible. Colonies are perishing and dispersing in a spray of inconceivable beauty and terror which some malignant power illuminates. Ash and violet are the colours of its decay. From every quarter human beings come flying—clergymen, school children, invalids in bath-chairs. They fly with outstretched arms, and a vast sound of wailing rolls before them, but there is neither confusion nor dismay. Humanity is

rushing to destruction, but humanity is accepting its doom. . . . The Empire is perishing; the bands are playing; the Exhibition is in ruins. For that is what comes of letting in the sky. (1989)

For all its subsequent, less vainglorious, history, the imperial association was never lost on those for whom it mattered. A neo-Jacobite version of Woolf's apocalypse inspired generations of Scottish soccer fans on their annual pilgrimages to the site, bent on the post-match mission of tearing up the turf, followed by the desecration of the imperial plaza of Trafalgar Square well into the night.

Even if Wembley had not evoked quite the wrong historical associations for New Labour, its location in the city's northwestern suburban settlements would have ruled it out of consideration as an Olympic centerpiece. Instead, the bid would win political support from Livingstone, and from Blair's inner circle, only when it became a vehicle for supplementing the regeneration of East London, already declared a national priority under the aegis of the mammoth Thames Gateway project. The eventual Olympic plan focused on a five-hundred-acre swathe of land around Stratford in the heart of some of the most disadvantaged areas of the United Kingdom. The largely brownfield site, in the Lower Lea Valley, ran through the four boroughs of Hackney, Waltham Forest, Tower Hamlets, and Newham (the poorest in the entire country), and it had already been slotted for revitalization, as had Stratford City itself.

The Thames Gateway scheme was the most ambitious regional regeneration plan in Europe and had been approved under Conservative rule back in the early 1990s. Its portfolio of infrastructural development included transportation (the Channel Tunnel Rail Link, a new bridge across the Thames, and other major road and rail projects), several townships with up to two hundred thousand new homes, a high-density City East with a half million residents, and a plan for the creation of tens of thousands of new jobs (Buck et al. 2002: 84–85). However controversial as Tory models of regeneration, the spirit that conceived its most visible fruits, in Docklands and Canary Wharf, had not been appreciably contested; if anything, it had been amplified by the New Labour administrations that followed. For the Thatcherite Canary Wharf project, planners were responding to the needs of blue-chip City banks and brokerages. This time around, the catalyst was the urgent need for new housing for vital service workers, like nurses and teachers, who had been squeezed out of the London property market.

The Olympic site would simply be part of this larger synchrony. Indeed many of the capital improvements for the Leaside had already been assured funding by the London Development Agency (LDA) to the tune of £250 million, irrespective of the outcome of the bid. The Olympic development would be "going with the flow," to cite the original unofficial motto of the Docklands authority. That phrase had been a perfect logo for the neoliberal times. Adopting the ecologically resonant reference to the confluence of the river, it suggested that the redevelopment of the Thames corridor was more like an organic force of nature, in tune with equally organic market forces. Subsequently, the Tory design for the city's eastward turn would be effortlessly absorbed into Livingstone's 2004 London Plan, a spatial development blueprint for the metropolis that placed all land use within a comprehensive framework of environmental sustainability. As a component of the London Plan, the Olympic site itself was proposed as an environmental showcase, creating the biggest new urban park in Europe in over two hundred years.

As part of the lavish patriotic propaganda that infused the Greater London Authority's "Back the Bid" campaign, the poverty of the local population was stressed, in large part, as a way of neutralizing criticism. How could anyone oppose a scheme that would help to counter deprivation? By contrast, in their pitch to the IOC, the London bidders tended to depict the site as derelict, suggesting that it could be developed without any messy population displacement. Naturally, Newham residents perceived this as a slight. Public sightings of "Fuck Seb Coe" graffiti (in reference to the slick, Tory Olympian who fronted the bid) were quick to follow. In addition, the bidders' depiction of East London as a vibrant multicultural center, where hundreds of languages are spoken, uncomfortably evoked the long, racialized history of perceiving, and treating, the East End as an "internal Orient."

But disdain was the least of the Eastenders' worries. Despite the bid's provisions for building in affordable housing (50 percent is mandated in the London Plan) and the promises of new jobs, very few locals were persuaded that the Olympics would not accelerate economic polarization in the region. Barcelona, Seoul, and Sydney had all seen a mercurial rise in property values in the run-up to the games, and especially near the Olympic zones themselves. Studies of the Barcelona games, officially heralded as a success, showed that prices of housing and commodities in the city were the only economic indicators that went up in the long term; after the games were over, there was no discernible increase in jobs or tourism

(Del Olmo 2004). Some degree of gentrification was virtually guaranteed. As for the promised employment, there would be an obvious disconnect between the occupational character of the service industries expanding into the area and the traditional skills of its longtime inhabitants. Even the bulge of temporary jobs in the high-tech stadium construction task would require the importation of specialized workers, as had previously been the case with the Millennium Dome construction (when only 12 percent of the jobs went to locals) (Kornblatt 2006: 16). The bulk of unskilled construction jobs would likely be taken by migrant workers from Eastern Europe who form the core of the industry labor pool today. In May 2007, a detailed report from the Center for Cities predicted a lean harvest for a project whose boosters had promised an employment bonanza: less than 8,000 pre-games jobs would be created in East London itself, while only 311 would be added after the event (Kornblatt and Nathan 2007). On the other side, the region would see the loss of over 30,000 manufacturing jobs as a result of displacement of industry (Blake 2005).

So, too, the recent regeneration schemes in the region had largely been aimed at aesthetic improvements to catch the eye of prospective investors and home buyers. They had delivered only a trickle of jobs for traditional residents (unemployment in Newham and Tower Hamlets remained as high as ever) and had seen many of those residents displaced by rents and prices only within the reach of affluent professional service workers. No one expected the outcome of the Olympic development to be much different. Apart from some strategically located home owners who looked to make a killing from selling their property, few residents anywhere near the zone foresaw tangible benefits for themselves or their communities. Moreover, in the aftermath of 2007's summer floods on other English rivers, rapid climate change merged as a clear threat to the Thames Gateway housing slated to be built on an increasingly vulnerable flood plain.

The funding formula for the games was not without its critics, either. While the £2 billion operating budget of the Olympic Organizing Committee was drawn almost entirely from the private sector, the Olympic Delivery Authority, charged with delivering the venues, infrastructure, and legacy, drew its initial financing from a £2.375 billion public-sector funding package negotiated between the government and the mayor. The bulk of these capital costs were to come from National Lottery funds. The commitment of such a large chunk of lottery revenue would undoubtedly take its toll on projects outside London, and it was unlikely that any other

East London project would be able to secure funding in the near future and for some time after 2012.

In addition, no one believed that the public-sector bill would not rise considerably, as it has done in every other Olympic city. A significant slice of the population saw little point in squandering a public fortune for two weeks of elite sports and a white elephant legacy in the sorry New Labour tradition of the Millennium Dome. Indeed, within a few months of winning the contest, senior officials estimated that the bidders had seriously underestimated construction costs and that London's games would cost twice as much to mount as the government had projected (Mathiason 2005). Livingstone's pledge that Londoners would meet the cost of any overruns in their council taxes already sounded like a political gamble gone awry. By July 2007, when a parliamentary public accounts committee lambasted the government for miscalculating costs, the price tag for the games had already tripled, to well over £9 billion and the private-sector investment—originally estimated to cover a quarter of the cost (at £738 million)—had failed to materialize (Culf 2007). By January 2008, when an additional £675 million was diverted from lottery funds (for a total of £2.2 billion) to make up for the shortfall, local authority leaders around the country reacted with fury.

Resistance to development of the site centered on the displacement of pockets of residents and the annexation of ancient Lammas Land bequeathed to the commoners of the region by Alfred the Great. These commons lands, which had carried customary use rights since pre-Roman times, were now newly prized for new housing development—affordable homes on the marshes and luxury stock on higher land (Iles 2007). However cogent and however widely shared, the opposition to the bid was steamrollered by a development consensus fully backed by several layers of government. In a way that would have been impossible in New York, local, metropolitan, and national authorities were fully aligned in their political support for the bid. Nor had such a synchrony been evident in earlier British bids on behalf of second cities: Birmingham in 1992, and Manchester in 1996 and 2000 (Cochrane, Peck, and Tickell 1996). As for the sources of popular support for the bid, they were equally numerous, not least among them a yearning to make a global impact on the sports landscape, which has been thwarted by the national record of decades of losing in so many top-flight athletic contests.

While this impressive alignment of governmental authority was necessary to stage the bid, it was not sufficient to win it. A more gripping story was required—at least if the argument that every games is simply bought by a cocktail of bribery and supplication is left aside (Jennings and Simson 1992). As Phil Cohen has described, the London bid met the IOC requirement that a modern Olympics should serve as a unique catalyst for some significant act of social and technical progress, such as the regeneration of an unloved metropolitan region, or else as a means of bringing a newly industrializing contender—the case of Beijing in 2008—more fully into the orbit of the global capitalist economy (Cohen 2005). In order to qualify, the story line has to be dramatic enough to generate oodles of press before and after the event. London's proposed Olympic zone was being folded into a grand project with truly regional, rather than merely civic, ambitions, and it therefore had the potential for a narrative with epic dimensions. Indeed, London 2012 is likely to be seen as a significant opportunity for the IOC to raise the bar. To be successful, future bids may now have to emulate this grand regional scale of aspirational development.

Bidding for What?

Like so many of the aesthetic arts, the Olympics are no longer simply promoted as an abstract ideal of individual accomplishment, or as an expression of the humanistic (and quasi-religious) principles of Olympism. Increasingly, the games have to be approached and appreciated as a top-level social service—an instrument of urban advancement that will somehow benefit the world at large. It would be difficult to come up with a profile better tailored to stimulate the managerial imagination expected of global, or would-be global, cities. Indeed, the process of bidding for the Olympics is not only obligatory, but it has become the acid test of municipal health and repute. The failure of Paris in the 2012 bid was its third defeat in recent years, which occasioned a massive crise de conscience for the bureaucratic mind in that status-conscious country.

From the perspective of members of the city's growth machine, there are myriad, gilt-lined, economic opportunities afforded by staging the games, and most carry little risk that cannot be offloaded anyway onto the public purse. A wide range of city elites sees their interests mirrored in a win-win proposition (Burbank, Andranovich, and Heying 2001). All urban development associated with the bid, no matter how corrupt and self-serving, promises to be irradiated with a rosy glow. Politicians and place makers stand to see their reputation embellished by the legacy of a successful mega-event. Not least, the popular glamor of the event helps to override opposition from grassroots groups and can even blind the public to the stark estimate of how lopsided the distribution of benefits almost always turns out to be (Cashman and Hughes 1999).

For those who profit from an urban symbolic regime (as opposed to a growth regime) that feeds off image creation, the opportunities are greatest of all, but they also carry the biggest risks. Exposure of overt corruption, incidents of state repression or terror, and infrastructural catastrophes can obliterate overnight the symbolic capital accumulated over several years of careful buildup. So, too, the more that is invested in the use of the event for image boosting, the less chance that city communities will see any material improvements. All available capital will be expended on the prettification, both physical and demographic, of the Olympic footprint. This was the pattern set by Los Angeles, when the host city was kept out of the picture entirely, and Atlanta, when the city had plans to leverage some of the private funding into urban development but did not have the power to prevail.

New York's plans for 2012 involved substantial physical improvements (more than in LA or Atlanta), and most of them could have linked together into a larger story about the renovation of its waterfront. Like the Thames corridor schemes, waterfront revitalization has been ongoing for almost a decade. New York 2012 could have gone with the flow, too, but it would not have had the same heroic resonance as the Thames Gateway, nor would it have been able to muster anything like the combination of government powers to support the narrative. Structural inertia over the World Trade Center (whose destruction offered a once-in-a-generation opportunity to mount a regional plan around Lower Manhattan) was living testimony not only to the chronic conflict of powers among city, state, and federal governments, but also to the ease with which a single commercial developer—WTC leaseholder Larry Silverstein—could hold the whole congeries to ransom.

Ultimately, however, the New York bid was held hostage by a *national* interurban contest—over regional stadium politics—that was on a lesser scale than the contest between global cities required of the competition for the Olympics. As if to underline this fact, the alternate site conjured up by Mayor Bloomberg to save the bid was little more than a generic deal to build a new stadium for the Mets in Flushing next to its existing Shea Stadium. The city and the state pledged about $180 million in public financing, while the team would enjoy the use of tax-exempt bonds (which will further reduce the club's tax obligations by $11.2 million a year) to come up with the "privately financed" part of the deal (Bagli and McIntire 2005).

Because they had been waiting for this opening for long enough, uptown rivals the Yankees were not slow to follow suit. Just three days after the inking of the sweetheart deal with the Mets, and only ten days after the Olympic bid went south, Steinbrenner announced that the Bronx Bombers would be building a new ballpark next to Yankee Stadium, with the city spending about three hundred million dollars on infrastructure, and with untold perks built into the bond-based financing plan. While the new stadium is being built on existing parkland (not easy to come by in the Bronx), "replacement parkland" is being created—over a parking garage. Having given up on his long-cherished dream of a stadium in Manhattan itself, the Yankees owner seemed to be doing his best to further antagonize his community neighbors in the Bronx. These neighbors had less clout and resources than the more affluent dwellers on the West Side downtown (who had a long history, inspired by Jane Jacobs, of successfully resisting large-scale projects, such as Robert Moses's Westway in the 1960s), and so their efforts to stop the plan were dwarfed by the Yankees' lavishly funded lobbying efforts.

In a sordid twist typical of stadium fiscal politics, Yankees lobbyists were subsequently revealed to have been paid with taxpayer money, thanks to a loophole in the club's city lease. The city, in effect, paid to have itself lobbied (deMause 2006). As is common with such projects, the full degree of public subsidies to the Yankees was well hidden and only came to light after exhaustive digging by investigative reporters. At the outset of the lobbying, Mayor Bloomberg had described the project as "the state helping the way, but George [Steinbrenner] footing the bill." At that time, the public tab for infrastructural improvement and replacement parks was estimated at a mere $135 million. In March of the following year, the subsidy watch group Good Jobs New York issued a report that raised that sum to $478 million; in July 2007 it updated the estimate of the cost to taxpayers to $663.5 million (Damiani, Markey, and Steinberg 2007). The combination of tax rebates, lease kickbacks, and tax-free financing all added up to what Neil deMause, expert watchdog in the field (see http://www.fieldofschemes.com), declared as "the most costly public stadium subsidy in U.S. history" (2007).

Once the mayor had broken his embargo on the Yankees and rolled over for the Mets, he could hardly deny the New Jersey Nets a new stadium in New York proper. Within a few weeks, real estate magnate Bruce Ratner announced plans for a Brooklyn stadium for his newly acquired Nets, vowing to restore major league sports to Brooklyn for the first time since the departure of the Dodgers. The Prospects Heights facility, which would be the anchor of a twenty-two-acre business and residential complex on the old Atlantic Yards, was also estimated to require hundreds of millions of dollars in public subsidies and the seizure of land by eminent domain. Built by Forest City Enterprises, the largest real estate firm in the country, the four-billion-dollar project sparked a fierce all-Brooklyn community protest movement against heedless development in the borough.

Ironically, the failure of the Olympic bid resulted in New York's acceptance of a stadium policy model that it had long resisted. New York's bid was imagined as a flight beyond stadium business as usual but was grounded by the relentless gravitational pull of a development formula with a lock on American urban policy. Moreover, New York's bid stood on its own, with little in the way of national-level backing. By contrast, London's bid was presold to political leaders on the basis of its capacity to mesh Olympic-zone development with national policymaking, especially in housing. Once approved, the New Labour formula for neutralizing opposition kicked in—a zealous push for modernization, couched in statist commitments, lubricated by private-sector stakeholding, and embellished by national-popular aspirations to see Britain's role on the world stage restored. After suffering the indignity of being pilloried as George W. Bush's dutiful poodle, the role of Olympic host was the perfect redemptive script for Tony Blair's ambition to retire from leadership on a more gracious, expansive, and world-approving note, not to mention the opportunity afforded to his would-be successor, Gordon Brown.

One of the most blighted of Britain's formerly industrialized zones would serve, once again, as a crucible for a new wave of capital investment and accumulation. Where greenfield sites are considered too expensive and politically fraught for large-scale public development, brownfield revitalization is a winning proposition for environmentally minded Olympians. After Sydney 2000 established the template for the "Green Games" (a moniker initially approved, and then disputed, by Greenpeace), all subsequent bids were obliged to build in sustainability initiatives and innovations. In this respect, London's bid was more than fortunate to coincide with the environmentalist vision promoted by the recently implemented London Plan.

But most local residents did not consider it so opportune that the rundown state of the Leaside fit with the needs of the bid. Imperial trade had driven the nineteenth-century urban development of East London, when its resident (partly immigrant) population served as a lightly administered "internal colony." Over several decades, the most polluting industries were located there, outside the regulatory limits of the GLC, in what was regarded as London's dumping ground. Modern Eastenders, who saw themselves and their communities as survivors both of the Blitz and of chronic deindustrialization, were no less assured of rough justice under the latest dispensation, aimed at consecrating London's new global fortunes. To have the Olympics hosted in their backyard, but not by them, was an ominous harbinger of their own local fortunes.

In conclusion, it could be asked whether the failure of its bid proved that New York is less of a global city than London. To some degree, this may be true, if global cities are defined by their autonomy, and thus their immunity to provincial or state power. The multisided politics of New York made it easier for a community coalition to intervene and block the plans of an elite power bloc. By contrast, the London bid revealed how national and regional elites can join in support of a city whose access to global markets, resources, and attention will act as a driver for their own economic interests. In this emergent, neoliberal scenario, the competition state solicits a winner to act as its national representative and carefully feeds the goose that lays the golden egg. Either way, the nobility of the Olympic purpose, combined with the tidal swell of patriotic fervor, is an effective cover for the fact that mega-event competitions are proving remarkably efficient in accelerating the transfer of vast sums of public money into private pockets.

Sustainability and the Ground Staff

4

Teamsters, Turtles, and Tainted Toys

NO ONE WHO toils in an offshore manufacturing facility needs to be reminded of the risks to life and limb that free trade delivers daily to their workplace. Thanks to the efforts of the anti-sweatshop movement, public consciousness has been on a slow but sure learning curve about these hazards. As long as the appalling conditions of low-wage offshore workers do not pose an immediate threat to consumers, however, they can always be glossed over as matters for the individual conscience to process. This is less the case when it comes to the compromised safety of thousands of products on the shelves manufactured or assembled in the loosely regulated production zones that host the modern sweatshop. Beginning in the spring of 2007, revelations about tainted products sourced from China made headlines in a way that threatened to dramatically change the conversation about free trade.

It doesn't take much to ratchet up the anxiety level of American parents. But reactions to the ongoing revelations about the tainted products took a seismic leap in August 2007 after Mattel recalled millions of toys found to be contaminated with lead paint. These included brands in the top rank of children's consciousness—Sesame Street, Dora the Explorer, Thomas and Friends, Barbie and Tanner, and Polly Pocket. As the recalls continued, the company's apologies came thick and fast, including to the government of China itself (and implicitly to the global business community) for having jeopardized the entire "Made in China" operation. Bob Eckers, Mattel's CEO, was forced to issue unusually strenuous assurances to consumers that the safety of children is of paramount importance to the company ("Because Your Children Are Our Children, Too" headlined one national ad).

Of course, no such assurance would ever be offered about the safety of workers in Mattel's South China supplier factories, who routinely handle toxic materials as part of their jobs. For every American child who might come in contact with a contaminated toy train, thousands of teenage girls toil twelve hours a day for a pittance, inhaling poisonous fumes in factories that are often firetraps. These workplace hazards have been well documented over the years by the Hong Kong Christian Industrial Committee (2001) and the National Labor Committee (2002). But anti-sweatshop activists in these organizations have been unable to prick the conscience of toy consumers as effectively as they have with garment shoppers.

That may now have changed, and not just because of the toy scare. The problems with Chinese imports began with mortalities caused by melamine-laced pet foods, retailed by Del Monte, Nestle Purina, and Menu Foods. Next to kids, pets are the most vulnerable and intimately loved of all family members, and so the anxiety hit home quickly. And the list went on, including dodgy drugs, defective automobile tires, poisonous toothpaste, combustible computer batteries, and toxic seafood. By the end of 2007, every product sent from China was suspect. Politically, the scandals were a godsend for China bashers on Capitol Hill and talk radio, where many smug lectures were offered to Beijing about how to put its regulatory house in order.

CEOs like Eckers had much more to worry about. The vast sums that they spend on building and polishing corporate brands are all directed toward winning consumer trust, which can evaporate overnight when tainted products show up. In addition, companies now shell out an estimated thirty-one billion dollars annually on PR known as *corporate social responsibility* (CSR), aimed, in large part, at redeeming brands that have been tarnished by sweatshop exposés. Yet headlines about contaminated goods in onshore shopping baskets are much more threatening to brand reputations than disclosures about substandard working conditions in offshore factories.

As the branding crisis deepened, officials in Washington and Beijing rushed to protect the lucrative U.S.-China trade. Congressional committees called hearings, the Consumer Product Safety Commission was asked to upgrade its procedures, and corporations that have long resisted third-party monitoring of their offshore suppliers' workplaces leapt to embrace independent testing and monitoring of their imports. Beijing, for its part, closed down some factories, beefed up inspections, and even executed its former chief of food and drug regulation. But all these measures were about containing the damage close to the point of consumption, and none of them got to the root causes of the problems, which lie in the factories themselves and in the contracting chain of command.

Citizens of affluent countries are used to thinking that their dirtiest and most dangerous industries (not to mention their waste products) can be sent offshore, out of sight and out of mind. But these risks are not exported to the global South on a one-way ticket. They return to us by way of what Ulrich Beck called the "boomerang effect," through their toxic side effects in consumer commodities or food produce (1992). Many environmental problems are local in character and can be contained, but unfettered free trade means that now almost everyone can be exposed to hazards that originate thousands of miles away. To cite one example of the chain of contamination, computers manufactured in China and used in North America are sent in the e-waste stream to be broken up in Guangdong province; the result poisons the ground water and soil, and sends toxics into the produce supply, some of which makes its way back to the United States.

Thirty years ago, ecology pioneer and Citizens Party founder Barry Commoner argued that environmental protections have to be assured at the point of production. It is ineffective to deal with products' environmental impact further along in their life cycle, and least of all at their endpoint, in waste disposal (1971). In the decades since Commoner pointed this out, global manufacturers and their subcontracting chains have emerged as the most destructive example of how to ignore his lesson. Abdicating responsibility for protecting workers at the bottom is a threat to life and limb all the way up the chain.

If consumers want assurances, there is no point in waiting for Beijing or Washington to take effective action—that will not happen anytime soon. Companies have to be forced to recognize that the best way to guarantee consumer safety is to ensure adequate workplace protections and benefits in the lowest of their supplier factories. If you sicken workers there, chances are you will sicken, and alienate, your precious customers here. This elementary fact, magnified by publicity from the tainted products scandal, has given labor activists a new opportunity to focus public attention on working conditions offshore. Just as important, as long as consumer relations are in flux, long-standing arguments can be made about the common concerns of labor and environmental advocates. Thanks to the global warming scares, more and more people acknowledge the global character of environmental problems, but few act on the understanding that food chains connect all over the earth, that pollution crosses zip codes and national borders, or that nuclear, chemical, and genetic hazards have little regard for the hierarchies of class and power.

Social justice advocates have striven to show how this geography of risk is connected to the distribution of hazards among low-wage workplaces in different parts of the globe. Indeed, part of the promise of the anti-globalization movement has been to bring the labor and environmental movements closer together in order to achieve this goal. The much-lauded unity of 1999's anti-WTO protesters in Seattle was memorialized in the slogan "Teamsters and Turtles—Together at Last!" Yet these movements still have too much to learn from each other to make common cause, and their divisions are exacerbated wherever possible by corporate foes, dead set on protecting their brand equity. As much as progress has been made, it has been diminished by the PR successes of the CSR industry. With their formidable war chests, CSR experts can redeem tarnished brands almost as fast as activists can sully them (Ballinger 2008).

Because this topic is too broad and deep to survey concisely, this chapter looks at two particular strands of environmental and labor advocacy— the anti-consumerist and the anti-sweatshop movements—and suggests how and why they could integrate more of the other's philosophies and goals. The record of attention to labor abuses within the history of the consumer rights movement confirms that there has been a longstanding dialogue between organized groups on both sides, but it is equally a history of missed opportunities. In return, labor advocates have been slow to question the dominant materialist lifestyle of a consumer civilization, preferring to promote ethical reforms in consumption patterns that will sustain the existing jobs of goods and service producers. For all their efforts to engage consumer politics, anti-sweatshop activists have stopped short of foundational challenges to the prevailing system. As for the anti-consumer activists who evangelize sweeping changes in lifestyle, trading, and modes of subsistence, they tend to see ethical consumption as little more than a way to greenwash the status quo. Further, they are not especially sensitive to the immediate needs of the working masses whose livelihoods are tied to the existing system, however corrupt it may be. They ought to view production workers and labor-based organizations as likely allies rather than as hapless victims of false consciousness. But this can only happen if their concerns about the unsustainability of a consumer civilization are addressed, quite literally, at Commoner's point of production, in decisions that fully involve workers.

The Quandaries of Consumer-Based Labor Activism

How long does any social movement have to make its mark on public consciousness? Given the ballooning pace of competition on today's information landscape, the window of opportunity is somewhere between five and seven years. If a movement is to achieve the status of an unavoidable moral cause, then it has to clearly register its message within that time frame through some innovation for capturing media attention. So, too, the targets of the movement are under similar pressure to respond by publicizing effectively the self-directed remedies for their sins. Their task, in other words, is to leave the public with the impression that the problem for which they are being blamed has been solved.

For the sake of argument, let this curt description be accepted as a template for the conduct of modern, media-oriented activism. Among recent candidates, the anti-sweatshop movement appears to fit the bill quite well.[1] Emerging in North America and Europe in the mid-1990s, it raised to a fine art the tactics of shaming global consumer brand firms through exposés of the substandard workplaces of their suppliers, and it succeeded in building a fully international network of well-connected activists and NGOs. By 2002, its goals were more or less normalized in the public mind. The moral shock value of its tactics could no longer command headlines with quite the same dramatic ease. For consumers, however, the global sweatshop was now a real, albeit distant, concept to live with, and some measure of guilt at the "labor behind the label" had become a factor in the psychology of consumption. A small, but significant, production sector based on fair trade opened up and found a buying public. The cause of fair labor had also made it to the negotiating table in global and bilateral trade agreements, even though it was invariably shunted into a backseat as proceedings got underway.

But multinational corporations, their brands sullied by ties to labor abuses, had also waged a capable PR campaign in response. Pressured by activists to reveal factory locations and adopt workplace codes of conduct for their suppliers, they worked hard at spinning these limited policy changes into a cloak of respectability for their brands. In a series of PR moves now paradigmatic for the burgeoning CSR movement, firms like Nike, the Gap, and Reebok strove to repair their damaged images, emerging from the fray as born-again paragons of social justice. For many informed consumers attentive to the PR, the truism that some of their favorite brands had taken steps to eradicate sweatshops would prove an adequate salve for their consciences. In their minds, labor atrocities might still exist, but buying Nike wares, rather than boycotting them, was somehow now helping to address the problem.

This, at least, is one of the more deflationary narratives that has circulated around the anti-sweatshop movement in recent years. It has some traction among weary activists, and understandably so, because they have been up against some of the most powerful, and wily, corporations in the world. It is also echoed by armchair leftists, who specialize, on demand, in the business of explicating traditions of despair. For reasons that will be explored here, it is not a narrative that I fully accept. The impact of anti-sweatshop campaigns on the labor movement itself (not to mention the much broader, global justice movement) has yet to be fully assessed. These campaigns not only helped turn a whole generation of young people toward labor politics for the first time since the 1930s, but they were also pioneering efforts in the emergent field of transnational labor organizing. So, too, the capacity of global corporations to prevail over markets and public opinion alike can no longer rely, as it once did, on the oxygen of free trade. The neoliberal game is not yet up, but its rules of play have been widely discredited (not least by the public hullabaloo about sweatshops) and nascent alternatives are beginning to form all over Latin America.

On the face of it, the narrative I sketched out was a rather predictable result of activists pursuing movement goals aimed at securing labor rights for global South workers through political tactics that appealed primarily to the conscience of global North consumers. The fragile connection between such unequal communities is not easy to maintain beyond the duration of a few news cycles. So, too, the experiential legacies that framed the campaigns were a heavy burden to bear. On the one hand, there was the experience, widely shared within the labor movement, of being consistently outmaneuvered by runaway employers. On the other, there was the equally gloomy experience, on the part of consumer activists, of seeing tactics being co-opted by corporate PR adepts. Purists, on the left or in the more ascetic anti-consumerist circles, could well conclude that under existing conditions of capitalism, any effort to push for "fair labor" standards is hopelessly reformist and doomed to end in frustration. How many workers on the ground, it is often lamented, truly have been helped by the vast energies expended by activists?

But even if this judgment were valid, the lessons of anti-sweatshop activism would not stop there. The trajectory of the movement continues to offer crucial lessons about the current and future shape of global organizing in the face of obstacles that can often appear insurmountable. And for those bent on integrating labor concerns more into the sphere of environmental politics, it is a case study that cannot be comfortably ignored.

If the goals of anti-sweatshop campaigning were to lay the groundwork for the eradication of the global sweatshop, then they could just as well have been achieved through morally persuasive appeals to legislators and regulators, or through mass worker organization in key locations. They were not dependent on reforming patterns of consumption significantly, or even on raising consumer consciousness to some critical plateau. The leverage afforded by the vulnerability of brand names to bad publicity, however, proved irresistible. The topmost profits in the apparel industry hinge on the repute of the label being sustained through each cycle of seasonal turnover. Nothing exposed corporate greed more than highlighting the gulf between the meager wages paid to production workers, toiling under life-threatening conditions, and the lavish profits enjoyed by brand firms and top retailers on the basis of label recognition and consumer loyalty. The general consumer was the natural audience to reach with such exposés, and this brought into play some of the tactics of, and debates about, the mobilization of consumer power familiar to veterans of consumer politics.

This was hardly the first time that labor-based campaigns had strayed into the realm of consumer politics. The International Ladies' Garment Workers Union pioneered the labor movement's "Look for the Union Label" pitch to working-class and progressive consumers in the 1960s and the 1970s (Tyler 1995). To this day it remains a cornerstone, albeit greatly diminished, of the AFL-CIO's public education policy. Buy-American populist campaigns have a much longer history, and while trade unions have generally supported them out of expediency, these movements were often fomented by antiunion crusaders like William Randolph Hearst. Dana Frank, the historian of these campaigns, has analyzed the virulent racism that accompanied their expressions of economic nationalism (Frank 1999). For the unions that supported them, the overt goal of protecting jobs was often inseparable from implicit antiforeigner sentiment (viz. the Japan bashing of the 1980s or the more recent galvanizing against the "China threat").

As for those targeted for exclusion, labor advocates have turned specific boycotts of consumer products to their advantage. Most famously, the spectacular success of the California table grapes boycott (1965–70) was key to winning contracts for the United Farm Workers. In recent years, a national consumer boycott of Mount Olive Pickle products helped guest workers in North Carolina win union representation and a contract. A similar boycott of Taco Bell helped the Coalition of Immokalee Workers win improvement in wages and conditions for Central Florida farmworkers. So, too, the boycott-based Killer Coke campaign (organized in protest against the corporation's complicity in brutally suppressing union organizing in Colombia) is directing a whole new generation of scrutiny against the labor economy of Coca-Colonization. Though anti-sweatshop activists have generally not endorsed boycotts (they do little to protect workers), informal consumer boycotts have nonetheless been proven to affect corporate revenue. For example, Nike's North American sales were down noticeably for five years after the controversy over their supplier sweatshops went public and before the public impact of their CSR machine took effect (Ballinger and Ziegler 2007).

Protecting the Consumer

Nor has the consumer movement itself been inattentive to labor conditions. Indeed, the origins of the National Consumer League (formed in 1899) lay in the call for consumers to leverage their buying power to raise the starvation wages of the "girls behind the counter" in retail stores (Storrs 2000). Florence Kelley, the league's first executive secretary, led the organization full tilt into the first anti-sweatshop movement in the early 1900s, and, throughout the twentieth century, the league remained consistently attentive to working conditions, lobbying hard for passage of the Fair Labor Standards Act in 1938, helping to create the Child Labor Coalition in the 1980s, and participating in the Fair Labor Association from the late 1990s onward.

In the 1920s and 1930s, consumer advocates such as Stuart Chase, Frederick Schlink, Arthur Kallet, and Colston Warne focused primarily on food safety and fraud, but concerns about fair labor were not sidelined (Chase and Schlink 1927; Kallet and Schlink 1933). The company exposés undertaken by Ralph Nader in the late 1960s, and the subsequent investigative reports issued by Nader's Raiders in the early 1970s, uncovered a structural pattern of corporate abuse and corruption, aided and abetted by government collusion, that placed workplace exploitation clearly within the chain of non-accountability that endangered consumers. The citizen action groups, founded by Nader, which demanded corporate and governmental responsibility, were prototypes of the kind of civil society activism that has flourished in recent years, especially in the alternative globalization movement.

The progressive thrust of Naderism, with its systematic critiques of power, can be distinguished from the mainstream of the consumer movement, which tends to see its mission as rationalizing consumer choice— that is, consumers ought to have the information they need to make safe choices, and market producers ought to respond with ethical practices. But what about the more radical strain of thought and action that describes itself as anti-consumerist? It challenges the existing patterns of consumption as fundamentally destructive and unsustainable while proselytizing for sweeping changes in lifestyle, trading, and modes of livelihood (de Graff, Wann, and Naylor 2001). Anti-consumerists see ethical consumption as little more than a Band-Aid for a fundamentally dysfunctional way of life and flatly reject any kind of politics that grounds civil rights in the purchasing power of consumers.

When it comes to labor issues, the anti-consumerist injunction to consume less is often accompanied by the appeal to work less. Why indeed should we work such long hours to win possession of so many consumer goods? As it happens, this impulse speaks to a longstanding debate within the labor movement about the moral virtues of hard work. The great crusades of the Knights of Labor in the nineteenth century for the eight-hour day, and of the AFL-CIO in the twentieth century for a forty-hour week with paid vacations, coexisted uneasily with the U.S. labor movement's own version of the Puritan work ethic based on appeals to the dignity of labor and the right to work. The push for reduced hours, based on the right to leisure, eventually ran out of steam in the capital-labor truce of the postwar years. The so-called Treaty of Detroit (1949) between the UAW and the Big Three automakers established a contractual understanding about how increases in productivity would be tied to incremental wage increases for primary-sector workers in manufacturing. Henceforth in the United States, reductions in the workweek would only be seriously considered during periods of recession and high unemployment as a way of sharing work around. Until the 1970s, the paid vacation days and logged work time of core American workers compared favorably with their European counterparts, but their fortunes have diverged radically since then. Today, Americans work harder and longer than any other industrialized country, enjoying a fraction of the paid vacation time of Europeans, who typically take up to eight weeks off. One-fourth of American workers have no paid vacation at all, and half of all private sectors are not even afforded paid sick days (Moberg 2007).

While the working week was reduced to thirty hours in 2000 in France (home of a vigorous anti-work tradition dating back to Paul Lafargue's 1883 *The Right to Be Lazy*), and while many EU governments require employers to make workers take vacations, pressure to expand the working day through *flexible* work arrangements has been a universal feature of neoliberal reforms. Income polarization in the United States has left the vast majority of working people, stranded by real-wage stagnation, with little choice but to work longer, and often in more than one job. The capacity to "downshift" from a fast-track corporate career has been a preserve of the relatively affluent, in much the same way as the anti-consumerist's commitment to "voluntary simplicity" is widely viewed as an option for secure middle-class people who can afford the status loss that results from eschewing materialism (Schor 1998).

Arguably, the greatest legacy of the anti-consumerist counterculture of the 1960s has been in the reform of nutritional habits among the middle class (Belasco 2006). These reforms lie at the heart, today, of an organic food industry that is the mainstay of gourmet-class consumption. While organic agriculture is a real alternative to the corporate system of food production, and is now being taken up by mainstream wholesalers like Wal-Mart, its labor practices have not proved appreciably different. Exploitation of farm workers (on organic, as opposed to factory, farms) does not tend to register as a priority concern, except among the most politically conscious of food consumers. The most radical expression of anti-consumer food consciousness appears in the movement known as freeganism, which endorses scavenging for discarded foods in supermarket dumpsters and wild foraging for non-industrially grown food. The movement dovetails with a number of autonomous practices, based on the sharing and bartering of skills and resources, such as free stores and the temporary swap meets known as Really Really Free Markets. Practitioners reject the path of pressuring corporations to improve conditions and elect instead to opt out of a system that systematically exploits workers, displaces communities, and despoils ecosystems. Taken together, their practices are an effort to imagine an alternative economy to industrial consumerism, though there is a tendency, common among utopians, for freegan devotees to see mainstream consumers as pitiable dupes of mass advertising and status dependency.

As is typical of social movements, there exists a reform tendency that is often sharply at odds with radical efforts to operate outside the system. In this case, the more reformist response has been aimed at ethical consumption—supporting fair trade consumer foods and goods that sustain the livelihoods of economically disadvantaged artisans and farmers worldwide (Raynolds, Murray, and Wilkinson 2007). Ethical consumers are in a position to reward retailers for working with small, low-income producers who have been squeezed by large-scale agribusiness and corporate manufacturing. Fair trade is broadly understood to observe environmental principles while ensuring the health, safety, and economic buoyancy of workers and their communities. The integrity of fair trade labeling varies, but its adoption as an international goal by NGOs, and some governments, has been a significant hedge against the chronic impact of unregulated competition in global commodity markets in recent decades. As neoliberal policies took hold, prices for the primary agricultural exports of developing countries plummeted, and governments, constrained by WTO and IMF policies, were forced to abandon small producers to the rough justice of a market stacked against them (Zaccai 2007).

Given the ambitions of the movement, many fair trade alliances entered into partnerships with multinationals and mass retailers (Nestlé and Starbucks are prominent examples), with the result that fair trade products are now among an array of available choices in mainstream consumer outlets (Barrientos and Smith 2007). Not surprisingly, this pact with the devil is widely reviled by anti-consumerists as a reinforcement of, rather than a critical alternative to, the unsustainable nature of the trading system. So, too, the preference of fair trade alliances for small producers or cooperatives means that the vast majority of workers, who work on plantations or large family farms, are not assisted at all. The nobility of the small, struggling independent—a favored profile in the iconography of progressives—trumps the more sordid panorama of wage dependency occupied by the proletarianized mass of global workers in the agricultural sector.

Beyond the Nation

Anti-sweatshop labor campaigning has been more firmly in the fair trade camp than in the anticapitalist corner of radicals opposed to the existing system. So, too, its approach to consumer politics triggered a move beyond nation-based action that matches the global strategy embraced by fair traders. In each of the areas described earlier—buying to protect domestic jobs, mounting boycott coalitions, and organizing for sustainability around an anti-work/pro-leisure platform—the mentality and tactics of activists were altered significantly by the accelerated rate of economic globalization that began with the passage of NAFTA in 1994 and went into overdrive with China's accession to the WTO in 2001. Indeed, it was implicit in the spirit of anti-sweatshop activism that the field of engagement had to be expanded to encompass the challenge of global organizing.

In this respect, it was clear, from the mid-1990s origins of the movement, that protectionist appeals to the livelihoods of domestic workers, or to the national interest for that matter, were no longer as relevant or useful as they had been in earlier decades. Goods that are wholly produced in one country are few and far between, and a "Made in the USA" label might only refer to one small part of the production process. Almost all the major brands targeted by activists were produced offshore, or else moved offshore when sweatshop activists targeted their domestic production facilities and wages. Most realists in the apparel industry acknowledged that the outmigration of labor-intensive U.S. jobs (beginning as early as the 1960s) was virtually impossible to stem (Howard 2007). By the mid-1990s, the garment union UNITE was looking to other sectors to organize and eventually merged with HERE, the hotel and restaurant employees union, in 2004 to facilitate this diversification.

That is not to say that economic nationalism did not prove expedient in politically minded appeals to consumers. The National Labor Committee (NLC) (a linchpin of the movement) made its name with the 1992 report *Paying to Lose Our Jobs* by exposing the promotional activities and the economic support offered by U.S. government agencies, under the USAID program, to induce American corporations into moving production to maquiladoras (NLC 1992; Krupat 1997). The theme of American job loss continued to be an effective point of reference, especially when offshore outsourcing began to take its toll on more skilled, high-value livelihoods. Protectionism also played well in tabloid reporting and was a perennial favorite among grandstanding politicians. So, too, legislative measures aimed at stemming job loss have been welcomed by small businesses, unable to move offshore and operate on a global scale like the multinationals that controlled the free trade policy agenda of the National Association of Manufacturers.

Indeed, the most successful of the American garment companies that sprang up to trade on sweat-free reputations was named American

Apparel, ostensibly to reinforce its claim that all company products were made domestically, in factories located in downtown LA. While its owner aggressively resisted a union organizing drive, the firm profited, in its advertising strategies, from the fact that it paid fair wages to its production workers (well above the city's own living wage) (Ross 2004). Most recently, it launched a pro-immigrant advertising campaign that praised the efforts of the workers, mostly undocumented, who staff domestic garment shops like theirs.

Even more significant, however, its success in the youth retail market has derived from its savvy design and edgy style quotient. Ethical producers who were its U.S. competitors—TeamX (which produced the SweatX brand before going under) or Bienestar International (which still produces No Sweat)—marketed to progressive individuals or to liberal institutions, such as unions or colleges. By contrast, American Apparel tested itself and its wares on the open market in order to prove that it could compete on style while also being sweat-free, rather than prove that it could compete *because* it was sweat-free. The distinction has not been readily acknowledged within the anti-sweatshop movement, where opinions about the company have been fatally colored by the owner's antipathy to unions, or by the perception that its sweat-free reputation has been exploited for commercial ends rather than celebrated for its own sake (Dreier and Appelbaum 2004). Along the same lines, while the firm's success has demonstrated that it is possible to compete with global offshore producers by paying fair wages to domestic workers, the appeal of the brand name, American Apparel, arguably lies less in its invitation to patriotic consumption than to the perceived hipness of its prosaic, neo-generic character, distinguishing it from the flash monikers chosen for other commercial brands. By contrast, most other firms in the ethical clothing business tend to call attention to political consciousness in their brand names—Made in Dignity (Belgium, France, and Italy), Ethical Threads (United Kingdom), Dignity Return (Bangkok), Oko-Fair (Germany), People Tree (United Kingdom and Japan), Just Garments (El Salvador), and The Working World, Justice Clothing, Just Shirts, Traditions Fair Trade, No Sweat Apparel, and Maggie's Organics (North America).

Notwithstanding the common-sense appeal of protectionism—every community surely has the right to protect the livelihoods of its members—the fundamental lesson preached by the (second) anti-sweatshop movement lay in the global challenge of the struggle against worker exploitation. Just as the first movement, in the late nineteenth and early twentieth century, sought to establish national labor standards, the second wave clearly saw its goal as setting standards for the global economy (Bender and Greenwald 2004; Bonacich and Appelbaum 2000). This meant accepting that the rights of workers in Lesotho, Guatemala, or Guangdong were on a par with those in the global North whose jobs may have been transferred offshore. The only alternative to a free trade order built on what economists euphemistically call global labor arbitrage was to build networks equally global in scope, based not on short-term profit and plunder, but rather on the principles of fair trade, sustainable economics, internationally recognized labor and human rights, and socially conscious investment. For trade unionists reared on the a priori injunction to protect their own members, global reach has been a hard lesson to swallow, especially because the challenge is so daunting (Howard 2007). Trade liberalization in India and China in the last decade has effectively doubled the global workforce available to capitalist investors—a clear recipe for maximum exploitation in labor-intensive sectors. The task of establishing enforceable global labor standards under these circumstances is formidable. It has not been easy to persuade union members of the benefit of global organizing when the prospect of harvesting short-term results was minimal, but the first steps toward creating global unions are being taken (Bronfenbrenner 2007; Brecher, Costello, and Smith 2006).

There existed a long prior record of international solidarity campaigns against companies operating in different countries, but they were mostly in unionized core sectors of advanced economies: dockworkers or auto workers, for example, taking sympathy actions on each others' behalf, often through the agency of the international trade secretariats formed to coordinate unions in the large industrial sectors, or through UN agencies like the International Labor Organization. In addition, and especially in the American labor movement, the push for unions to go global was often underwritten by institutional complicity with the expansionist interest of state capitalism (Herod 1997). When capital and labor were partners during the Pax Americana, it was implicitly acknowledged that whatever was good for American business abroad was good for the domestic workers who enjoyed the world's highest standard of living. Accordingly, the notorious anticommunist activities of the AFL-CIO's regional labor organizations (especially the American Institute for Free Labor Development, directed at suppressing radical labor movements in Latin America and elsewhere) were prime examples of labor in the service of Cold War imperialism (Radosh 1969; Kelber 2004). The legacy of that period of U.S.

labor internationalism has not been easy to shake off, and it has bedeviled the efforts of independent labor advocates to build relations of trust in developing countries.

Nonetheless, anti-sweatshop campaigning broke new ground by demonstrating that attention to, and links with, unorganized workers in these developing countries—the most marginalized and vulnerable workers of all—might be an effective way to pressure high-profile firms to take responsibility for the whole chain of dispersed production that goes into the making of their goods (Bullert 2000; Ross 2004; Armbruster-Sandoval 2004). What had hitherto been perceived as a firm's strength—the ability to produce in locations that lay beyond the orbit of regulatory scrutiny—could be turned into a major liability when consumer brand imagery was threatened by association with sweatshops.

The movement's iconic moment came when an especially vulnerable celebrity figure, Kathie Lee Gifford, fell into the trap and was exposed by the NLC in 1996 for her Wal-Mart clothing line's reliance on sweatshop suppliers in Honduras. The Gifford campaign established a formula that could be replicated as long as celebrity cultural capital was used to sell the brand. To cite a more recent example, from 2004, the NLC, in conjunction with sweatshop activists at New York University, was still able to work the formula with ease to pressure the Olsen twins, enrolled in the university at the time, into supporting maternity leave for Bangladeshi workers producing their Wal-Mart clothing line. No institution is too sacred to be tainted, as the NLC proved with its 2007 Christmas campaign about crucifixes produced in Chinese sweatshops for St. Patrick's Cathedral and Trinity Church in New York. Given its proven potency, the need to avoid an NLC-style exposé has been widely acknowledged and absorbed in the corporate world. In the course of field interviews I did in East China in 2003, managers and executives of multinational firms regularly referred to "the Kathie Lee Gifford affair" as shorthand for their worst fears.

The opportunities for exposure multiplied in the case of parent companies with several brands, where PR damage to one brand can affect the entire group. In 2002, for example, the major trade union federations of France, the Netherlands, and the United States joined together to target Pinault-Printemps-Redoute (PPR), the French multinational apparel company known for major brands like Gucci, Brylane, FNAC, Yves Saint-Laurent, and Ellos. The union campaign linked substandard conditions in PPR supplier factories in India and the Philippines to union busting at a

Brylane distribution center in Indianapolis. As the most vulnerable link in the publicity chain, it was the Gucci name that offered the most traction, and so activists focused on sullying the luxury goods brand. As a result of the international pressure, the Indianapolis workers won the right to union representation in February 2003, but the firm was able to cut and run from the Asian suppliers whose employee abuse had been publicized. The offshore workers simply lost their jobs. In a similar case, an international union campaign targeted H&M, the Swedish-based global fashion company, for its antiunion policies in U.S. outlets. Once again, the poor record of the firm's Asian suppliers was used to shame the company and win union rights for workers in North America. As for the workers in the offshore supply chain, the company's PR wing had other plans for them. In common with other apparel giants, H&M took steps to beef up its ethical production and trading profile. Its 2004 CSR report announced an ominous shift from "policing the supply chain to working with it." For activists familiar with the on-the-ground impact of such strategies, this was telltale rhetoric for policies designed to pressure suppliers to fake compliance with corporate codes of conduct.

A successful alternative strategy to the Kathie Lee Gifford formula was to center an activist campaign around an institution associated with high ethical standing. The movement among American college students to put pressure on licensees of varsity names exploited the need for universities to uphold the integrity of their name, even when it appeared as a logo brand on clothing. The efforts of United Students Against Sweatshops (USAS) to create a sweat-free zone for college licensing contracts turned a small but significant sector of the garment industry into a closely fought war of position among sportswear giants like Nike, Adidas, and Reebok, regulatory NGOs, and the labor movement (Featherstone 2002). The Workers Rights Consortium (WRC), which emerged as the monitoring institution of choice for USAS, helped to win some concrete victories for workers in free trade zones in Central America and Southeast Asia by leveraging the collective clout of its members—more than 170 institutional licensors (Esbenshade 2004).

In Europe, the Clean Clothes Campaign (CCC) selected international sporting institutions like the Fédération Internationale de Football Association (FIFA) and the International Olympic Committee (IOC) as the bodies of ethical integrity around which to organize. Nike, Adidas, Reebok, Fila, Lotto, Umbro, and Puma are all top sponsors or suppliers of quadrennial mega-events like the UEFA European Football Championship, the World Cup, and the Olympic Games. Building on a landmark 1996 Code of Labor Practice for all products with a FIFA logo, CCC launched a Play Fair campaign to pressure sponsors to live up to this code of compliance and others. The campaign drew the support of top athletes and hundreds of organizations in over thirty-five countries in advance of the 2004 Olympics, and a broader initiative to monitor suppliers to the Beijing games in 2008 was launched at Athens with the cooperation of the International Confederation of Free Trade Unions and the International Textile, Garment, and Leather Workers' Federation (see http://www. cleanclothes.org).

Frequently Asked Questions

In the public sector, the movement to pass ordinances mandating sweat-free criteria for city and state contractors has been widely successful (see http://www.sweatfree.org). But what about the open markets, where the only ethical court of appeal is the individual consumer's conscience? With nationalist purchasing an increasingly irrelevant, or unattractive, option for consumers, the opportunities to promote "positive buying" have been limited to the handful of small firms (previously mentioned) that sprang up from fair trade circles to offer an ethical alternative to the industry leaders.

In response to a damaging November 2007 exposé by *The Observer* of child labor employed by Indian suppliers, the Gap announced plans to pioneer, along with the Global March Against Child Labor, a sweat-free label for its clothing. To date, little, if anything, has come of the plan. No global apparel company has earned the right to be considered sweat-free, clothing labels convey little useful or accurate information, and consumers looking to do their own research are likely to run into a tide of PR about the socially responsible practices of any choice brand. The more determined, or sophisticated, researcher would have to sift through the claims, records, and case studies of companies that participate in multi-stakeholder initiatives like the Ethical Trade Initiative in the United Kingdom, the Fair Wear Foundation in the Netherlands, or the Fair Labor Association in the United States (terms of participation involve commitment to supplier codes of conduct and a willingness to be investigated if the workers of a supplier report violations of the code). The results of such research would be murky, to say the least.

The absence of a list of recommended clean top-rank brands limits any follow-up to the urgent appeals that activists make to the public consumer. Because individuals of conscience tend to want to use their consuming power in a tangible way, the appeal of negative purchasing then becomes a powerful one. For many people, wearing a swoosh has come to be as abhorrent as wearing a fur coat. The more acute their animus against the brand, the more seductive the prospect of hurting it financially through reduced sales. Yet it has not been considered useful to encourage the boycott of specific apparel brands. Unlike in the case of commerce that involves animal abuse (such as the fur trade), where boycotts have been very effective, the same strategy can be harmful in cases that involve worker abuse. More often than not, the company will seek to clear its name by cutting contracts with the offending supplier and the workers will be laid off. Workers' rights and livelihoods are better served by public pressure on the brand to rectify the abuses by improving workers' pay and conditions. Ultimately, a boycott that succeeds in significantly reducing consumption can lead to an increase in price pressure on the entire production chain by the brand firm, which only worsens worker conditions.

Without follow-through directed at the conditions of specific workers, high-visibility exposés, by their nature, all too often result in the company cutting and running. This is by far the easiest way for firms to dissociate the brand from any problem, especially when there is no shortage of suppliers. If corporate PR handles things expediently, the brand can actually be enhanced by the appearance of having reacted quickly by punishing an abusive supplier through the termination of its contract. In reality, the abuses invariably stem from the pressure put on small contractors by a brand or retailer to deliver faster and cheaper; prices paid to factories for production have decreased in most global locations over the last several years. The favored corporate scenario of the humane manager from the North teaching lessons about worker respect to the callous contractor from the South is entirely illusory.

Northern activists also faced critiques from their global South counterparts when they failed to follow through with production workers whose abuse had been featured in their campaign (Kabeer 2000). Offshore workers, in quasi-militarized free trade zones, put themselves at great risk when they speak out about abuses, and there is little insurance to be found in the vague footprint of attention left by a media splash in the global North. A politics based on the volunteer conscience of affluent consumers is a thin guarantee of justice for workers at the mercy of footloose foreign investors and the hardscrabble local contractors whose ability to compete rests on squeezing more out of their workforce. Campaigns that featured images of downtrodden offshore sweatshop workers not only reproduced the industrial division of production from consumption sites, but also reprised a paternalist history (from abolitionism onward) of using the iconography of poor people in the South to manipulate the scruples of northern liberals (Brooks 2003). Immigrant women employed in domestic U.S. sweatshops tended to eschew the media image campaigns in favor of organizing their own workers centers, usually independent of the trade union movement (Louie 2001; Fine 2006). So, too, student groups shifted their own strategies in response to the criticisms.

The most obvious alternative was for these activists to devote themselves to helping offshore workers build unions—the most effective, long-term solution to improving conditions. Students involved early in USAS chapters had focused their energies on pressuring corporations to establish factory codes of conduct, and then on forming an independent network of local monitors (as opposed to the multinational auditing firms that corporations preferred) to check enforcement of the codes. It became clear, however, that the codes were virtually impossible to enforce; manufacturers simply asked their suppliers to fake compliance, which CSR reps spun into positive publicity. The only practical way of stopping the spin was to convert the anti-sweatshop movement into a union-building program in free trade supplier zones. Using the monitoring capability of the WRC to combat union busting in the factories of licensees, workers were able to get independent union contracts signed in strategic locations—most famously at KukDong, a Mexican factory producing for Nike and Reebok, and at BJ&B, a collegiate cap-making factory in the Dominican Republic that supplies major brands. Conditions for union organization at several other factories were nurtured. But these initial gains have been difficult to sustain against investor flight in the labor-intensive apparel sector, where transnational bidding auctions ensure that orders will go to the cheapest, and most illegal, suppliers. Even when the WRC has succeeded in soliciting cooperation from big brand members of the rival Fair Labor Association, getting results on the ground has been tough going. Contractors prefer to shift their investment elsewhere than work with an independent union or listen to lessons about ethical practices from CSR reps whose sourcing managers are, at the same time, demanding delivery prices and schedules quite at odds with the humanitarian messages. After five years of operations, the WRC estimated that only eight out of the several thousand overseas factories producing clothing with college logos were in compliance with the consortium's standards (Jaschik 2006). Clearly, it was time to change tactics (Ross, Robert 2006).

Accordingly, the WRC/USAS adopted a successor policy whereby colleges demand that their licensees contract from a list of designated suppliers (who host unions and/or pay living wages) in the Dominican Republic, Kenya, Mexico, Thailand, South Africa, and Indonesia. The manufacturer has to pay a reasonable sum to help factories comply with the codes and labor provisions. The policy is an ambitious effort to close the loopholes in the old system and create the prototype for a durable sweat-free sector. A wave of student hunger strikes and campus protests in 2005–6 brought as many as nineteen colleges into the program, and, to date, forty-five are in support.

The new program has the potential to reverse the pattern of seeing factories that have hosted model unionizing efforts closed down, as happened in March 2007 with the BJ&B facility in the Dominican Republic. When this occurs, activists' hard-earned morale plummets, and there is little recourse to media-oriented campaigns when the managers of the brand name can claim, as Reebok and Nike did at BJ&B, that they intervened on behalf of the workers. Those laid-off are especially embittered, and other workers in the same labor market are less emboldened to undertake an organizing effort. Even if the latter are strong-willed, they are unlikely to risk losing their livelihoods unless they can rely on the support of a more powerful institution—either the state or a larger union movement. Whether this will change as a result of the shift in power leftward in regions like Latin America remains to be seen. As for the larger union movement, it continues to face, on a global scale, exactly the same technical problem as the first anti-sweatshop movement at the turn of the twentieth century—a contracting system that is an effective, and resilient, capitalist tool for dividing labor and dispersing labor power.

Recognition of the intractability of this problem has resulted, primarily, in a diversification of activist energies. Attention to living wage campaigns, on campuses or in cities and metropolitan regions, has afforded activists more local control over events, while responding to criticisms, for example, that white, middle-class students care more about the rights of workers within the developing world than about those of workers who clean their dorm rooms, cook their meals, and dispose of their garbage. So, too, the channeling of energy into the crusade to expel Coca-Cola products from campuses has been a finite, winnable, and therefore gratifying campaign. Above all, the appeal of the movement coalition against Wal-Mart has been irresistible. Unlike, say, Nike or the Gap, the retail colossus is not simply a leading competitor in an industrial market; Wal-Mart's monopoly on trade and consumption makes its ability to organize labor and markets equivalent to an entire *mode of production*, affecting everything from local patterns of land development to the worldwide sustainability of resource utilization (Lichtenstein 2005). In facing down Wal-Mart, sweatshop protesters find themselves in a much broader coalition of activists, integrating many different interests and constituencies in the fight against a common target. In this diverse company, labor exploitation is no longer a single-issue struggle, but rather one of an array of concerns that the public cannot easily ignore. Moreover, the opportunity (not available in the case of Nike) to link Wal-Mart's exploitation of its large domestic workforce with labor abuses among its offshore suppliers demonstrates all too clearly that the fight for fair labor can and should be genuinely transnational.

Nothing's Too Good

Given that sweatshops are a structural by-product of capitalist growth, how much anti-sweatshop activism has actually come out as anticapitalist in orientation? To what end should anyone fight for fair labor without demanding a redistribution of power within the workplace or an alteration of the property regimes by which corporations subsist and thrive? Like the communists who organized in the CIO unions in the 1930s, many activists have responded by submerging their long-term critiques of the capitalist system in the interest of building a sweatshop movement around uncontroversial, short-term goals, such as basic labor rights. As each new reformist strategy falls short, they are then in a position to press for stronger, more radical moves. Consciousness, and support for their goals, builds on the steady erosion of the belief that capitalism can be a munificent system for workers if only they are treated fairly and given some stake in the system.

As with the Popular Front against fascism in the 1930s, it has also proved more strategic for the left to unite against a particular version of capitalism—neoliberalism—rather than capitalism as such. A similar choice confronted many sectors of the anti-globalization movement. While some global justice protestors (and, curiously, some mainstream media organizations) favor the moniker "anti-capitalist," the dominant spirit among activists, if it is at all possible to define such a thing in this "movement of movements," leans toward pushing for alternatives to neoliberalism. In practice, that means targeting the multinationals along with those who write the rules of neoliberal trade for them, and building coalitions around more sustainable and democratic forms of trade and development.

While anticapitalist critique tout court is often considered too redolent of the old left, anti-consumerism is one of the most visible, culturalist faces of the global justice activism, embodied in the rallying cry of *No Logo*, the title of Naomi Klein's generative 2000 book. As a tendency, anti-consumerism cuts a broad swathe—from the "pure church" advocates who extol the virtues of an alternate economy (based on barter, recycling, second-hand consumption, and self-sufficiency) to the more urbane "adbusters" and "culture jammers" who do battle on the field of commercial icons and symbols. For the former, the calamity of commodity overproduction and eco-collapse is a direct result of "our" addiction to consumer goods. A ready cure beckons if only we can wean ourselves off our dependency. For the latter, global brands and their advertising support systems are the new demonology; the Rousseauian impulse to exorcize them from our lives will bring relief (Heath and Potter 2004). The internationally observed social marketing campaigns to "uncool" consumerism—Buy Nothing Day or TV Turnoff Week—are moratoria on our addiction and the first steps down the road of downshifting to a simpler life (Lasn 1999).

Though sweatshop politics has its place within anti-consumerist circles, the obverse is not so certain. Appeals to reduce consumption, or to redirect production into sustainable channels, are not a high priority, and are still likely to be seen as an awkward fit, for most labor activists weaned on the gospel of raising standards for workers. A June 2005 article in the satirical organ *The Onion* showcased some of this dissonance in "reporting" the sentiments of Chen Hsieh, a South China factory worker, who "expressed his disbelief over the 'sheer amount of shit Americans will buy.'" Among the items that he was often asked to manufacture were "plastic-bag dispensers, microwave omelet cookers, glow-in-the-dark page magnifiers, Christmas-themed file baskets, animal-shaped contact-lens cases, and adhesive-backed wall hooks." Chen questioned the need for superfluous kitchen commodities: "I can understand having a good wok, a rice cooker, a tea kettle, a hot plate, some utensils, good china, a teapot with a strainer, and maybe a thermos. But all these extra things—where do the Americans put them? How many times will you use a taco-shell holder?" His brother works breaking down computer waste sent from the United

States and had asked Chen to join him. Despite the hazards involved in handling highly toxic components, it might be a more attractive work option for Chen than "looking at suction-cup razor holders and jumbo-dice keychains all day." He decides to turn down the offer, however, adding, "Somehow, the only thing more depressing than making plastic shit for Americans is destroying the plastic shit they send back" (*Onion* 2005).

To achieve its comic effect, the article mimics the generic template for news reporting about labor exploitation in southern China's labor-intensive export factories. It even cites a representative from the Hong Kong–based labor advocacy group China Labor Bulletin (a leading source of regional information about labor conditions) to the effect that "complaints like Chen's are common among workers in China's bustling industrial cities." In real life, a complaint of this sort would be an eminently rational response to the overproduction of dubious items. Indeed, it resonates with a long tradition of critiques about the waste of labor expended on producing useless goods for status display (Morris 1886; Veblen 1899). Alienation in the workplace has often been tied to the resentment of worker participants in an economy they perceive to be absurd or irrational. Because China is fast developing its own consumer markets (already under immense pressure from the problem of overproduction), Chen's complaint could just as well be directed at production for domestic consumption.

Yet it is improbable that a critique like Chen's would register on the public media landscape, nor would it be likely to take precedence on the agenda of the labor movement over complaints about basic working conditions and pay. When set alongside the task of alleviating the misery of those at the very bottom of the global labor market, foundational challenges to the prevailing system of production and consumption are considered to be the privilege of the relatively secure. Calls for reducing or limiting production are more likely to be viewed simply as invitations to take away jobs. Indeed, the history of labor politics is littered with lost opportunities to join movements that dispute, or alter, the gospel of growth that pervades the business world. Time and time again, the prospect of delivering material abundance has been an easier path for labor leaders to take, no less than for the "captains of consciousness" in the advertising game. Who would risk the ridicule that comes with preaching self-restraint? After all, for those who have been socially and economically denied, a lifestyle of voluntary simplicity holds little immediate attraction. As the maverick IWW organizer Big Bill Haywood once replied, when asked why he smoked oversized cigars, "Nothing's too good for the proletariat."

On the other side, moralistic critics of consumption are invariably in-
sensitive, or even oblivious, to the livelihoods tied to servicing the goods
economy. In these circles, production workers are likely to be seen as the
last source of social change. Instead, that task is allotted to an enlightened
vanguard with little inclination for respecting popular opinion and even
less time for institution building. As the manifesto of the flagship *Adbusters* magazine put it, "You don't need a million people to start a revolution. You just need a passionate minority who sees the light, smells the
blood and pulls off a set of well-coordinated social marketing strategies"
(*Adbusters* 1998).

For the devotees of Adbusters, an image campaign critical of sweated
Nike sneakers is primarily an assault on consumerism as an immoral way
of life, hostile to the natural environment and human psyche alike (Lasn
1999). Secondarily, it can be an opportunity to push Adbusters's own,
earth-friendly Blackspot "unswoosh" sneaker (made with vegetarian
leather and hemp, recycled soles, and designed to give Nike a "swift kick in
the brand"), which trades on its alternative anti-logo status. For the sweatshop activist, the same kind of image campaign would be viewed as an opportunity to push Nike to raise labor standards among its supplier workforce. Given the power of an industry leader to alter global market norms,
holding Nike's brand to ransom is regarded as potentially a more effective
multiplier of labor benefits than investing activist energy in a politically
correct shoe for consumers who may be seeking socially conscious status.

These two impulses are not mutually exclusive; they are both distinctive efforts to exploit the cultural power of a global consumer brand by
appropriating some of its accumulated value. But their respective advocates would each benefit from integrating more of the others' philosophies
and goals. Concerns about the unsustainability of a consumer civilization
have to be addressed at the point of production. Thus, anti-sweatshop
campaigns would be less vulnerable to co-option by the CSR juggernaut
if they were able to broaden the definition of fair labor and fair trade to
include environmental factors that are all too often "externalized." At the
very least, wages and workplace standards should be adequate enough
to protect the social and environmental well-being of communities both
in the host location and elsewhere. It is more difficult for corporate PR
agents to spin the brand out and away from socio-environmental relationships with communities than from wage contracts with individuals. But
labor advocates should also be looking beyond bread-and-butter issues.
Questions about the utility of a product or a production process have to

be asked even if the outcome jeopardizes some jobs. Sectors of production don't have to be ethically weak or harmful—weapons, narcotics, SUVs— to be subject to this kind of scrutiny.

On the other side, anti-consumerists have not taken seriously enough the needs or livelihoods of those employed in a system that they consider immoral. Approaching production workers and labor-based organizations as potential allies rather than hapless victims of false consciousness would make anti-consumerists less vulnerable to critiques that they appeal solely to individual acts of moral volunteerism. So, too, they could learn how to hitch their wagon to progressive institutional forces with proven records of trust among communities and popular constituencies. While advocates of ethical consumption like fair trade are more labor-conscious, they are often quite selective in their choice of which workers to assist, elevating the noble artisan over the industrial employee in the ranks of labor, thereby replicating the exclusivist mentality of the AFL's craft unions of yore.

As always, the challenge is to link movements of ideas with movements of action, and to persuade different populations that they have overlapping, if not exactly complementary, goals. When it comes to labor and environmentalism, their potential alliance is one of the great unfulfilled legacies from the twentieth century. Economic globalization, and the geographic spanning that it has engendered, has only made the spirit of this alliance all the more urgent. The push for "green jobs" is only just getting underway, but it promotes the eventual possibility of mass employment in clean energies, ecologically appropriate technologies, and organic agriculture. Because we are at the outset of this era, the opportunity now exists for sustainability to be addressed at the point of production rather than at the wasteful end of the consumption cycle.

5

Learning from San Ysidro

THE MIGRATION OF people in search of a subsistence livelihood is an abiding feature of world history. In modern times, the dispossession of peasant land is one of the chief factors that has set populations in motion, and in the era of neoliberal free trade, these patterns of displacement have intensified as migrants from developing countries make the trip to the global North, across borders and oceans in ever-increasing numbers. One of the triggers for this movement is the arrival of foreign capital in their home lands and the exposure of their livelihoods to unfair global competition. Livable incomes can no longer be eked out of small farms, and industrial jobs in the new free trade zones suck the daughters and sons of farmers into a precarious urban residence (Bacon 2008). Since the end of the Cold War, an estimated 200 million people have moved from their homes to find opportunities in other countries. In-country migration has also stepped up. In China, the movement of peasants to the cities of the developing coastal regions has numbered over 150 million alone, while 18 million Chinese have moved overseas, to 150 countries in all (Kwong 2007). The expansion of the European Union has freed up the movement of workers to Western Europe, while most member states have seen an influx from outside the bloc. The rate of South-to-South migration also continues to accelerate. As a result, the mega-cities of the global South—Mexico City, Sao Paolo, Dhaka, Lagos, Shanghai, Mumbai, Cairo, Bangkok, Jakarta, Manila—are likely to continue swelling for decades to come, and it is their version of slum life—where one billion are already living in substandard housing—that will define the urban future for the majority of the planet's population (Seabrook 1996; Davis 2006).

Once people are in motion internally, they often keep moving, en route to the affluent regions of the world that export the capital. In North America, where NAFTA has rendered national borders especially porous, campesinos now undertake the journey directly from their rural homes, without any passing sojourn in Mexico City, San Salvador, or Guatemala City (Bacon 2006). They arrive in U.S. cities that have themselves been reshaped by neoliberal investment and policies. In the course of a single generation, the job economies of Los Angeles, New York, Chicago, Miami, Houston, and Phoenix have been transformed, just as sharply as in the Mexican and Central American cities mentioned above, and in ways that are inextricably linked. Nor are these linked fortunes restricted to cities. Migrants drawn to work in U.S. rural regions may find themselves working in a heavily subsidized agribusiness franchise whose corporate global reach could well have been responsible for sealing the fate of their own family farms.

The public is increasingly familiar with this new geography of work, but there is widespread disagreement about the rights and responsibilities owed to these new generations of transnational workers. In the aftermath of decolonization, immigrants to European colonial cores, when asked, however impertinently, to rationalize their presence, could justifiably say, "We are here because you were there." In neoliberal times, the new arrivals could say, with equally good reason, "We are here because your corporations are there." But today's circuits of migration are more complex by far, especially when so many of its travelers are truly transnational in their outlook and operations, retaining allegiances to their home countries, or else subsisting through transborder networks of contacts (Levitt 2001). Moreover, there is as little public knowledge or concern about the varied impact of capital overseas than there was of colonial occupations.

In the pre-NAFTA decades, the mass of immigrants were refugees from civil wars sparked and promoted by U.S. foreign policy, especially in El Salvador, Guatemala, and Nicaragua (Garcia 2006; Teitelbaum 1985; Loescher and Scanlon 1986). Like the free trade agreements of the 1990s, these conflicts were largely the product of Washington's efforts to control the economic and political affairs of Central America, and the migration streams they generated were sometimes locally as large as the post-NAFTA ones. But limits were placed on the available political will to welcome the refugees, lest Washington's proxy wars be officially acknowledged as the main source of regional instability (Crittenden 1988; Golden and McConnell 1986). The same kind of double standard is responsible today for the disconnect that exists between public knowledge about NAFTA's devastation of Mexican livelihoods and the all-too-obvious impact on immigration.

Regardless of whether the migrants have been political or economic refugees, domestic U.S. employers have exploited their plight at every

turn, exercising their business clout to maintain and protect a cheap labor supply who can be hired and fired at will, and who lack the rights
and social supports they need to win some basic security. The injustice
of this arrangement is only one part of the broader pattern of inequality
that is a consequence of corporate free trade. When it comes to assessing
the economic impact of neoliberalism, the record of benefit and loss has
become impossible to ignore: the winners in the game of corporate-led
globalization have been far outnumbered by the losers. Even neoclassical
economists—the court poets of free trade—are beginning to break ranks
with the iron consensus of their profession that liberalization is a win-win
game. One of the reasons for the erosion of fundamentalist faith in neoliberalism is the public abhorrence at atrocious labor conditions in sweatshops in overseas free trade zones. By contrast, it has not been so easy to
prick the public conscience when it comes to the use of immigrant labor
in our own backyard. The psychology of denial surrounding low-wage service jobs in the domestic economy rests on a formidable coalescence of
guilt and personal economic interest.

   If the public is accustomed to turning a blind eye to domestic sweatshops on farms, construction sites, food factory floors, and in restaurant
kitchens, there is even less attention to the housing conditions of most
low-wage immigrant workers. The right to housing was one of original
nine rights proposed by FDR in his 1944 bill of rights, and indeed the
1948 Housing Act promised a "decent home in a suitable living environment for every American." But there has been a notable decline in U.S. political support for this position since the 1960s (Hartman 1988). In 1996,
in response to the cumulative pressure of numerous international human
rights documents, the State Department asserted that it "must make clear
for the record that the U.S. does not recognize the international right to
housing," and that it prefers a weaker recognition that decent housing is
simply an ideal to be pursued (Moses 2005). But the erosion of support
for the right to housing is not simply a neoliberal reflex, or a typical ploy
on Washington's part to position the United States outside of international
neo-legal norms. Progressive critics have argued that, practically speaking,
most government efforts to respond to this obligation have made matters
worse, if only because the policy of most public housing agencies has been
to simply put a roof on poverty. Instead, the critics argue, the provision of
housing has to be approached in tandem with guarantees of access to employment, health, and education. Otherwise, social housing is little more
than a Band-Aid (Carr 1998).

In recent years, ecological factors have entered the picture. How can sustainable land-use practices be encouraged in the face of mass migration? From an environmental standpoint, the acceleration of migrant streams into metropolitan areas is most often viewed as a problem. The powerful neo-Malthusian impulse behind so much environmentalist thought—the idea that limited resources keep populations and economic growth in check—automatically positions population increase as a threat to sustainability. As a result, shortages of available affordable housing are often interpreted as a confirmation of the scarcity of resources rather than an expression of social inequality. In fact, zoning and lending regulations, engineered to protect the property value of upscale populations, are far and away the primary factor in creating housing scarcities, severely restricting the ability to build what is needed. Wherever the requisite political will exists to amend these regulations and implement adequate housing policies, it seems quite clear that poor people will get the job done—with or without their advocates.

Where no secure shelter exists at all, migrants in the global South tend to settle on the most fragile ecologies—riparian corridors, for example, where degradation occurs most rapidly, or in dried-up riverbeds, thereby impeding efforts to restore rivers. Environmental advocates often find themselves at odds with affordable housing advocates in such situations, and the poor are caught in the middle. Yet it has often been noted that squatters at the edge of the mega-cities improvise their shelter and their lives in extremely efficient ways. Even while they are victims of petty economic cruelty, they are making housing, to paraphrase Marx, under conditions not of their own making. Forty-five years ago, the anarchist architect John Turner was energized by the ingenious examples of housing construction undertaken, on his administrative watch, by residents of *barriadas*—urban squatter settlements—in the Peruvian city of Arequipa after the earthquake of 1958. The self-motivated building efforts of these poverty-stricken people proved more practical and efficient than the applied knowledge that he, as a professional, working with the Peruvian bureaucracy, could have offered (Turner 1972). The squatters at the edge of the city were first- or second-generation migrants and their rural habits of cooperation in building roofs and walls were still quite strong (Chavez, Viloria, and Zipperer 2000). This powerful image of mutual aid in action, buttressed by Turner's own anarchist ideas about local autonomy, helped to promote the self-help housing movement on a highly visible international stage.

Self-help had found an earlier standard-bearer in the Egyptian architect and planner Hassan Fathy, who restored architectural credibility to Nubian mud-construction techniques by training locals to use mud bricks to build the ambitious though ultimately ill-fated community of New Gourna, near Luxor (Fathy 1972). More successful were the extensive government resettlement programs initiated in the 1940s and 1950s in Puerto Rico (whose manual Turner distributed in Peru to facilitate the rebuilding of ten thousand homes). In 1976, the core principles of mutual aid would inspire the founding of Habitat for Humanity, which has drawn on volunteer, in addition to occupant, labor to complete the most extensive self-building program of low-income housing in the United States over the last few decades (Stevens 1982).

Turner's influence, and the showcased successes on the ground in Peru, helped push self-help onto the policymaking agenda of the World Bank, which rapidly became the chief actor in Third World housing after the formation of its urban department in the mid-1970s. Convinced of the economic efficiencies to be gained from helping the poor to help themselves, officials at the bank shifted their funding, previously earmarked for direct housing construction, into the provision of sites and services, the basic armature around which people could build their own shelter. While democratic in spirit, there were many technical problems associated with this model. Most of the bank's projects, for example, involved locations on the urban periphery, far removed from likely sources of employment (Ward 1982). Nor was the case for economic efficiency fully borne out— the capacity of a public agency to purchase building materials in bulk trumped the cost of piecemeal construction on an individual basis. But there was also a larger ideological issue at work. Over time, and in the hands of an institution that worked, as a good cop to the IMF's bad cop, in imposing privatization in developing countries, Turner's ethos of learning from the poor was transmuted into a recipe for withdrawing the state from most of its responsibilities for housing the poor and marginal, let alone providing them with jobs. Self-help proved an easy pathway toward letting market forces prevail in the informal sector of housing and employment— a natural complement to the more widely publicized rollout of neoliberal deregulation in the formal sector (Davis 2006).

Allowing market dynamics to prevail in informal urban settlements only accentuated their highly exploitative economies. In a world teeming with sweatshops, slumlords, gangsters, and fiefs whose wealth rests on small tributes paid by the poorest in return for the most miserly resources, nothing comes cheap. Fresh migrants are preyed on from the moment they arrive. Some of the most venal slumlord practices take place among immigrant slum dwellers themselves, where squatters with established claims on space use this leverage to extract rent from the newest, and most vulnerable, arrivals. It is by no means easy to extract Turner's lessons about mutual aid from environments and populations so carefully and ruthlessly squeezed for any available profit margin.

Just as the informal sector emulates the formal one, so, too, the IMF/World Bank programs known as "structural adjustment" were first introduced in affluent countries like the United States. In the case of housing policy, they were likewise stimulated by a progressive critique of the status quo in planning. At the same time as Turner and others advocated alternatives to top-down expertise in housing the poor, Jane Jacobs was launching her celebrated attack on the arrogance of large-scale planning, especially evident, at the time, in the programs of slum elimination known as urban renewal. Rather than clear out the overcrowded slums by decanting and decentralizing, as the Garden City devotees had preached and the postwar urban renewers had practiced, Jacobs argued that residents had the capacity to "unslum" neighborhoods themselves, with just a little in the way of resources, while retaining the social, cultural, and economic benefits of their density (1961). Aside from her own Greenwich Village in New York, Jacobs cited Boston's North End (a classic European immigrant community), Rittenhouse Square in Philadelphia, and Telegraph Hill in San Francisco as examples of dense, inner-city neighborhoods that had been or were about to be slated for clearance. If only they were spared the bulldozer, each promised its own renaissance, at the hands of residents themselves.

Yet, over time, Jacobs's faith in self-motivated community revitalization suffered a fate not unlike Turner's when it was taken up as a neoliberal prescription for privatizing housing solutions. According to this new paradigm, government planning and intervention could only ever do harm and were best kept at bay. Instead of fulfilling obligations to all its citizens, the state's resources would henceforth be directed to stimulating and assisting entrepreneurial efforts at boosting property valuation in depreciated neighborhoods. When subsidies were offered to the most eligible takers, long-established residents no longer had control over the fate of their community. The result, all too familiar today, is gentrified urban enclaves cleansed of the diverse income mix that was key to Jacobs's concept of vibrant urbanism.

It is unfair to hold Jacobs or Turner responsible for the unanticipated uses made of their respective legacies by antistatist ideologies. Both of them promoted practical ideals that can still inspire the provision and preservation of affordable housing. Cooperative, human-scale building, resource conservation, and local knowledge are perfectly sound principles. But the record shows that, in a purely entrepreneurial policy climate, they are all too often wielded as weapons of incumbency or as tools to exclude, to block any new land-use proposal or population influx, or to create and protect a property-value haven. As this chapter argues, the integrity of these principles stands its best chance of being tested in the case of new immigrants, who have the least to lose and who are most likely to be current with the wise application of sustainable building knowledge.

In common with the concerns about internal migration in developing countries, the outcry over immigration in the contemporary United States has been fed by neo-Malthusian concerns about the scarcity of resources. But all too often the racist underbelly of such concerns reveals the threat of white populations becoming a demographic minority in many regions of the country. In response to anti-immigration sentiment and legislation, advocates have mostly argued on the basis that immigrant labor brings considerable economic benefits to the nation. It is more rare to hear a positive environmentalist argument made on behalf of immigration. Yet the case for it must be investigated, not for its pragmatic value but because the exigencies of the ecological crisis demand that we think about land development, population movement, and urban planning from all potentially helpful angles.

Jobs, Sprawl, and Conservation

If you had to name some hot-button issues that rouse, if not inflame, American public opinion, undocumented immigration would be up there alongside land-gobbling sprawl. Scour the public media spectrum for efforts to link these two issues, however, and you might come away empty-handed. Given their many points of connection, this is surprising. Both anti-sprawl and anti-immigration advocates are all too easily portrayed as partisans of the status quo, with a zeal for barring new entrants and blocking new growth. So, too, concerns about the sustainability of both ill-planned land development and unregulated population growth appear to overlap. More Americans living wastefully on the land is the last thing the world's energy budget needs. There is high public recognition, globally, about the ecological cost of maintaining the American engine of suburban land development, dependent as it is on the free flow of cheap oil. From the perspective of many global citizens, resistance to George W. Bush's war in Iraq boiled down to a very simple question. Why should the rest of the world be held hostage by the energy budget of the three-car American suburban home?

Much of the debate about sprawl—the term most often used to describe unplanned low-density suburban development—has focused on its grabby consumption of open space and wasteful dependency on automobile use. The remedies on offer—smart growth, high-density settlement, greenbelts, highway suppression, and urban growth boundaries—have all been subject to the kind of extensive cost-benefit analysis that can support arguments on both pro- and anti-sprawl sides (Burchell et al. 2005; Gillham 2002; Bruegmann 2005; Frumkin, Frank, and Jackson 2004; Duany, Plater-Zyberk, and Speck 2001). Yet virtually none of the eco-cost accounting that has been applied, tirelessly, to sprawl development has factored in the housing needs of the immigrant workers hired to build and maintain the infrastructure of low-density suburbia as well as provide long-term services for its residents. Large-scale developers and their contractors benefit directly (and rapaciously) from the ready availability of their undocumented labor. Indeed, some of the loudest notes in the pro-immigrant chorus have been sounded by managers of the home-building industry. Their data shows how much of the recent construction boom relied on cheap immigrant labor and, to a much more disputed extent, home buying by immigrants (Belsky 2006). (It was no coincidence that Home Depot branches across the country became recruitment centers for day labor.) With housing starts sharply down in most regions and merchant-built growth on the urban peripheries stalled as a result of the realty recession, the opportunity now exists to rethink land use along different lines.

Undocumented immigration is not going to stop anytime soon, though it is being pushed further underground. It might be best, then, to start thinking about balancing the housing, employment, and commuting needs of immigrants in a more or less permanent way. With economic mobility sharply reduced, new arrivals, if they stay, are likely to reside at their point of entry for longer periods of time. From a design perspective, this challenge of semipermanence is a new one. It differs sharply from the response to distressed, migrant communities typified by the organizational work of Architecture for Humanity, where the task of engineering shelter solutions is triggered by the emergency conditions of humanitarian crises (Architecture for Humanity 2006). Even so, there are lessons to be learned from design approaches to the problems faced by these displaced peoples. Refugees from, and victims of, famines, wars, natural disasters, and epidemics have needs that are, first and foremost, driven by survival. Once the danger point has passed, this temporary status cedes to a transitional one, where the goal is to reconnect them to livelihoods. Architectural solutions to these problems are mostly brokered by an army of NGOs, which have assumed the burden of humanitarian response to crises in the global South engendered, for the most part, by the political shortcomings of more affluent states. The most successful designs tend to make use of cheap, locally available, or recycled materials—rammed or compressed earth, adobe, rubble, hemp, straw bales, pallets—and deploy customary building methods that make it easier for the displaced residents to participate in construction. The most ingenious of all utilize materials that can be dismantled and reused in permanent housing. Though the majority of the emergency sites are in poor countries, there is no reason why these cheap, sustainable approaches, and many of the techniques themselves, cannot be applied to housing in regions of the global North.

Architects engaged in emergency housing abroad bring back valuable knowledge to their home countries. As Sergio Palleroni, founder of University of Washington's Global Community Studio, which began its work in Mexican squatter zones next to maquiladoras, put it: "I realized I needed to take students out of the United States into these areas so they could see how they could be rethinking their profession as designers—to become citizens of the world, to be aware of the social, cultural, and environmental impact of architecture" (Architecture for Humanity 2006: 267). But professionals are not alone in retrieving this knowledge. Although immigrants to the United States, especially those coming directly from rural areas, bring know-how that is immediately relevant to their housing and livelihood needs, it is rarely solicited. They are the last population to enter the minds of planners, the last in line to be considered as a group from whom some things might be learned.

When it comes to their housing needs, low-income immigrants are all too often placed in the same mental category as refugees—that is, as displaced peoples who require temporary or transitional shelter. It is expected, moreover, that they will move on and up, as immigrants have traditionally done. Yet while many immigrants did improve their lot, the substandard housing stock of their neighborhoods did not improve, nor did it change all that much, as it played host to each succeeding generation of overly vulnerable settlers. Barrios and other customary immigrant settlements have long outlasted their expiration date at the core of American cities. Furthermore, as property value has steadily risen in other city neighborhoods, the traditional ability of immigrants to move up has declined rapidly. For many new arrivals, their first home in the United States is more and more likely to be their only one. Indeed, given the rate at which historic barrio and ghetto areas (Harlem and Spanish Harlem in New York City, for example) are now being encroached on by gentrification, immigrants are increasingly hard-pressed to hold on to that first home (Davila 2004).

Given that the employment landscape is morphing so quickly, it might also be said that any emphasis on permanence would be imprudent. But the demographic and employment patterns suggest that in the future, changes may well reach those in high-wage sectors, increasingly affected by the march of outsourcing up the skills ladder, more than low-income groups, whose services cannot be outsourced and will always be needed (Ross 2006a). Workers in the latter category are more likely to stick around, especially when the opportunities for occupational mobility are being closed off by an economy geared to go on shrinking its middle class. In the era of the industrial city, blue-collar housing was more likely to be proximate to places of employment or conveniently linked by mass transit. When factory owners relocated plants outside cities (by 1950, half of all manufacturing jobs were suburban in location), they did so to escape the concentrated and organized power of urban workers to halt production through strikes and other forms of industrial action. In the more dispersed suburban landscape, workers' power was diffused (Gordon 1978). In addition, there was an underlying political motivation to the home ownership offered to workers as part of the postwar program of mass suburbanization. As William Levitt, the grandee of Cold War suburbanization, famously put it, "No man who owns his own house and lot can be a Communist. He has too much to do" (Jackson 1985: 231) Most inner-city families of color were excluded from this highly subsidized program, and so their access to decent employment opportunities steadily eroded during the second half of the twentieth century (Abrams 1955; Sugrue 1996; Jackson 1985). The growth of low-wage service-sector jobs, in tandem with the rise of urban professional services, has been a draw for many new immigrants, but this precarious work, along with other informal jobs filled by the undocumented, is often at a considerable distance from places of residence.

For sure, cities and less dense regions absorb immigrants in different ways, but the need to design a more effective job/housing balance is consistent. So the questions facing designers and planners are readily apparent. How can decent, affordable housing be designed or upgraded in a sustainable way—in particular, close to jobs? How can commute times for low-wage workers be reduced? How should zoning and coding regulations be revised to enable this? How can these efforts be financed when most of the funding structures for affordable housing stand in the way? Most challenging of all, perhaps, how can designers and architects get immigrants involved meaningfully in the design and planning process at a time when fear of deportation keeps them out of sight? Surely, somewhere in the design and/or planning professions there are people dedicated to addressing these questions. But most evidence suggests otherwise. The immigrant populations who build and who keep everything running are almost as invisible to architects and urbanists (even those trained in community design programs) as they are to the average middle-class American who would rather not acknowledge the indispensability of their labor.

Eco-Design from the Bottom-Up

What is the current wisdom in eco-design? Focus on clients at the top end, whence, it is assumed, the good ideas and practices will trickle down. For the architectural profession, this means that the rewards of visibility and prestige go to those who can claim to have designed the "greenest" among the sprouting forest of signature luxury-housing buildings. And on the landscape of single-family housing, New Urbanist efforts are aimed at upper-middle-class suburbanites with "choices" about how and where to locate their families and material assets. But what if sustainability were approached from the other end, from the perspective of new immigrants—a ballooning population with chronic housing needs and conservation habits formed from long experience with meager resources? Adopting the standpoint of those with the fewest choices and the most efficient lifestyles might help refocus the debate about sprawl while redefining the character and uses of urban infill development.

There is no need to unduly romanticize the conservation-minded culture of this population. Indigenous peoples, for example, have not always been well served by being depicted as the wisest and most unimpeachable stewards of the environment (the closer to nature, the further from civilization). Anyone who lives and works close to the subsistence level, making do with scarce resources, is a conservationist by necessity. These habits are not just budget-wise requisites: they are embedded in the customary ways of communities for whom mutual aid often goes well beyond the networks of extended families. Immigrants who come bearing know-how about turning scarcity into a virtue have lessons and knowledge to impart. When global corporations outsource technology and skilled jobs to developing countries, the euphemism they employ is "knowledge transfer," but the onshore countries are also taking in immigrant skills that are not always put to the best use. Reverse knowledge transfer of this sort is typically squandered. It is common to encounter taxi drivers or domestic workers who had professional careers in other countries, and there are similar mismatches in every corner of the workforce.

The same applies to the housing sector. Immigrants are sometimes viewed as heroes of inner-city renovation, fixing up decaying neighborhoods with sweat equity and colorful ethnic gusto (Davis 2000). In some shrinking northern cities, the new arrivals have stemmed a steep population decline and have salvaged nearly abandoned neighborhoods. These are notable achievements, though public perceptions of their success are often fed by the psychology of American racialization. According to this racist hierarchy, Mexicans and other Central American immigrants, along with islanders from parts of the Anglophone Caribbean and most Asians, are understood to possess a superior work ethic, relative to immigrants from the Dominican Republic, Haiti, Jamaica, Puerto Rico, and Colombia, and certainly to Puerto Ricans, with citizen rights, and native-born African Americans (Smith 2006). The "good immigrants" in the former category, even when they are undocumented, are perceived to be capable of virtuous feats of self-help that will put them on an upwardly mobile path. Whether immigrants or native-born, the others, according to this public stereotyping, are more likely to be overly dependent, in the long term, on the state and its social services.

Immigrants encounter this formidable filter of ethnic stratification upon arrival in the United States and learn to live with the knowledge that it has, to a large degree, predetermined the respective limits of their social mobility, along with their chances of securing loans, decent employment, and housing credit. For this racist psychology to persist, it requires the visibility of some model immigrant minorities as proof that the American dream is available to those who work hard and respect the law. It is by no means necessary to deny or minimize the successful examples of community revitalization to acknowledge that this practice feeds into profiles of model minorities. Yet statistics tell a different story. Overall, immigrants are more likely than any other demographic to be trapped in substandard housing that is overpriced, illegal, and dangerous. Though their median income is about the same as the median income of native-born working families with critical housing needs, immigrants tend to settle in more expensive housing markets, so they are more likely to be paying higher prices and to be living in crowded conditions (Lipman 2003). In addition, because they are the most vulnerable clients, they are often preyed on by those only slightly less poor than themselves. For most, the opportunity to invest sweat equity in revitalizing a home and a neighborhood, never mind the freedom to make decisions about dwelling, is systematically denied.

Before the lavish system of federal incentives for building suburban sprawl and upmarket urban development was established, the business of constructing housing for immigrants was among the most lucrative sectors of the housing industry. In the era of the industrializing city, sizable returns were extracted from investments in settling new arrivals who had limited shelter choices. Until recently, the immigrant market in barrios and other low-income enclaves was a highly bankable prospect (DiMento and Graymer 1987), and rent gouging from inner-city substandard housing is still among the more profitable forms of land speculation. Though the history and persistence of these exploitative practices are shameful, they blow away the given wisdom that there is no money in low-income housing and that heavy government subsidies are required to build.

Socially responsible design groups have adequately demonstrated that decent, aesthetically significant housing can be built at low cost. To drive home the point, Auburn University's Rural Studio, founded by the legendary Sam Mockbee, produced the 20K model—a two-bedroom, stick-frame house that is energy-efficient, meets federal standards, and can be built by any commercial contractor for twenty thousand dollars, including materials and labor. This cost puts the house within the range of mortgages available to the lowest-income rural households. The Rural Studio has also pioneered personalized custom design for the rural poor of southwestern Alabama, shaping a respectful, interactive client relationship with residents (Dean and Hursley 2002, 2005). Likewise, Seattle's Housing Solutions Studio innovated the use of straw-bale construction in

Indian housing on the central plains of South Dakota and Montana. The use of this material, locally abundant and energy-efficient, made it easy for residents to learn low-cost building techniques as they participated in the construction of their new homes (Palleroni 2004). When Bryan Bell's Design Corps built housing for migrant farmworkers in Pennsylvania, it was designed for the taste and needs of the workers but also with an eye to the budget of the growers. The result was a significant upgrade of the traditional migrant worker cabin, notorious for its vulnerability to the elements (Devereux 2004; Bell 2003).

Further innovations in the design of this housing type are needed to reflect shifts in the culture of migrants. For example, Bell designed most of the units to meet the mobility-based needs of seasonal migrants, primarily single males. But he also designed units for families (increasingly common in the migrant stream since the 1986 Immigration Reform and Control Act), whose goal is more likely to be one of permanent residence. This reorientation toward permanent settlement, triggered by the New Right's legislative fondness for "family values," requires a quantum shift in responsible design, because it involves access to educational institutions along with a whole range of social services. Housing, in this context, is just one link in a network of support that can and should be designed together, from a sustainable standpoint. Yet, in urban areas, where new immigrants are the fastest-growing population segment, little attention has been paid to their ecological footprints, either by planners or environmentalists.

The latter tend to fall into two camps: pastorally minded "greens," who are largely committed to combating exurban housing development for the well-heeled, and environmental justice advocates, who are focused on the prejudicial distribution of hazardous waste sites among minority populations or the dangers posed by inadequate brownfield conversions. Scholars like Devon Pena have begun to change the conversation, by arguing that the recent immigration of indigenous Mesoamerican communities into southwestern cities is not only a recolonization of El Norte, but also the key to restoring the ecologies of the region. The impact of their land-use practices and ethno-cultural views on food and watershed sovereignty have already registered sharply in the informal spatial map (street, alley, and marketplace use) and on the agronomy (urban farms and community gardens) of these cities (Pena 2009, 2005a, 2005b).

As for the planning establishment, low-income immigrants routinely do not register as target constituents, either because they don't qualify as eligible clients or because they lack public clout in the sphere of city politics. New Urbanists, who have led the charge toward sustainability through their promotion of Traditional Neighborhood Development (TND), take the prewar, Euro-American small town as their blueprint, unmindful of the long history of compact towns that thrived in the Southwest, first in indigenous pueblo settlements, then in Mexican-origin urban villages of the nineteenth century. Indeed, David Diaz and Michael Mendez have argued that the true conceptual roots of New Urbanism are more readily located in those sustainable southwestern forms, which morphed into the densified urban barrio of the twentieth century (Diaz 2005; Mendez 2002, 2005). The customary preferences of Latino immigrant communities today are already congruent with the basic New Urbanist principles—mixed-use and high-density interaction of private and public space—though the low-budget, hybrid outcome is usually too messy for the approved TND aesthetic taste.

Dumb Growth

Traditional immigrant gateways, like New York, Boston, and San Francisco, which do not have room for easy peripheral expansion, cannot absorb new arrivals in the same way that the sprawling cities of the Sunbelt can. The latter are the most rapidly expanding American cities, where immigration is a big factor in the population growth, and where anti-immigrant sentiment is often strongest. Apologists for sprawl argue that cities like Phoenix and Houston, with highly permissive land-use policies, have done a better job of accommodating the poor than "smart growth" strongholds like Portland, which tend to be high-priced and racially exclusive bastions, and where immigrants settle outside of the city. In addition, they point out that in almost half the country's large cities—including many with sprawl-friendly regulations and large immigration streams—urban densities have been rising for some time now. Indeed, in the period when the anti-sprawl movement has been most active, the rate of sprawl, far from accelerating at a disturbing pace, has been on the decline.[1] Indeed, the much-maligned Los Angeles basin was recently revealed to be the densest metro region in the United States (it has always had small lot sizes and its residential ground coverage is quite comprehensive) (Bruegmann 2005).

Yet, when looking at how low-income people have fared, economically, over this period of time in the most rapidly growing U.S. cities, the picture is not so rosy. The explosion in urban property value has squeezed the poor most, fast outpacing their income increments. Indeed, the biggest increases in the percentage of income that residents spend on housing are in the fastest-growing immigrant destinations in states like Texas, California, and Colorado (American Community Survey 2006). The geographic patterns of the mortgage crisis are also pretty clear, because the culture of many immigrants is to sink savings into housing equity as soon as they can. Immigrants with limited English language capacity and restricted access to information networks have been especially vulnerable targets of the predatory lending practices that flourished until recently in many cites and first-ring suburbs, and so they have been left, disproportionately, holding bad subprime loans and facing foreclosure.

Largely because of the vestigial influence of frontier values, western and Sunbelt cities are often seen as exemplars of dumb growth. They exhibit the clearest contradiction between the pro-growth mentality of their chambers of commerce, the coding and zoning regulations of their planning agencies (crafted to protect established interests within the housing industry), and the often-virulent anti-immigrant sensibilities of the general incumbent population. Take the county with the biggest population growth in the United States for several years—Arizona's Maricopa County, which includes Phoenix and is as large in area as New Jersey. It added seven hundred thousand residents between 2000 and 2007, most of them new immigrants and migrant retirees (U.S. Census 2007). The Maricopa County sheriff, Joe Arpaio, claims to be "America's toughest sheriff" (standing out among a highly competitive field in the South), having revived the use of chain gang labor (while instituting it for women and juveniles) and pioneered prison conditions aimed at both fiscal efficiency and punitive severity. Arpaio uses his office to recruit volunteer citizen posses to hunt down undocumented immigrants, whom he incarcerates in his widely publicized "tent city" jails (where services are stripped to the bone, thirty-five-cent meals are served, pink underwear is issued, and temperatures approach 120 degrees) (Arpaio and Sherman 1996). In 2007, he earned additional national-publicity points by asking the Los Angeles authorities to transfer Paris Hilton to Maricopa County to serve her jail sentence (Lemons 2007).

Though Arpaio is very popular among the frontier-minded, he is a source of embarrassment to government officers, whose job it is to attract business to the county; he is also an annoyance to housing contractors concerned about maintaining their cheap labor supply. Nonetheless, the popular support for his profile has been parlayed into a series of tough anti-immigrant measures—the 2007 Employers Sanctions Bill authorizes country attorneys to revoke the business license of an employer who knowingly hires undocumented workers. Fear of deportation, allied to the downturn in the building economy, has begun to generate a small, but significant, population exodus on the part of undocumented residents in a state whose foreign-born population surged from 270,000 in 1990 to over 900,000 (half of them undocumented) in 2005.

Planning departments in swelling southern counties like Maricopa have also tried to appease popular sentiment about immigrant control by introducing restrictive and unconstitutional legislation to restrict housing occupancy. A Manassas, Virginia, law ordained that occupants had to prove consanguinity or a direct family relationship to the homeowner, while Cobb County, in Atlanta's metro north, proposed legislation limiting occupancy of a housing unit to no more than four unrelated dwellers (*Washington Post* 2005; Jonsson 2006). Such measures are targeted at both the expanded family households favored by many immigrants as well as the proliferation of "drop houses," which are filled with bunk beds for use by multiple families. To evade charges of discrimination, drop houses are enacted in the name of controlling density—a longstanding obsession in the planning profession that has, over time, become fully institutionalized in the housing market. Some cities, like Escondido and San Bernardino in Southern California, Hazelton in Pennsylvania, and Palm Bay in Florida, have gone even further, by trying to ban outright the renting of apartments to undocumented immigrants.[2]

At the same time that their suburban and county counterparts introduce demographic control through housing policy, pro-growth city managers are generally happy to trumpet any available statistics of population increase. While pro-growth sentiment ensures that immigrants are somewhat more welcome in urbanized areas, the population growth does not usually translate into better housing conditions, let alone better job opportunities. For low-income communities in cities like Phoenix, the steady influx of residents means ever-expanding barrios, which suffer from the typical symptoms of underdeveloped immigrant housing: deteriorating stock, land speculation, chronic underinvestment from both public and private sectors, restricted access to financing for home buying and home improvement, and overcrowding and overpricing. In 2003, one of every four households in the county was spending more than 50 percent of its income on housing (Voas 2001).

Historically, barrios in southwestern cities were located near centers of employment, but that is no longer the case. Manufacturing plants transferred from northern states are generally not close at hand. A variety of low-wage service employment exists in Maricopa's central commute shed (the employment locations of workers who live in the core urban areas), serving the cities of Phoenix, Scottsdale, Mesa, and Tempe. But those working in construction or as domestic employees travel long distances daily to exurban subdivisions that are increasingly encroaching on high-risk flood plains and other Sonoran Desert lands subject to severe erosion and sediment damage. Settlement patterns in Maricopa have long exhibited the telltale signs of speculative leapfrog development, which leaves unusually large acreages of bypassed land: by 1980, a full 40 percent of the city of Phoenix was vacant (Heim 2001: 1).

Leapfrogging, where a developer builds on only the most choice pieces of land, generates a host of problems for sustainable land use. In 2001, a report for the Maricopa Association of Governments forecast that the number of vehicle miles traveled would increase at a rate much faster than that of the swelling population. It also noted that the spatial mismatch between suburbanized jobs and the central city poor was more likely to be alleviated by improving transit commutes than by the politically volatile move of building affordable housing in the suburbs. The mismatch has helped reinforce the county's skewed income differentials, one of the highest in a state already ranked number two in the nation for its income disparity (Maricopa Association of Governments 2001). Another consequence is the deterioration of air quality in most of the county's commute sheds. Indeed, the National Wildlife Federation has alerted the county that dozens of animal and plant species are now imperiled (National Wildlife Federation 2005). In a county beset by water shortages, the result is a bizarre cocktail, with very American ingredients, guaranteed to deliver a nasty ecological hangover.

One eminently rational solution, initiated by Phoenix planners in 1995, was to start an infill program, whereby tax credits, incentives, and waivers were offered to those willing to build in central city areas. Yet the program was aimed exclusively at owner-occupied, single-family homes and included no mixed-use provisions. So, too, planners shied away from higher densities when faced with political opposition from the frontier-values mentality that still drives regional growth (Heim 2001: 11). In addition, the program put no caps on the price of qualifying homes, so many of the recipients of the subsidies turned out to be well-heeled (Silverman

1995). In more recent years, business tycoons who are members of the Downtown Phoenix Partnership have made a fine art out of harvesting for private developments, public tax dollars loosely designated for infill (Dougherty 2003).

Phoenix's effort was a typical lost opportunity for combining efficiency, sustainability, and affordability in one package. Ideally, an innovative infill program could have delivered construction jobs with short commutes, along with decent self-built housing for the workers themselves. What better way of harnessing the sweat equity that has been the creative elixir of immigrant homesteading elsewhere? A more far-reaching effort at planning would map and coordinate employment, commuting, and housing patterns, but there may be too many political and regulatory obstacles for such a top-down planning process to succeed.

Learning from San Ysidro

The situation in fast-growing cities and counties cries out for more ingenious community-based efforts in which sympathetic architects are able to broker the dialogue between government agencies, housing advocates, nonprofit developers, implementers, and populations in need. The Sunbelt model for this kind of brokering has been pioneered by Teddy Cruz, who is uniquely positioned—working across what he calls the "laboratory" of the San Diego/Tijuana border—to facilitate culturally appropriate responses to affordable housing in both cities. Indeed, it would be more accurate to approach this border region as if it were one metropolis, however strictly divided, with two centers, only twenty minutes apart. The steel wall that is the divider effectively renders San Diego into what Cruz calls "the world's largest gated community."

Cruz has been inspired by informal settlements on the Tijuana periphery that are typical of the new Mexican *barriadas* swelling with rural migrants. There, design is mostly about self-building with materials—tires, garage doors, siding, packing crates, and whole bungalows—recycled from the American city to the north, which exports its infrastructural waste to the Mexican city in the south (Cruz 2007b). The Tijuana authorities are legally obliged, after the fact, to supply infrastructure and utilities to these piecemeal, unplanned settlements, which are then protected from demolition. Cruz has grasped, and praised, the democratic essence of this makeshift process. Further, he has tried to upgrade and regularize it by calling for officials and NGOs to pressure Tijuana's large *maquila* employers, who take advantage of the migrant labor, to play a more responsible role by manufacturing self-help housing kits. To date, he has persuaded at least once such employer (a Spanish-owned *maquila* that makes jumbo industrial shelving) to produce a prototype building frame that occupants can use as a housing skeleton to accommodate the recycled materials. Ideally, the frames would come as part of a kit, with an assembly manual and a snap-in water tank, in a spirit not unlike the early twentieth-century concept of the Sears catalog house (Cruz 2005, 2007a).

North of the border, the building possibilities are already heavily predetermined by zoning and coding regulations and by public policies directed toward boosting private-sector entrepreneurialism, business growth, and luxury housing. As a result, almost no affordable housing has been built in San Diego in the last decade. Clearly, self-help in and of itself is not an option for low-income communities like the predominantly Latino border town of San Ysidro, where Cruz has undertaken his most innovative housing projects. Partnering with Casa Familiar, a nonprofit developer with respected community origins and relations, ensured grassroots participation in the plans. Affordability is facilitated through a managed micro-credit system whereby owners can barter their services, bank their time, or earn credit through sweat equity rather than relying on the single loan structure typical of subsidized housing projects. In addition, Cruz was able to help the developer petition successfully for a waiver of San Ysidro's zoning codes—especially the density ordinances—as the opening salvo of an ambitious campaign to take on all of San Diego's building codes. These codes (which otherwise protect developers and enforce home owners' discriminatory aversion to density) are a clear, technical obstacle to Cruz's self-avowed task of making the best, sustainable use of leftover urban space for the communities that need it. The spaces, and the uses made of them, are nonconforming in every sense, but they are much more plentiful and practical as affordable housing prospects than those few that qualify as infill sites under the city's building ordinances. Planning regulations assess density numerically, as units per acre; Cruz, on the other hand, likes to define density as a matter of social choreography—the number of "social exchanges" per acre. The emphasis here is on the social sustainability of a community project—that is, what component parts (beyond mere housing) are needed to guarantee that residents can adequately support one another.

The first phase of the San Ysidro project ("Living Rooms at the Border") called for a mixed-use, high-density complex built around an old church that would be transformed into a community center. The plan included housing units, a community garden, and a central market plaza that would serve as a multipurpose social gathering place for the community as a whole. The second phase, for senior housing and for child care largely undertaken by grandparents, is connected by an alleyway and includes a restaurant counter and gardens. The housing units, in particular, are designed for flexibility, with interlocking rooms that can be broken down or pieced together to house expanded families as needed. In these designs, Cruz's approach has been to allow the community's existing patterns of use (private, semipublic, and public) to serve as a beginning template (Solnit 2007). This incremental approach emulates the illegal additions that families customarily append as companion units when they expand or when they open a micro-business. The result is a model of informal densification that has organic roots, quite unlike the unloved high-density apartment complexes that affordable housing agencies allow developers to drop into poor neighborhoods.

Cruz sees housing as "less about a collection of objects and more about participatory community processes and the resourcefulness and organization of people" (2005). This definition (under which the community exercises some ownership of the project from the outset), and the practice it entails, blends the improvised south-of-the-border ethos with the best lessons learned by U.S. designers of affordable housing over the last few decades. Indeed, its promotion of user empowerment harks back to the advocacy planning movement of the 1960s and 1970s while being realistic about the political obstacles that lie in the path of today's designers. Housing is a verb, as John Turner declared in his most influential essay, and in today's U.S. immigrant enclaves, where individuals are too vulnerable to act on their own, it is best approached as a form of community organizing (Turner 1972).

How does this impinge on the mentality of the professional? When you are designing for affordability at the community level, there is little room for the self-satisfied belief that good design in and of itself will improve peoples' quality of life, let alone promote better citizenship. Designer fundamentalism of this sort has to cede to lessons about the social ecology of a community's needs. Moreover, the feat of cracking a local zoning code may be a necessary key to opening the door to more sustainable building, but it is not a sufficient demand to make on public policymaking. Truly sustainable shelter for low-income residents, as affordable housing innovator Michael Pyatok of Oakland has insisted, may depend on the existence of a robust network of social supports—a secure job base, a decent public school system, accessible public transit, housing subsidies in the form of rent control or inclusionary zoning, and some palpable sense of community respect (1999). Without these, the greenest or best-designed housing won't help low-income occupants make it, let alone be in a position to adopt an environmentally sustainable lifestyle. Brian Bell's Design Corps promotes similar lessons about "inclusive" design, geared to respond fully to the social, economic, and environmental priorities of communities (2003). Community Design Centers have proliferated in a variety of cities, brokering the dialogue between local activists and design professionals in neighborhoods damaged by the cumulative impact of urban planning policies. So, too, the upsurge of community design programs in many of the nation's architecture schools is a heartening sign that the message may finally be getting through.[3]

Cold-weather Challenges

Pyatok is fond of recalling his Brooklyn tenement childhood in neighborhoods served by a wide range of public supports. But New York City today is a different place, all but unaffordable and increasingly bereft of attention to public interest, never mind public affluence. Its much-vaunted public housing system is struggling to maintain existing stock, while the continuing construction boom is almost wholly devoted to upscale development (Housing First! 2005, 2006). In 2006, the official figure for the city's foreign-born population was nearly 37 percent, but the number of nonnatives had increased by only sixty thousand, or 2 percent, over the previous five years, while the biggest rate of demographic change was occurring in first- and second-ring suburbs in the tristate area. Unofficial estimates put the foreign-born as high as 60 percent in a city where half the renters (who make up two-thirds of the population) pay more than 30 percent of their income on housing, and in some locations more than 60 percent (Roberts 2006). The housing market tends to be the tightest and the rent burden the greatest in low-income communities. Despite the efforts of the city's numerous nonprofit community developers to mitigate the affordable housing shortage, as many as one hundred thousand illegal units have flourished (according to the Citizens Housing and Planning Council). Overcrowding, code violations, and firetraps are legion in this kind of housing, which is least equipped to meet the highly variable needs of immigrants (Galvez and Braconi 2003).

Even if they had access to a fully loaded system of social supports, the city's global South immigrants would face cultural and economic challenges that were spared the second-generation white ethnics of Pyatok's Brooklyn. Their capacity to move outside the poverty trap is severely limited by racial marginalization and by the loss, in recent decades, of several rungs on the ladder of American mobility. In addition, unlike previous generations of European immigrants, they have only limited access to subsidized housing, and none at all to the city's prized stock of over a million rent-controlled apartments, which are cheaper than market dynamics would normally determine. For the foreseeable future, the social and economic isolation of the vast majority is assured—the cultural distance from neighborhoods like Flushing or Brownsville to the golden cores of Manhattan is immeasurably greater than it was in Pyatok's childhood. While New Yorkers pay loud lip service to the City Hall credo that theirs is a city of immigrants, the pride wears thin rapidly when judged against the meager resources that city agencies actually devote to ensuring new arrivals a safe, let alone civilized, place to call home. Given these obstacles, the built environment claimed and customized by an immigrant community can take on a particularly stabilizing significance.

In this respect, the cold weather climates of northern cities like New York pose an additional challenge for design efforts at dignified and sustainable solutions for immigrants. In Southwestern communities like Cruz's San Ysidro, the warm climate makes it easier to maintain or reinvent the ecological frameworks—horticultural, social, and physical—that are meaningful to the survival of transplanted communities from the South. Constructing a loggia, for market commerce or public intercourse, or a laying out a community garden plot for Oaxacan heirloom seeds, can go a long way toward building a fully imagined community. Such efforts to transfer immigrant know-how in efficient, sustainable living to a country infamous for its inefficiency can serve as environmentally positive examples. Moreover, design details of this sort take on a crucial significance in the face of external threats—whether from government authorities, property speculators, or land developers. To survive the rough justice of urban America today, a community needs to draw on all of its resources and assets—financial, physical, or symbolic.

Cold-weather examples of transcultural design are less numerous, however, and more often have a symbolic, rather than a material, impact. One celebrated example is the South Bronx casita known as Rincon Criollo, a tiny wooden bungalow that thrived for thirty years on a vacant street-corner lot as a community center with its own garden. The Rincon Criollo typology evoked the Puerto Rican campo in frankly nostalgic ways, but the serviceable use of its space for dances, musical performances, and regular social intercourse was also a source of Nuyorican community pride (Flores 2000). The fight to save it was increasingly pit against the need for affordable housing in the Melrose neighborhood, especially as the revitalization of the South Bronx picked up steam.

The Melrose section had been among the hardest hit by the wave of disinvestment and housing abandonment that swept through the South Bronx over the course of the 1970s. An urban renewal plan, which comprised 35 contiguous blocks and included 2,600 units of new housing, was conceived by the city in the late 1980s to reverse the damage. But the plan's provisions for bulldozing the existing housing stock would have displaced a significant number of residents, while the old housing would have been replaced with more upmarket units, out of reach for most residents in a neighborhood that had a median family income of less than twelve thousand dollars a year. Nor had the conception of the plan included anything in the way of community consultation. Riding the resentment with which advance word of the project was received, a citizen group called Nos Quedamos ("We Stay") won approval from city agencies to transform this top-down plan into what would become a widely respected model of large-scale design through community participation. The redesign of the plan emphasized services—health, cultural, and educational—not otherwise available in the neighborhood, along with an expansion of job opportunities. No residents were to be evicted, and the provision of affordable housing was established as a priority (Garcia, Bautista, and Olshansky 1996). In the ensuing years, the Melrose Commons project has become a showcase for city authorities in how to turn around a neighborhood (in the poorest congressional district in the nation) that was a byword for urban blight in the 1970s and 1980s.

When the original plan threatened to move residents out of the neighborhood, the Rincon Criollo was there as a potent reminder of earlier evictions and cultural losses. Nos Quedamos mobilized these sentiments as part of their successful effort to revise the plan by incorporating community needs. But, over time, sharp differences opened up between enthusiasts of the low-tech casita ethos and the housing advocates, who collaborated with power elites in city government and well-connected architectural firms. The casita was eventually moved a few blocks to make way for the new housing, but the community garden was lost along with several others in the neighborhood; the elderly especially mourned the garden, which was a living link with their former livelihoods as farmers.[4] Indeed, it was the local conflict over the fate of the gardens that proved the most instructive. The bulldozing of community gardens, built lovingly on vacant lots all over the city, had been one of the most bitterly contested policies of former mayor Rudy Giuliani. In many poor neighborhoods ripe for real estate speculation in the 1990s, these leafy products of mutual aid stood as an affront to the greed and insouciance of the gentrifying developers, who were being aided and abetted by City Hall. For the South Bronx, a community with a sky-high incidence of asthma, the eradication of green space added a public health concern to the list of reasons why the gardens were so cherished. When the public tenor of the Melrose debate was reduced to whether the community most needed affordable housing or gardens, the outcome was a foregone conclusion. But there was no end of resentment that a community action group, committed to sustainable design, had allowed it to be framed that way.

The working ethos of Cruz's San Ysidro project preempts these kinds of community divisions by working in cultural, social, and physical considerations from the outset. But can this mix be replicated elsewhere, especially outside the Sunbelt? In 2007, Cruz drew up plans for his first cold-weather project, in the Hudson River Valley town of Hudson, which is increasingly divided between western wards that house African Americans and new immigrants (primarily Ecuadorian, Caribbean, and Bangladeshi populations), and eastern wards occupied by more upscale, white, exurban newcomers, clustered around the town's surging antiques economy. Cruz had been invited by the nonprofit PARC Foundation to design mixed-use affordable housing complexes on several vacant lots (including public amenities like a swimming pool and an ice rink). The parcels, owned by the city, county, or by the foundation, bridge different wards. Though Hudson's client population is much less homogeneous than that of San Ysidro, the project's public forums and workshops, conducted in four languages, focused some early agreement around culturally specific demands. For example, one of these demands—coming, primarily, from the Ecuadorians and Bangladeshis—was to make provisions for communal cooking spaces.

But the more pressing concerns were about jobs and the need to build in an infrastructure of direct links to social services. In response, some of the early propositions included artisanal workshops to help jumpstart livelihoods and office space for other micro-business start-ups. So, too, several social service organizations were drawn into the partnership, persuaded by the dangling of advantageous tax credit programs to enter a domain—housing production—that they had not considered their bailiwick. Relatively unhampered by the rigid coding regulations enforced in San Diego, the Hudson project has a real chance of bridging some of the town's separate-but-unequal economies, demographies, and cultural sensibilities. It also promises to soften the bitter legacy of a long fight over the proposed—and ultimately thwarted—siting of a large cement plant (low-income groups wanted the jobs; the antique and second-home communities inveighed against the environmental impact). Above all, it offers another model of how a community, in Cruz's words, can come closer to being a developer in its own right, while redefining the meaning of infill along the way.

In February 2008, the mayor and the city council accepted the proposal and issued possession of the sites, mostly owned by the city or the county. For a town whose tourist identity was branded by its well-preserved nineteenth-century facades and streetscapes, community acceptance of a centrally located project that included modern-style buildings was a notable achievement. More important, a coalition of nonprofit groups, accountable to a variety of the town's populations, expressed interest in serving as a de facto developer for the project. Hudson, a boomtown whaling port in the nineteenth century, had successfully reinvented part of itself as a kind of "creative city" in the 1990s. With the adoption of Cruz's plan, it was signaling an openness to remedying some of the inequalities generated by that model of urban turnaround.

Do Cruz's small-scale local initiatives add up to a programmatic endeavor? Not yet, but they soon may. After all, the gap between the emergency needs of immigrants and the existing supply of housing provisions is immense, and the roster of workable ideas for plugging the gap is negligible. If Cruz's formula coheres, city planning agencies ought to show as much interest as they did in responding to pressure from New Urbanists to revise their zoning codes. In the absence of a "movement" with foot soldiers, disciples, and resources to apply, the uptake is likely to be much less extensive. The proponents of New Urbanism set out to show how existing planning building codes outlaw the kind of compact mixed-use development that would be energy-efficient and socially vibrant. They initiated their program on the high end of the suburban landscape for a well-off client population rich in resources, but they have seen their templates adopted in low-end locations such as Hope VI public housing or in post-hurricane New Orleans reconstruction in the form of the Katrina Cottage. The lessons of San Ysidro come from the communities most starved of social and fiscal capital. In time, and with the right kind of knowledge transfer, they might offer more upscale solutions to reducing the ecological burden that American land-use imposes on the rest of the world's population.

Instruments of Knowledge Capitalism

6

The Copyfight over Intellectual Property

POLICIES LIKE THOSE I discussed in the first three chapters—appealing to creative industries or mega-events—are aimed at place-based development. On the face of it, they promise to anchor good jobs and retain investments that would otherwise be globe hopping. The evidence suggests, however, that the distribution of benefits from these policies is far from evenhanded. This chapter will survey the efforts of elites to use intellectual property (IP) legislation to further direct and control the globe-hopping traffic of jobs, knowledge, and trade. A goodly portion of these efforts result in a flagrantly unequal property grab, and so the ownership shares are being contested in the name of public access by a coalition of experts with the legal access and resources to do so. Their response is both cogent and admirable. But what are what are the prospects, in a burgeoning knowledge economy, for those who have no immediate claims to make on intellectual property, let alone the resources to enter this contest?

As free trade agreements continue to lower or abolish entry barriers to the world's cheapest labor markets, most globe-hopping employers have turned to beefed-up IP regulation to facilitate the transfer of work from one location to another. In the manufacturing sector—where moving the physical plant of factories is still the name of the game—investors weigh the cost of shipping machinery against the returns to be harvested from setting up in a trade zone offering tax holidays, free land, discounted overheads, and a ready pool of dispensable labor. Even in the high-tech industries, where the cost of installing an semiconductor fabrication plant often makes it prohibitive to pick up and move, fierce competition at the top requires leading players to move their technical operations to cheaper locations as soon as the technology matures. In the absence of political will to protect their livelihood rights, most manufacturing workers, whether in labor- or skill-intensive sectors, have had little alternative but to accept that their prospects are tied to the footloose industrial conduct of investors, while their own mobility, by contrast, is much more limited.

In the service industries, where bulk machinery is less of a factor, the development of advanced workflow software has made it increasingly easy to break down tasks, assign them to different global locations, and reintegrate the results. In this manner, a substantial volume of skilled work, knowledge, and IT technologies has been migrated to the cheapest available labor markets. The result has been an explosion in the outsourcing of knowledge work, as project managers can now rely on around-the-clock delivery of input from time zones all over the world. Because knowledge is a far from fungible quantity and cannot be relayed effectively through automation, often employees are asked to train in person those who are destined to be their offshore replacements—needless to say, a much-resented task. Either way, the goal is to extricate employers from their reliance on fixed supplies of regional talent and set them free to roam in search of emergent labor pools.

Technically speaking, these transfers of knowledge and technology can be accomplished at will, but they are far from seamless. Even with the most tightly controlled system of reporting and integration, leaks are sprung in subcontracting industrial chains that snake all over the world. Employees can walk off the job with expertise in their head or with digitally stored information in their pocket. Company data can be easily copied and passed on to competitors or government officials. In the era of digital networking, industrial espionage is no longer about stealing or photocopying physical blueprints. Piracy, leakage, and viral diffusion are stock features of the new business landscape. Several years ago, while doing research in China, I witnessed the dismay of the offshore business community when a Chinese car company (Chery) unveiled a new model at a premier annual trade show that was almost an exact replica of a prototype developed by General Motors. Quick to mount a lawsuit, GM eventually dropped its case in order to preserve its business interests in China. The impact of piracy is even greater among end users of products made for digital consumption. Each new generation of file-sharing technologies foils the efforts of those seeking to profit from the business of making information scarce so that consumers can be held to ransom. Trying to preserve control over the authorized use of digital products is like collecting gas in a porous container.

Digital rights management (DRM) engineering is the latest corporate effort to retain control by technological means, but it is a desperate rearguard action, offering temporary fixes that are destined to fall apart over time. Corporations are increasingly relying on legal regimes that govern the licensed or authorized use of products. IP legislation has emerged as the leading weapon in their arsenal, the preferred form of regulation for firms that otherwise profit handsomely from the general deregulation of trade. The campaign waged by the WTO's trade representatives and by the World Intellectual Property Organization (WIPO) to harmonize the IP laws of member nations is currently the leading edge of efforts to protect and expand the large corporate monopolies of the knowledge economy. Deregulatory legislation is crafted to increase the holdings of large private property owners, but nothing has more hastened on the march to privatization than the rush to propertize everything in nature and culture.

Advocates of the public domain are active in their resistance to this massive property grab. As I will show, a loosely organized coalition has emerged in the "copyfight" over intellectual property. Their efforts to protect the public domain coalesce with concerns about the monopolists' appropriation of IP from creative workers. But there has been much less attention to the impact of IP claims on the livelihoods of those who are not in the creative professions. This chapter will survey that impact and consider how and why it is important to remedy the neglect.

Don't Shoot the Piano Player

Kurt Vonnegut published his first novel, *Player Piano* (1952), at a time of high dystopian anxiety about the abuse of technology by the state and industrialists alike. The novel—which depicts an unsavory future in which new technologies make everyone's skills obsolete—dutifully channeled these public concerns. Player pianos do not really figure in the novel, but the title was an explicit allusion to their contribution, historically, to the technological disemployment of musicians. Nor was Vonnegut the only writer of his generation to draw attention to the mother of cultural automation. The threat posed to artists' livelihoods by the mechanical player piano was also shared by William Gaddis, who developed a lifelong obsession with the technology (2002a, 2002b).

It is worth recalling briefly how and why the player piano, which had a short-lived but legally significant career, should have earned such a reputation as the original sinner. Its fin-de-siècle development was arguably the first salient example of an industrial technology designed, in large part, to cut the costs of creative labor. The subsequent player piano boom came at a time when the American Federation of Musicians (AFM) had scored some significant successes in negotiating wage scales and other conditions for its members. Indeed, the union's bristling response to this new technology marked the beginning of the AFM's long struggle against the automation of the jobs of live performers. By 1909, an estimated 330,000 of the pianos produced in the United States were mechanized, and by 1916, 65 percent of the market was still monopolized by player pianos (Ehrlich 1990: 134; Gaddis 2002a). The roll industry, which serviced the boom, had become one of the chief factors driving the music industries as a whole. While it was promoted as a great equalizer (create your own music in the home!), the player piano met the industry's need to find a less durable consumer product than the standard piano. Aside from the instrument's direct threat to live performers, the production of the player rolls created a low-wage manufacturing industry that offered compensatory factory-style employment to the displaced performers and others who could not find work in vaudeville or in one of the many traveling dance orchestras of the time. As a result, the work of pianists was imperiled and degraded on all sides.

The pianist workforce took further hits with each new commercial technology for recording or broadcasting performances. While the advent of silent movies provided employment for piano accompanists in the theaters, the sound film process introduced by Vitaphone and the use of canned music in motion pictures would put them and thousands more movie and theater pit musicians out of work.[1] Jukeboxes and other uses of phonographs took a further toll. In the space of two decades, pianists, who had been the mainstay of virtually all commercial and domestic entertainment, were reduced to bit parts in the Fordist assemblies of orchestras and big bands. By mid-century, the piano was more ubiquitous in households as an item of furniture than as an active complement to the hearth. It is fair to say, in keeping with the spirit of Vonnegut's title, that the player piano set in motion a machinery of disemployment that continues to transform the craft of music making to this day.

But the player piano is more likely to be remembered, and cited, today as a key case study in copyright law. Pianists, after all, were not the only group whose livelihoods were threatened by the mercurial rise of these machines. Their use also deprived composers of profits from sheet music sales. The U.S. Congress was asked to adjudicate whether the Aeolian Music Company (maker of the Pianola) had to pay copyright holders for permission to play their content. In their landmark decision of 1909, the legislators resolved that whoever wanted to record the music and make subsequent copies of it had to pay for the content, though not at a price set by the holder. Instead, the fee paid to the composer or the relevant copyright holder was set by law (at two cents for each copy).

This is a favorite dispute for scholars of IP to revisit, because its resolution set the precedent not only for ASCAP's licensing and royalty system, but also for the regulation of the radio and cable television industries, and may yet prove to be a viable model for regulating the use of peer-to-peer file-sharing technologies. For the most part, however, legal scholars' accounts of the case—Lawrence Lessig's treatment, in his book *Free Culture*, is a good example (2004: 55–56)—have nothing to say about the human piano players whose livelihoods were affected both by the mechanization of piano playing and by the congressional ruling. The only "musicians" who figure are the composers whose full authorial rights were being compromised by the industrial piracy of the day.

There is much to be learned from this exclusion. Constitutional scholars and First Amendment activists have assumed a natural leading role in the battle against corporate IP monopolies, but the history of creative property and its relationship to technology cannot be left in the hands of law professors to write, nor should it be. Too much is left out, if only because legally minded coverage of IP disputes tends to revolve exclusively around the interests of claimants: creators, copyright holders, or the more general public of users and consumers. The state also figures in these accounts, because its judges and legislators have to decide not only whose interests will prevail in the resolution of disputes, but also how to weigh factors that advance national interests, such as high-tech innovation, symbolic prestige, or the IP export trade that garners revenues from other countries.

By contrast, there is little room for those without an immediate legal stake in the disputes. Legal analysts of landmark cases rarely have anything to say about the multitude of jobs and livelihoods affected by the judicial treatment of IP-based assets and new technologies. Not only does this offend our sense of cultural and social history, but it also weakens our capacity to understand, and react to, the vast changes occurring today as a result of the technology-driven IP property grab that has resulted in an aggressive expansion of copyright, patent, trademark, or publicity rights. Labor issues should be a more obligatory component of the extensively documented public debates about new technologies, yet they are rarely a concern on the minds of opponents of the corporate enclosure of the "information commons" (Bollier 2002, 2004; Lessig 2001; Perelman 2002;

Shulman 1999; Vaidhyanathan 2002, 2004; Bettig 1996; Thierer 2001; Drahos 2002). We ought to acknowledge that efforts to regulate or propertize new technologies have the potential to drastically alter the landscape of work. Yet these consequences tend to go unexamined, whether in case analysis or in the realm of public opinion making, where libertarian concerns about the freedom of consumer choices hold sway.

It is easy to see why the libertarian response has taken precedence. Because the profits of IP monopolists depend on the creation of information scarcity, corporations such as Time Warner, Microsoft, and MGM have declared all-out war on innovative technologies that can reproduce and disseminate information to users at a cost approaching zero. Consequently, these IP bullies are perceived as blocking our rights to information that "wants to be free." Yet the historical ironies evoked by this assault speak directly to how labor has been discounted in the race to propertize. Consider that the legal vehicle for the new property grab is an expanded version of the limited monopoly rights granted to authors under eighteenth-century copyright laws so that they could pursue an independent living in the marketplace of ideas. Because U.S. law permits corporate entities to be artificial persons, most of the "authors" seizing the copyright and patent claims in the twenty-first century are global firms in multimedia, IT, and biotechnology. Likewise, the technologies under attack—file sharing and other peer-to-peer programs, decryption tools for picking digital locks, and each successive generation of reverse-engineering techniques for overriding proprietary measures and "improving" original products— are the brainchildren of the kind of whiz-kid innovators that patent laws were initially intended to encourage and assist. The early beneficiaries of patent grants, like their writer peers, were also breaking free of the rigid patronage of monarchs or states to make their own way in the industrializing world.

In the Lockean tradition, property rights have retained a formal, if distant, association with the labor for which such rights are understood to be a reward. In the case of IP, the attachment is increasingly tenuous. Legal scholars have explained why entitlement in IP disputes is limited to a relatively small number of economic actors who have some plausible claim to be authors of the creative property in question (Boyle 1996; Litman 2001; Fisher 2004). But if the impact of these disputes on the means of production is as profound as some commentators have described, then clearly an infinitely greater slice of the workforce has a legitimate interest in their resolution. Can the claims of those larger constituencies be represented in any adequate way in the current legal wrangling over IP? If the answer is no, then what can scholars and activists do to highlight and remedy this neglect?

The overwhelming evidence from IP law suggests that American courts have little interest in thinking outside of the box of singular authorship. They will not recognize the potentially legitimate IP claims of participants in the kind of collective creative work that is the norm in the culture, IT, and other knowledge-intensive industries, and they have even less interest in hearing the argument that the true source of most creative works is the public domain itself. Instead, judges are increasingly fixed on assigning monopoly rights (and lots of them) to single, indivisible authors, who are more than likely to be corporate entities. As several scholars have observed, the courts have invested more and more exclusive rights and privileges in the category of proprietary authorship at a time when cultural critics have been doing exactly the opposite—dissolving the Romantic mystique that supports any such notions about the extraordinary rights of creative geniuses (Jaszi and Woodmansee 1994). The state has obliged the courts' interpretation by passing punitive legislation to protect these privileges.

In the court of public opinion, corporate IP warriors can always win points by broadcasting the claim that they are defending the labor rights of vulnerable artists. Yet the historical record and the experience of working artists today confirm that the struggling proprietary author has always been more of a convenient fiction for publishers to exploit than a consistent beneficiary of copyright rewards. Culture-industry executives are able to masquerade as the last line of protection for artists, when in fact they are systematically stripping them of their copyrights; of course, their corporate employees are well set up to fend off claims on their IP assets from broader constituencies.

By contrast, what vision of labor has been put forth by the opposition forces in their public campaigns to raise the alarm about IP monopolies? Liberal advocates of the public domain who argue for a "free culture" (free as in "free speech" [liber], not "free beer" [gratis]) have petitioned for the fullest rights of access to information for users and consumers, while continuing to recognize copyright as a valid way of ensuring that individual creators receive their moral desert.[2] As the foremost public domain proponent (and instigator of the widely used Creative Commons license), Lessig has compared this campaign for "free culture" to the antebellum free labor movement that fought against chattel and wage slavery alike (Roberts 2003). It is a lax analogy, and so perhaps it is not entirely fair to observe that this preindustrial ideal of self-reliant artisans—who wanted to sell their products, not their labor—is hardly the most practical response to the broad reality of the hierarchical divisions of labor that knowledge industries command today. On the other hand, it is an ideal that speaks to those whose labor rank puts them closest (but no cigar) to the entitlements due to "authors." Thus, Lessig's analogy rings most true for the thwarted class fraction of high-skilled and self-directed individuals in the creative and knowledge sectors whose entrepreneurial prospects are increasingly blocked by corporate monopolies. If there is an aristocracy of labor today, they have some of the strongest qualifications to join its ranks.

It is no surprise, then, that the widely networked ranks of high-tech workers and cognoscenti who rally behind the umbrella term FLOSS or FOSS (Free/Libre/Open Source Software) are in loose alliance with public domain advocates like Lessig (Stallman, Lessig, and Gay 2002; Raymond 2001; Weber 2004; Williams 2002; DiBona, Stone, and Ockman 1999). The production credo of these employees, who are opposed to most proprietary restrictions on the use of information and information technologies, is cooperative in nature, with deep roots in the hacker ethic of communal shareware. Volunteerism and mutual support is central to their labor ethos. Because they are generally indisposed to state intervention, FLOSS engineers, programmers, and their advocates have not explored ways of providing a sustainable infrastructure for the gift economy that they tend to uphold. Nor have they made it a priority to speak to the interests of less-skilled workers who lie outside of their ranks. For the most part, labor consciousness among FLOSS communities (whether in the relatively distinct "free software" or "open source" subcultures) seems to rest on the confidence of members that their expertise will keep them on the upside of the technology curve that protects the best and brightest from proletarianization. On the face of it, there is little to distinguish this form of consciousness from the guild labor mentality of yore that sought security in the protection of craft knowledge.

Neither the public domain advocates nor the FLOSS evangelists have actively considered the consequences of IP disputes for the mass of workers and employees who do not come close to the legal category of copyright/patent holder. It is odd that such labor concerns have not been more on the agenda. Consider the volume of public anguish expended on the post-9/11 "jobless recovery" or on the impact of skill-intensive outsourcing. Ranking politicians have reserved some of their most heated rhetoric, though not their fullest legislative powers, for the purpose of stemming job loss, especially in IP-driven industries regarded as strategically important for the national interest. But this backdrop has not insinuated itself very far into the IP wars. The crusade against the IP monopolists continues to be dominated by strains of techno-libertarianism that lie at the doctrinal core of the information society, obscuring the labor that built and maintains its foundations, highways, and routine production. The result? Voices proclaiming freedom in every direction, but justice in none (Forsook 200).

Today's contest over technology-driven copyrights and patents cannot be only about protecting the claims of top-flight knowledge workers, or safeguarding the future of technological innovation, or guaranteeing consumer access to a rich public domain of information. The outcome has far-reaching consequences for the global reorganization of work, and these consequences need to be subjected to a serious line of inquiry. Otherwise, it will be safely concluded that the IP wars are simply an elite copyfight between capital-owner monopolists and the labor aristocracy of the digitariat (a dominated fraction of the dominant class, as Pierre Bourdieu once described intellectuals) struggling to preserve and extend their high-skill interests.

The Acquisition Race

Though the idea of intellectual property has been around for several centuries, IP entered the lexicon of state and corporate bureaucracies only after the 1970 founding of WIPO. Hitherto a relatively stable niche of property law, IP legislation in the United States began to proliferate after the 1976 revision of the 1790 Copyright Act. No doubt, this development reflected the consensus of the nation's economic managers that IP-driven technology growth was becoming the primary industrial asset of the United States.[3] Though it was soon a leading factor in the balance of trade—weighted on the export side by the copyright-based and patent-rich industries of information, media, entertainment, software, and high-value manufacturing—the concept of IP did not fully enter public currency until the 1990s. The 1998 passage of the Sonny Bono Copyright Term Extension Act and the Digital Millennium Copyright Act brought the problem of excessive IP protection to the attention of a wide range of public interest groups. Finally, after 2003, when the recording industry's zero-tolerance crusade against Napster and its users hit the courts, the term became all too familiar to the hundreds of millions engaged in online file sharing.

The corporate clampdown on the ubiquitous practice of downloading music and other entertainment products was a sobering initiation for many into the tawdry reality of the IP grab. As a result, everyone has a horror story to tell. There's the one about ASCAP suing the Girl Scouts for singing some of its members' songs around the campfire; George Clinton being sued for singing some of his own songs without permission from the copyright owner of his back catalog; the "Happy Birthday to You" song, now owned by Time Warner, and restricted to licensed uses until 2030; or the betrayal of class consciousness perpetrated by the litigious copyright owners of Woody Guthrie's "This Land Is Your Land" and the Fourth International's flagship song, "The Internationale." Beyond the music ghetto, things only get more surreal: Donald Trump has tried to trademark the expression "You're fired," along with his accompanying hand gesture, from the reality television show *The Apprentice* (McLeod 2005).

These stories now belong to the demonological archive of consumer folklore. But the truly chilling ones apply to the lifeworld itself, where multinationals like Syngenta, AstraZeneca, DuPont, Monsanto, Merck, and Dow are engaged in a cutthroat race to patent seeds, livestock, plant genes, and other biological raw materials that have been the basis of subsistence farming in the developing world for centuries (Shiva 1997, 2001; Rifkin 1998; Lewinski 2004; Brown 2004). The corporate privatization of biodiversity is a colossal act of plunder, infinitely more damaging to the basic income and health of mass populations than the petty street piracy of movies in developing countries is to those who work in the Hollywood entertainment system. Neoliberal pillage of nature and indigenous knowledge is an imminent threat to food security and livelihoods across the global South.

From the perspective of countries with few IP assets, the demand, on the part of rich nations, to respect and protect the IP rights of foreign multinationals is little different from the traditional imperial call on a vassal to pay tribute. Nor, as an economic arrangement, is it much of a departure from the colonial pattern by which the periphery supplied raw materials to be processed and branded in the core. Today, the materials come in the form of traditional knowledge—seeds, folklore, healing remedies— and are converted into IP by the likes of Monsanto, Disney, and Pfizer.

A revolt against this arrangement surfaced at a WIPO meeting in August 2004 when the Argentinian and Brazilian representatives pushed for a Development Agenda focusing on the use of intellectual property to assist in the development of global South countries. A subsequent statement from the Indian representative laid out the case, in fighting words, albeit in the jargon of progressive policy-wonk diplomacy: "No longer are developing countries prepared to accept this approach, or continuation of the status quo. . . . Given the huge North-South asymmetry, absence of mandatory cross-border resource transfers or welfare payment, and absence of domestic recycling of monopoly profits of foreign IP rights holders, the case for strong IP protection in developing countries is without any economic basis. Harmonization of IP laws across countries with asymmetric distribution of IP assets is clearly intended to serve the interest of rent seekers in developed countries rather than that of the public in developing countries" (Saha 2004).

The IP-rich countries resisted this proposition, but their desire to continue imposing IPR protection without helping to build a developmental infrastructure was challenged by a coalition known as Friends of Development. The rationale behind this uprising was plain enough. Why should poor countries spend their scarce resources on IP-policing operations for foreign multinationals? They see none of the benefits of Sony, Bertelsmann, Microsoft, or Aventis's profits, nothing in the way of technology transfers, and precious little that could be viewed as a development asset (Correa 2000; Drahos and Mayne 2002; May 2000). By contrast, their underground pirate economies do a passable job of providing much-needed drugs, software, consumer technologies, seeds, and all manner of cultural products at affordable prices, and at cost margins that filter into the pockets of local producers and distributors. Piracy, from this viewpoint, is just another form of distribution, and often one that is able to cater to community needs while staving off predatory outsiders.

The 1960s saw a similar revolt against the prevailing Western copyright laws. These laws had been promulgated in the multilateral Berne Convention of 1884 and were largely written to benefit the major IP exporters. The intervention, staged by African nations at a Brazzaville meeting in 1963, resulted in the Stockholm Protocol Regarding Developing Countries. Like the Development Agenda initiated at WIPO in 2004, it was vigorously opposed by Washington. The world's leading pirate nation for two centuries, the United States had lately become a net exporter, and though it would not become a full Berne signatory until 1989, it was beginning to flex its muscles as a global IP bully. The outcome of the wrangling—the Paris revisions of 1971—preserved intact the broad international membership of Berne but relaxed restrictions on IP uses for scholarship, teaching, and research in developing nations (Goldstein 2003: 153–54). The outcome of WIPO's Development Agenda remains to be seen (it was finally established in June 2007), but copyright powers in the North will be less likely to agree to concessions on educational materials than they were thirty-five years ago. In the intervening years, higher education has become a key site of capital accumulation in the knowledge economy.

Academics don't have to hail from Africa or India to see the evidence in their own workplace. The chilling effects of the IP clampdown extend into every corner of campus. Institutions increasingly claim ownership of traditional academic works—from syllabi and courseware to published research—that had hitherto been assigned to the independent copyright jurisdiction of their faculty creators. Now these materials are increasingly regarded as "works for hire," prepared by employees in the course of fulfilling their contracts, in much the same way as an industrial corporation asserts ownership of its employees' ideas and research (Gorman 1998). Well-established trends confirm that the research university is behaving more and more like an adjunct to private industry: the steady concentration of power upward into managerial bureaucracies, the abdication of research and productivity assessment to external assessors and funders, the pursuit of intimate partnerships with industrial corporations, the pressure to adopt an entrepreneurial career mentality, and the erosion of tenure through the galloping casualization of the workforce (Slaughter and Leslie 1997; Slaughter and Rhoades 2004; Washburn 2005; Aronowitz 2000; Martin 1999; Kirp 2004; Krimsky 2003; Nelkin 1984; Krause et al. 2008). From the perspective of increasingly managed academic employees, the result is systematic deprofessionalization: the value of a doctoral degree has been degraded, while new divisions of labor have emerged that are corrosive to any notion of job security or peer loyalty (Johnson, Kavanagh, and Mattson 2003; Nelson and Watt 1999).[4]

As Clark Kerr once prophesied, academics are now more like tenants than owners within their university institutions, but today's university is not quite the high-tech "knowledge factory" that he, and his critics, described (Lustig 2004). The research academy—with its own bulging portfolio of patents, copyrights, trademarks, and corporate funding contracts— is undoubtedly a conduit for capitalizing and transmitting knowledge to the marketplace, but it is also an all-important guardian of the public domain. As Corynne McSherry points out in *Who Owns Academic Work?* the academic workplace is characterized by a tension that lies at the heart of knowledge capitalism. As the academy increasingly hosts property formation and incorporates the customs of the marketplace, ever-greater care must go into maintaining its function as a guarantor of objectivity and unreservable knowledge (McSherry 2001; Newfield 2004). This is not just window dressing or money laundering. Without an information commons to freely exploit, knowledge capitalism would lose its primary long-term means of reducing transaction costs. Nor, if all knowledge were propertized, could faculty entrepreneurs poach on the community model of academic exchange to advance their own autonomy and status as knowledge owners. Consequently, the traditional academic ethos of disinterested inquiry is all the more necessary, not just to preserve the symbolic prestige of the institution, but also to safeguard commonly available resources as free economic inputs, in much the same way as manufacturing, extractive, and biomedical industries all depend on the common ecological storehouse for free sources of new product.

High-tech IP and Outsourcing

Though the academy is the natural home of this tension, its side effects are familiar to all knowledge professionals who enjoy a degree of autonomy in their workplace. This is because the collegiate model of the self-directed thinker has steadily migrated to knowledge-intensive industries, where no-collar employees emulate the work mentality and flexible schedules of disinterested research academics on corporate campuses or in surveillance-free work environments. Arguably, the diffusion of this temperament is much better evidence of the character of knowledge capitalism than are departmental water-cooler tales about the corporatization of universities.

As the knowledge and work customs of the academy infiltrate the high-tech corporate world, they are employed to extract IP-rich value from employees in ways that were impractical in more traditional, physically bounded workplaces. In return for ceding freedom of movement to workers along with control over their schedules and work initiatives, employers can claim ownership of ideas that germinate in the most free, and downtime, moments of their employees' lives (Ross 2002). New mobile technologies aimed at ubiquitous computing and telecommunications have directly facilitated employers' annexation of that free time. In principle, employers can now harvest IP returns from their employees anytime, anywhere. With the advent of globally networked technologies, the value collecting has extended its reach even further.

This new geographical scope has opened the way to a wave of high-skill outsourcing that cuts costs drastically and (just as important) imposes labor discipline on each end of the transfers. Under pressure to hold on to their hard-earned skills, onshore employees struggle to keep their jobs above the red line, while their offshore counterparts are warned that their new jobs could move to a cheaper location at any time. The process of outsourcing, moreover, depends on an implicit understanding that the skills and every other facet of the work being migrated are the property of the employer. IP, in this context, is much more than technology-driven legal entities such as patents, copyrights, and trademarks; it is the whole range of assets—processes, techniques, methodology, and talent—required to operate and make use of technologies, which business analysts often refer to as "intellectual capital."

Knowledge transfer is the preferred corporate euphemism for the outsourcing of skilled work. Though it increasingly depends on advanced technologies, and is tied to new capitalist opportunities to globalize IP, knowledge transfer is hardly a recent innovation. It is really only the latest version of the de-skilling undergone by craft artisans in the nineteenth century, when industrialists deployed factory technologies to extract and automate the knowledge and rules of their trade. Control over their own work rhythms and schedules was wrested away, and they were forced to submit to factory time. Transferring the artisans' knowledge to a fixed asset was also the most efficient way of claiming that knowledge as the property of the employer.

In many respects, the factory ethos was as alien to these artisans as the mind-set that accompanies outsourced work is to today's overseas beneficiary of job transfers. Offshore employees have to learn how to think and behave in ways that fit with capitalist rationality, adapt to the customs of a Western business ethos, and wean themselves off native knowledge practices. In those parts of the developing world that host the footprint of corporate globalization, this narrowly defined package of skills lies at the core of what a knowledge economy means. Hot to attract foreign investment, local governments commit all available resources to education that serves this definition. All other genres of knowledge are shunted aside, including indigenous knowledge traditions that have sustained populations for innumerable generations (Ross 2006a).

Even when it comes wrapped in the mystique of professionalism, white-collar outsourcing is simply the latest progeny of what garment and textile workers used to call the runaway shop. Managerial talk about freeing up onshore employees to concentrate on higher-skill jobs flies in the face of all empirical evidence that the loss of decently paid onshore jobs results in a sizeable wage reduction for most of those who find new sources of employment.[5] More significant, just the threat of offshoring serves to keep wages and salaries down in any given labor market. However transparent the employers' rationales, employee resistance tends to be limited, both by middle-class guilt (white-collar employees tend to blame themselves and not their employers when they lose their jobs—see Newman 1988) and by the shallow penetration of labor unions. Accordingly, one of the few sources of worker leverage, both onshore and offshore, lies in the threat of walking off with the company's IP.

In high-tech industries, where job-hopping is endemic among valued employees, managers have learned to build this risk into the cost structure. Yet engineers in these industries often perceive that they are the true, "dispossessed" authors of corporate IP, and this helps to explain why they are often the most enthusiastic participants in FLOSS projects during their downtime.[6] In FLOSS's cooperative, nonproprietary mode of production, they are less likely see the product of their labor as alienated. More to the point, free or open source software is a product that reflects their class consciousness; it is a flattering tribute to their collective labor, and the philosophical zeal for it to be used by everyone, with only minimal restrictions, endows the claim to universality to which any rising class must aspire.

For that reason alone, the much-lionized history of shareware and its maturation into the dual-track ethos of free software and open source can be seen as the narrative of a distinctive class fraction—a thwarted technocratic elite whose libertarian worldview butts up against the established proprietary interests of capital-owners (Wark 2003). While the engineers see their knowledge and expertise generating wealth, they chafe at their lack of control over the property assets. Their willingness to work against the proprietary IP regime is directly linked to their entrepreneurial-artisanal instincts, but, more important, it is a power test of their capacity to act on the world. The class traitors in their midst are engineer innovators who go over to the dark, Gatesian side of IP monopoly enforcement.

But what about those further down the entitlement hierarchy, who are not direct participants in this power struggle, and whose position in the chain of production does not extend to the profile of the master craftsman straining at the corporate leash? These employees are much more distant from the rewards of authorship, and they are less likely to feel personally disrespected when IP rights are expropriated from above. When their jobs are outsourced, they are simply told to retrain or seek occupational niches that are secure from flight. Alternatively, if they belong to unions, say, in the copyright industries (one of the few union strongholds in the private sector), their affiliates may find it strategic, for the purposes of job protection, to side with employers engaged in the punitive clampdown against IP infringement.

In any event, their interests do not coincide with the highly skilled auteurs manqués. Consider the example of adjunct teachers in the academic workforce. Full-time, tenured faculty, whose claim to authorial status is relatively strong, barely regard them as colleagues, rarely speak on their behalf, and are disinclined to oppose any expropriation of faculty IP rights that affects adjuncts disproportionately. This passivity is surely one of the reasons for the largely unobstructed growth of remote learning programs and private, for-profit, online institutions such as the University of Phoenix, Walden University, Kaplan University, Westwood College, and DeVry University (Keller 2003; Noble 2002). Lack of full-timer opposition also explains the steady march to outsource writing, or other "remedial," programs from four-year institutions to the underpaid staff at extensions or in two-year community colleges (Baringer 2005). It is also driving the overseas expansion of American collegiate brands, in the form of a global campus system, which I will discuss in the last chapter of this book.

Such initiatives are aimed at cutting teaching labor costs and establishing control over curricular materials and rights. Except at the height of the dot-com boom, when digital technology fever penetrated even the fantasies of Ivy League administrators, full-timers have generally viewed such developments as a threat only to those who do not share their own guild privileges. Even so, contingent faculty constitute strong, articulate voices, and they have sought to unionize in great numbers in order to protect their interests (Scott, Parascondola, and Bousquet 2003; Bousquet 2008). Compared to the marginalized in other knowledge industries, they are taking steps to clarify their relationship to IP rights in their workplace (Rhoades 2001).

Their counterparts in the technology industries have a harder time making claims on IP. Consider the landmark, decadelong court case brought against Microsoft by its "permatemps" (*Vizcaino v. Microsoft*, first filed in 1993). Thousands of longtime employees, who had worked along-side full-timers but were denied benefits because they were classified as independent contractors, sued the corporation for under-compensation. One of the biggest claims in the case revolved around their exclusion from the Microsoft Employee Stock Purchase Plan, which would have brought indirect benefits from IP assets that the permatemps helped to create. Faced with several rulings that established the workers as common-law employees, Microsoft settled out of court in 2002 and immediately established hiring rules designed to restore the status quo ante by circumventing the new legal and tax regulations that applied to long-term serial temporary assignments. This revised policy has been widely copied throughout corporate America. Temps are now more carefully segregated within corporate culture, further distancing whatever IP-related claims they might have on the products of their labor. In addition, the permatemp case helped spur corporate flight. Jobs hitherto assigned to pools of temporary workers were added to those of regular employees slated for overseas knowledge transfer.

But it is the entertainment industry and its hierarchy of craft unions that offers the clearest single example of the stratification of creative labor. There, performers, writers, and directors are commonly referred to as above-the-line employees. Their unions—the American Federation of Television and Radio Artists, the Writers Guild of America, the Directors Guild, the Screen Actors Guild, and the American Guild of Variety Artists—have negotiated successfully for residuals payments, which are basically royalties from rebroadcasts or reuse of film, television, or commercials. That these talent unions can extract such fees from the Alliance of Motion Picture and Television Producers, which represents most studios and independent producers, is the source of their strength and relative health. By contrast, below-the-line technician employees have been hit hard by a combination of de-skilling from new technologies and runaway production to nonunion locations (Gray and Seeber 1996). The most recent writers strike, initiated in the fall of 2007 over online residuals, highlighted the ability of creatives, however suppressed by their employers, to claim a share in the most technologically advanced means of distribution. To achieve this share, the union agreed to take off the table its demand that employees of reality shows (denied the status of "authors") have the right to organize.

Here are two sides of the impact of globalization. As the entertainment industry has expanded its ability to distribute overseas through each new technological generation of media formats, the additional residuals have brought handsome benefits to those above the line. Below the line, however, the capacity to produce overseas or in right-to-work states has decimated the livelihoods of technicians, set designers, sound engineers, cinematographers, and grips. While no one, either above or below the line, enjoys full authorial IP rights, the ability of talent to piggyback on copyright for its claim on royalties has made all the difference between the two classes of employees. Clearly, the development of the new technologies has only accentuated the uneven distribution of income governed by the line.

Union Resistance

In the 1930s, the American Federation of Musicians took a militant last stand against technological automation, establishing a Music Defense League to combat the use of canned music in movie theaters and calling a celebrated strike in 1936 against theater owners (Kelley 2001). But the union soon made its peace with the motion picture and other entertainment industries in the form of collective bargaining contracts. The advent of business unionism in these industries ensured a new intimacy between the interests of owners and their employees. Accordingly, the resistance of unionized musicians to new technologies that reduced their employment prospects now ran in tandem with the resistance of corporate owners to new technologies that undermined their control over IP.

In the annals of IP scholarship, unions, when they appear at all, are almost always portrayed in the role of anti-modernizers, instinctively set against the march of progress, rather like the fuddy-duddy folkies who famously booed and pulled the plug on Bob Dylan's electrified set at the 1965 Newport Folk Festival. Let me recount just one example. In *Copyright's Highway*, Paul Goldstein's generous history of copyright, the printer and bookbinder unions are fingered as the chief lobbyists behind the blocking of early twentieth-century efforts to conform U.S. copyright law to the international standards of the 1884 Berne Convention (2003: 15). For their part, these unions were defending the favorable position that their members had enjoyed as the chief beneficiaries of the trade in foreign titles during the golden age of American media piracy. But Goldstein's account sees the protectionism of organized labor as standing in the way of international agreements perceived to be more enlightened. As a result of this union intransigency, Washington was obliged to maintain its outcast status in the international copyright community for several more decades.

Yet there is another way to interpret the anachronistic feel of the unions' response. A variety of hands were once understood to have an equivalent stake in the production process. Martha Woodmansee has shown that in Germany as late as the 1750s, the author was still regarded as "just one of the numerous craftsmen involved in the production of a book—not superior to, but on a par with other craftsmen." Under its definition of "book," a dictionary of the time lists writers alongside papermakers, type founders, typesetters, printers, proofreaders, publishers, bookbinders, gilders, and brass workers as equal beneficiaries of "this branch of manufacture" (Woodmansee 1984). The subsequent crusade to elevate the authors' labor from that of craftsperson to originator of special value was the heady product of Romantic ideology about the singularity of artistic creation. A multifaceted response to the onset of industrialization and commerce in culture, this ideology was expediently taken up to justify the generous rights extended to authors under copyright law. In the European legal tradition, these inalienable or "moral" rights are limited to flesh-and-blood authors and cannot be assigned to corporations. By contrast, in the American legal tradition, which seeks to balance the interests of copyright holders against the needs of consumers, real authors have no such moral standing.

It is unlikely that the printers and bookbinders who opposed the U.S. move to join Berne were acting out of some high-minded principle about the maldistribution of copyright benefits. They were simply holding on to a good thing. But their formal claim on the trade, and the considerable influence that it carried for so long, demonstrates how union power can be used to effectively represent workers whom copyright law does not recognize as author-worthy contributors to cultural production.

In other contexts, union resistance can be a useful and persistent reminder that industrial technologies, especially those served up with a supersized helping of utopian modernization, are developed and programmed to control the labor process in every way possible. For the harried employee, new technologies in the workplace are invariably the bearers of speedup and ever more sophisticated forms of managerial surveillance. They are packaged and introduced with the warm promise of job enrichment but are more likely to be deployed as a way of de-skilling or disciplining a workforce.

In the case of creative technologies, this dark side is more difficult to distinguish, especially when the results are vaunted as important advances in the arts. Simon Reynolds, the pop music critic, once told me that the British musicians' union launched a campaign against the synthesizer in the 1980s, at a time when electronic dance music had begun its mercurial ascent to the status of a mass cult in European pop. The threat was clear enough, and, indeed, the subsequent reign of dance music proved to be a long, cruel season for performers of live musical instruments. In many quarters, they were as uncool and obsolescent as an eight-track tape; no one wanted to book them, especially if they came in the form of guitar bands.

As a devotee of these electronic genres, I could certainly count myself among those who believed that their inventive use of drum machines, samplers, and sequencers ushered in a quantum leap in musical progress. Indeed, it took some convincing to persuade me that the result had anything remotely in common with the worker layoffs that came with automated factories. Yet whenever I asked no-name working musicians who depended on live club and bar bookings what they thought of "DJ music," I was guaranteed to get an earful. There was no question in their minds that owners of live venues welcomed and encouraged a DJ-based economy of pre-recordings or musical acts because it cut their overheads and labor costs by eliminating drummers, keyboard players, guitarists, and vocalists. Killing off live music may have been sold to fans as a worthy crusade against the pretensions to authenticity of the rock aristocracy, but it was also a serious labor problem.

Labor concerns were also an issue in the early hip-hop scene. High-minded advocates of vinyl-based sampling argued that it was a way of paying homage to the ancestral archive. In the black musical tradition, according to this view, ideas, phrasing, and melodies were more likely to be seen as common property than as a matter of personal ownership; a version of someone else's music was a tribute, not an act of plagiarism. Even after the commercial introduction of the MIDI digital interface in 1982, which transformed hip-hop into a reliable recording industry product, the ancestor-worship theory endured as a worthy rebuttal to accusations that sampling was just a virtuoso form of theft. But sampling was just as likely to be viewed as disrespectful by the very elders who were supposed to be recipients of the tribute. In addition, for every layperson's casual dismissal— "It's not real music"—there was a musician who saw DJ-based hip-hop as a threat to his or her livelihood as a contract performer. Nor did it help when leading rap producers declared war on musicians. Listen to Hank Shocklee, from Public Enemy's Bomb Squad, the most formidable crew of sound engineers working in the 1980s: "We don't like musicians, we don't respect musicians . . . We have a better sense of music, a better concept of music, of where it's going, of what it can do" (Rose 1994: 81).

The legal clampdown that brought an end to the golden age of rap sampling in 1991 was hardly a victory for the musicians either. New York Circuit judge Kevin Thomas Duffy's infamous decision (in *Grand Upright Music v. Warner Bros.*) against Biz Markie—that he had "violated the Seventh Commandment" as well as the nation's copyright laws—ruled that unauthorized samplers were no different from common thieves. The decision, which could have been justly decided under the rubric of "fair use"—on his album *I Need a Haircut*, Markie had only sampled a few notes from Gilbert O'Sullivan's 1972 hit "Alone Again (Naturally)"—had nothing to do with the injunction of copyright law to encourage creativity. Indeed, compared to other periods of high creative ferment, the era of sample-based rap music would probably be up there in most music critics' top rankings. Nor did it change a thing for no-name working musicians. All the decision ensured was that, henceforth, only well-heeled performers or their record companies would be able to afford sample clearance (Miller 2008). Lawyers were authorized to have an increasingly important say in music making. Legal permission for almost any kind of cultural quotation is now an obligatory factor in artistic expression. By contrast, the doctrine of fair use increasingly is considered too weakly defined to be judged worthy of the risk of litigation.

The Labor Theory of Value

If those who labor are routinely neglected in the field of IP law, the concept of labor has hardly been absent from it. Indeed, one of the fundamental philosophical precepts informing the field is the labor theory of value classically laid out in John Locke's influential views on property. For Locke, property rights accrued to individuals as the fruits of their labor on resources held in common or unclaimed. For example, these property rights could be earned by improving an object of nature. This was the doctrine notoriously applied to justify the legal appropriation of commonly used native land by colonist settlers; Native Americans who had a view of land-use rights more akin to usufruct (the right to use and benefit from another's property as long as it is not damaged) were stripped of these rights when they signed agreements bound by European laws that honored exclusive individual property rights (Cronon 1983). Locke also argued that labor was a property of personhood, and that individuals had a right to own whatever they "mixed" with that labor. If the resources worked on were held in common, and "if there is enough and as good left in common for others" after the appropriation, then the result could justly be regarded as a natural property right (Locke 1980).

This latter proviso was a serious consideration for any attribution of physical property rights (about which Locke himself was writing) but appeared less consequential in the field of creative property, where ideas and facts are non-rivalrous goods whose value is not diminished, in principle, by their shared use by others. It was this acknowledgment, by Jefferson and others, that creative property was not like real property, that led to the special provisions made for IP in the U.S. Constitution. Though this was a relatively uncontroversial observation, it was destined to be abused in a market civilization in which monopolists depend on artificially imposed scarcity to generate wealth. No would-be monopolist will pass up the opportunity to exploit public confusion about the difference between physical and intellectual property or relinquish the invaluable, moral stigma attached to theft and piracy in order to do so. The development of IP-driven technologies has directly strengthened the hand of those in a position to profit from the outcome.

Industry gatekeepers like the MPAA's Jack Valenti, the voice of Hollywood's vested interests for several decades, could be depended on to never concede an inch on this distinction—VCR owners, for example, who copied a television show in the home were no less felons than the stickup artists at the local drugstore. Prone to grandstanding, Valenti often went much further. Indeed, in the 1984 case (*Sony v. Universal Studios*) that established the legality of the VCR, he testified to Congress that "the VCR is to the American film producer and the American public as the Boston strangler is to the woman home alone."

It was also Valenti who declared that the duration of copyright terms should be "forever minus a day." By perfect contrast, in a British parliamentary debate in 1841 about a proposed extension of the British copyright term, Thomas Macaulay argued that any form of monopoly is an evil, and "the evil ought not to last a day longer than is necessary for the purpose of securing the good." Copyright, in his view, was "the least objectionable way of remunerating" writers (1914: 23). It is difficult to imagine what possible labor theory of value could bridge the positions of Valenti and Macaulay, and yet the indeterminate labor proposition that underpins copyright law has been able to do so.

On the one hand, Valenti and other hired corporate PR guns shamelessly cite the labor of poor struggling artists in their efforts to expand the bundle of rights assigned by IP law. Celebrity actors and musicians are needed to front the corporations' cause; like striking baseball players on multimillion-dollar salaries, however, the stars run the risk of exhausting public credibility by claiming that their livelihoods are sufficiently harmed by unlicensed access to their performances. But the risk is easily borne because the Romantic concept of the artist as a neglected genius still holds sway over the public imagination. Its staying power overrides what people might otherwise know about the distinction between the creative labor of authorship and the copyrighted ownership of the product—which is primarily in the hands of a corporate entity. Indeed, invocations of the underpaid proprietary author were a charade in the eighteenth century (because most authors signed over copyright to publishers before publication) and are even more so today, when for legal purposes the entity that paid to have the work created is regarded as the author. Still, copyright's reward is a highly visible formal expression of the Lockean principle that individuals are not only naturally entitled to the fruits of their labor, but also that property is an appropriate, if not inviolable, part of the reward.

On the other hand, the moderate view of Macaulay leans toward a much more limited definition of just deserts. Creative work is not a special category of labor, deserving of extensive rights to collect rents. On occasions when authors have no other means to eke out a living, then limited copyright monopolies are justified to ensure some modest reward. Though the industrial economy of his day was characterized by wage slavery, Macaulay's position resonates with the liberal ethos of a society of possessive individuals. Property rights in such a society are easier to reconcile with another favorite rationale for copyright—the utilitarian injunction to maximize net social welfare. Indeed, this harmonious balancing act is the default position today of liberal opposition to the corporate IP fundamentalists. For pragmatic advocates of the public interest, the goal is to ensure just compensation for the honest labor of individuals but not at the cost of the broadest public benefit from that labor. In their view, careful copyright observance in statutes and case law was the key to preserving that balance for two centuries, and it must be restored.

Yet any demotion of creative work to an ordinary social status opens the door to other kinds of challenges. For one thing, the worth of that toil is now subject to a wider pool of critiques of the labor theory of value. In a 1970 essay by Stephen Breyer (intended, like Macaulay's speech, to oppose an extension of the copyright term on the part of a national legislature), the future Supreme Court justice questioned the natural-rights argument that authors—but no one else—deserve to reap what they sow. Compensation is not ordinarily awarded "on the basis of labor expended," he argued, and "few workers receive salaries that approach the value of what they produce." Why, then, he concluded, is "the author's moral claim to be paid more than his persuasion costs any stronger than the claim of others [like printers or publishers or booksellers] also responsible for producing his book?" Breyer could not find a purely economic justification for copyright that was not "weak" or shallow" (1970). Even so, his skepticism about the institution had little impact on the legal push to strengthen and expand IP laws, which began in 1976. In retrospect, however, his arguments are one of the many tributaries that feed into the main current of sentiment today against the continuing relevance of copyright.

Some of these are based on a more frank assessment of the relative worth of creativity. Many critics, for example, see no reason for retaining a system of individual ownership that enshrines notions of originality that are increasingly implausible and unworkable in an age of ubiquitously networked information. The abundant availability of information, ideas, and data makes it more and more transparent that "creators" really only add something to what their predecessors have thought or done. At times, what they add can be said to be truly original, but most of it is staggeringly mundane and almost entirely derivative of the public domain of ideas. In any event, this value hardly justifies granting an exclusive monopolistic property right, which can then be assigned to a multinational corporation, for up to an average of ninety-five years.

Other critiques are attentive to ethnocentrism. In non-Western societies where Anglo common law and the Continental legal systems were colonial impositions, the property traditions that these codes honor are not always the best fit. Individual IP rights do not resonate well in cultures where creativity and knowledge are more likely to be considered a community characteristic or collective expression. Western efforts to impose IP regimes on China, for example, have repeatedly foundered on a combination of Confucian legacies and statist pastoral rule (Alford 1995). In

India, analysts like those from the Sarai group in Delhi (see http://www.
sarai.net) and the Alternative Law Forum Bangalore (see http://www.alt-
lawforum.org) are striving to conceive how new forms of information networking can resonate with communal traditions to form a working basis
for economic policy in developing countries. Others have devised working
proposals for either the outright abolition of copyright or the adoption of
usufruct as a more suitable way of handling creative works (Schijndel and
Smiers 2005; Smiers 2002).

A third and more elemental source of opposition stems from the acute
embarrassment generated by laws that are quite simply untenable. Mass
use of peer-to-peer technology is crumbling the ground beneath existing
IP laws. No legal arrangement can subsist for long when it makes outlaws
of most citizens. Legislators feel uncomfortable when their laws are so out
of sync with customary practice, and so, increasingly, those appointed to
legitimize the social order will feel the need to find a practical substitute.

The General Intellect

Notwithstanding the travails of IP law in the age of digitization, one might
fairly ask of the entire Lockean tradition why private property should be
the reward of labor of any kind. Why would we expect to own what we
had mixed our labor with? Most workers, in any case, have not come anywhere near exercising that privilege. As James Boyle notes, copyright presents us with the blatantly unfair proposition that "property is only for the
workers of the word and the image, not the workers of the world" (1996:
57). Nor is there any reason why work, in and of itself, should have to be
ennobled, except, of course, to dignify it to those already burdened with
loathsome toil. As a pungent Haitian proverb puts it, "If work really were
such a good thing, then the rich would surely have found a way to keep it
for themselves."

Those who helped to idolize work in the nineteenth century were,
by and large, middle-class intellectuals, such as Thomas Carlyle, Horace
Greeley, William Ellery Channing, and, of course, Karl Marx (Glickstein
1991: 17). Yet it was Marx who saw most clearly that the labor theory of
value, pioneered by Locke, and developed by Smith and Ricardo, should
be viewed in the context of social division of labor as a whole rather than
as an explanation of individual acts of exchange, as classic liberalism prefers. Accordingly, he had a system-level response to the notion that labor

earned the right to property. Only collective forms of ownership could dissolve the exploitative inequalities that private property promotes.

Of necessity, Marx had much more to say about the direct labor of producers than about forms of input that we would recognize as intellectual in nature. Nonetheless, his musings on what he called "the general intellect" (in the "Fragment on Machines" in the *Grundrisse*) have been a stimulant to recent debates about property formation in a knowledge economy (Dyer-Witheford 1999: 219–38; Virno and Hardt 1996; Soderberg 2002; Terranova 2004). As the capitalist use of science developed apace, Marx saw that the generation of profit would depend less on direct labor time and more on the harnessing of mental powers and knowledge resources—"the general productive forces of the social brain" (1861). Technology, in the form of fixed capital, would be the most efficient way for owners to coordinate and absorb mental labor. Yet to the degree to which the general intellect is a collective entity, production would become more and more social in nature. Ever alert to evidence of the bourgeoisie digging its own grave, Marx imagined that this latter development might lead to the dissolution of wage labor and private ownership along with capital itself.

That moment is not yet upon us, but it is plausible to conclude that the conflicts manifest in the IP wars are, in large part, a consequence of the potential harbored within the general intellect. Consider the loosely organized coalition on the antimonopoly side. It is packed with lawyers eager to take on monopolists in the courts and artists unwilling to see their creative professions cede to full marketization. It includes high-skill engineers in the technology industries, whose professional labor ethos is opposed to any proprietary hold on information technologies, as well as overseas activists, many with advanced science degrees, fighting the efforts of multinationals to patent seeds, livestock, plant genes, and other biological raw materials. What is distinctive about the disparate members of this loose coalition is the high degree of brainpower involved. They are drawn from sectors that are key to capital accumulation in the new knowledge economy, and collectively, they represent a significant, dissenting fraction of the cognitariat.

On the other side, efforts to administer an effective division of labor within the knowledge industries increasingly depend on control over the IP inside employees' heads and the capacity to effect knowledge transfers without too much friction. Information monopolists have undertaken a massive property grab to prevent leaks in the system. But the leaks are

being sprung nonetheless, and the Internet, which teems with unauthorized content, is the most porous of all entities. Corporate managers bent
on disciplining rogue users, through the use of electronic locks or other
forms of digital rights management, are now in a running battle with the
ever-proficient hackers of the technocratic fraternity. Punitive policing
among the general population runs the risk of adding to the record of
case law that supports fair use and casts doubt on the legitimacy of all-out
privatization. And overseas, rent-seeking multinationals are running into
significant resistance in their efforts to impose global IPR harmonization
on terms most beneficial to themselves.

No one can doubt that their coercive efforts will continue apace. IP-
driven industries—from microchips and biomedicine to multimedia entertainment—stand at the commanding heights of a rapidly globalizing
economy, and their owners are bent on hammering out a property regime
that will keep them there for decades to come. As always, the ability of
elites to shape and create their own opposition makes it easier to recruit
their enemies. At least two generations of hackers have agonized over accepting lucrative offers of employment within corporate or government
IP security. That is hardly the model of job creation or income security
that we need—but it is clear that we do need one.

The cooperative labor ethos of the FLOSS initiatives has not yet become a practical inspiration for those without the resources to survive in
a gift economy. Moreover, the burgeoning corporate interest in the open
source alternatives to proprietary software is testing the clarity of FLOSS
idealism daily. Open source software is no longer a fringe option for corporate America. The outstanding technical performance of the Linux operating system (built with the volunteer labor of three thousand engineers
in over ninety countries) has attracted the widespread patronage of multinationals. Yet few can doubt that this interest in nonproprietary standards
is not driven by the opportunity to take advantage of unpaid, highly innovative labor (Terranova 2000; Berry and Moss 2005). As for the free
software movement, for all its admirable political advances, it has done
little to address the suspicion that a predominantly volunteer labor model
poses a threat to the livelihoods of future engineers. Nor have Free/Li-
bre Culture contestants in the IP wars made a priority of thinking about
the bread-and-butter interests of lower cohort employees in the knowledge industries, let alone those of workers whose service labor supports
the knowledge economy. Neither the reformists—petitioning to rescue
the IP system from the monopolists—nor the abolitionists—dedicated to

alternative forms of licensing—have so far been able to link their issues to the needs of those further back in the technology race.

In part, this has been due to the need to keep eyes on the prize. But if the IP wars are not a single-issue skirmish—if they are about altering the relations of production rather than just restoring the status quo ante— then it is time to ask questions about how the prize is to be distributed. How can we ensure that the interests of those who fall below the line are more fully represented in the resolution of disputes? How can the campaign for a free information domain take up the challenge of conceiving a sustainable income model? What kind of state action is required to ensure that inequalities in the private sphere are minimized by the establishment of a public sphere that is knowledge-rich and monopoly-free? Which new technologies and policies are best suited to furthering these goals? These are not easy questions, but the ability to answer them should not be beyond the conceptual limits of a technologically advanced people.

As I have described them in this chapter, the copyfight over IP has primarily been waged between high-end social actors and institutions. At best, the outcome may determine how the spoils are divided at the top, but it will not necessarily change the process by which the spoils are generated. One of the keys to a more sustained challenge to knowledge capitalism and its role in magnifying existing inequities lies in building cross-class coalitions. The first step in this process is fully acknowledging the experiences of below-the-line workers and learning from the resources they have developed to win rights, respect, and solidarity in the face of the most precarious circumstances.

7

The Rise of the Global University

THIS LAST CHAPTER of this book concerns the work sector to which its author contributes on a daily basis. Higher education has not been immune to the impact of economic globalization. Indeed, its institutions are now on the brink of channeling some of the most dynamic, and therefore destabilizing, tendencies of neoliberal marketization. On the domestic front, the stable professional securities of a teaching career have rapidly eroded, while competition in the global market for higher education has intensified, sparking an explosive rise in cross-border traffic among students, teachers, and investment capital.

In the medieval universities of Europe, academics were accustomed to intermittent employment. The lingua franca of Latin enabled itinerant savants and clerics to find contingent work in centers of learning far from their regions and countries of birth. "Wandering scholars," or *goliards*, who were usually unaffiliated with universities, partook widely of the largely unmonitored movement of ideas and educated people (Waddell 1989). This cosmopolitan culture of learning faded as secular and nationalist forces came to the fore. The rise of modern institutions for training professional elites, and, in particular, the growth of research universities with close ties to industry and government agencies, transformed higher education into national systems of heavily subsidized services and inputs, each with fiercely protected patterns of funding, credentialism, and employment cultures. Yet in recent years, as universities are increasingly exposed to the rough justice of the market, we have seen their institutional life driven more by the rate of change than by the observance of custom and fixed, professional expectations.

Few examples illustrate this better than the rush, in recent years, to establish overseas programs and branch campuses. Since 9/11, the pace of offshoring has surged and is being pursued across the entire spectrum of higher-education institutions—from the ballooning for-profit sectors and online diploma mills to land-grant universities and the most elite, ivied colleges. No single organization has attained the operational status of a global university, after the model of the global corporation, but it is only a matter of time before we see the current infants of that species take their first, unaided steps.

The WTO has been pushing trade services liberalization for several years, of which educational services are a highly prized component, with an estimated global market of two trillion dollars (Bassett 2006: 5).[1] Opponents of liberalization argue that higher education cannot and should not be subject to the kind of free trade agreements that have been applied to commercial goods and other services in the global economy. After all, WTO agreements would guarantee foreign service providers the same rights that apply to domestic providers within any national education system while compromising the sovereignty of national regulatory efforts. Yet the evidence shows that, just as corporations did not wait for the WTO to conclude its ministerial rounds before moving their operations offshore, the absence of any multilateral accords has not stopped universities in the leading Anglophone countries from establishing their names and services in a broad range of overseas locations. The formidable projected growth in student enrollment internationally, combined with the expansion of technological capacity and the consolidation of English as a lingua franca, has resulted in a bonanza-style environment for investors in offshore education.

As with any other commodity good or service that is allowed to roam across borders, there has also been much hand-wringing about the potential lack of quality assurance. Critics argue that the caliber of education will surely be jeopardized if the global market for it is deregulated. Much less has been said in this debate about the impact on the working conditions of academics or on the ethical profile and aspirational identity of institutions. How will globalization affect the security and integrity of livelihoods that are closely tied to liberal educational ideals like meritocratic access, face-to-face learning, and the disinterested pursuit of knowledge? Will these ideals (and the job base built around them) wither away entirely in the entrepreneurial race to compete for a global market share, or will they survive only in one corner of the market—as the elite preserve of those able to pay top dollar for such handcrafted attention? As casualization takes its toll offshore, will the ever-threatened institution of tenure—the only clear guarantor of academic freedom—become even more of a minority experience than it currently is? This chapter is an effort to address these questions in the face of the rise of the global university—a phenomenon that, for all its mercurial growth, is not well documented, let alone widely understood.

Lessons from the China Field

While researching my last book, *Fast Boat to China*, I conducted a year of fieldwork in several Yangtze River Delta cities. Once I had wangled a membership in Shanghai's American Chamber of Commerce, I spent a lot of time attending meetings and functions of that organization. It proved to be a wonderful research site to gather data about the offshore business climate, because almost every roving speculator on the planet eventually shows up there, expecting to make a fast buck. One of the best vantage points to watch this tawdry spectacle was at the chamber's social mixers, usually hosted in one of the city's toniest nightspots and crafted to ensure a frenzy of networking, promotional pitching, and deal making. Though I was a regular attendee at these mixers, I was invariably taken for a musician (no doubt, because I had shoulder-length hair at the time) circulating in the crowd before being called on to perform. How to dispel this perception? As an ethnographer who wanted to clarify his real identity, I often introduced myself thusly: "I'm not here to make money, I just study people who do." But, despite all such efforts, my interlocutors found it almost impossible to resist pitching their business models to me, just in case I might want to invest. Indeed, wherever I went on my research trips in China, I was treated as a potential investor (at least after it was established that I was not in fact a musician). It took me a little while to realize that this treatment had less to do with the fact that I was a foreigner than that I was an academic. My business card, after all, revealed my affiliation with New York University, a huge brand in China's private sector, much revered on account of its business school, which contributes in no small measure to that country's "MBA fever."

In addition, however, as I discovered after two or three mixers, some of the people most likely to be propping up the bar at these chamber events were representatives of American universities. A few were there for purely social reasons—to make friends and romantic connections—but all of them were ready to pitch their wares when the opportunity arose. Desperate for management expertise, the Chinese government, as early as 1991, began to authorize foreign universities to offer MBA and EMBA programs. Shanghai, earmarked for top-drawer development as Asia's new financial capital, became the epicenter for the jointly partnered or wholly transplanted degree programs offered by such universities, with Washington University and the University of Southern California leading the pack. In the last few years, other kinds of academic programs have followed suit, especially in industrial sectors crucial to China's economic growth: engineering, applied science, and tourism management. Skyrocketing tuition fees, long absences from home, the Asian financial crisis of the late 1990s, and post-9/11 visa restrictions have sharply reduced the flow of Asian students to the United States. Consequently, more and more of our revenue-hungry institutions have gone offshore to service these students in their home countries. Local government officials compete to acquire the foreign varsity names in much the same way as they court corporate brands.

After talking to these reps at the bar, and watching them interact with the corporate investors in the room, I came to realize that, as a representative of an American university, I was not at all out of place in this environment. My institutional employer and its brand were perfectly at home in this watering hole for profit-chasing, cost-cutting investors pursuing a lucrative offshore opportunity. It's one thing to joke in the faculty lounge about our universities going off in pursuit of emerging global markets, and yet another to be handed business cards in one such emerging market by corporate reps who want to do business. My personal experience in China helped me understand how easy it is, in practice, for our academic culture to meld with the normalizing assumptions and customs of modern business culture.

Certainly, it was easy to see how the academic reps might be influenced by the maverick mentality of these investors. But it is more important to grasp why the investors might feel that they have something to learn, and profit, from the successes of American higher education in the business of overseas penetration. After all, the history of foreign involvement in China in the nineteenth century was the dual record of missionary educators and businesspeople, the former pursuing a potential harvest of four hundred million minds and souls, the latter seduced by the lure of four hundred million consumer converts, each community providing cover for the other's activities. Arguably, the religious educators were more successful. Many of the colleges that American missionaries established have morphed over the decades into China's top universities, and, in addition, the lure of American higher education for Chinese students has proved to be quite enduring. Such things are not lost on the keen business mind.

Given the rate at which American universities are setting up shop in China, it is no surprise that NYU opened its own program in Shanghai in September 2006, bringing its list of study abroad locations to eight: the others are in London, Paris, Madrid, Berlin, Prague, Florence, and Accra

(Buenos Aires and Tel Aviv would shortly follow). The Shanghai site is one of several locations being considered as branch campuses of NYU that are registered to offer degrees to students who will not have attended the domestic U.S. campus. Plans for two of these were announced in 2007; the first in conjunction with the American University of Paris (AUP) at a site on the Île Seguin, and the second as a freestanding NYU campus in Abu Dhabi. Indeed, NYU-Abu Dhabi has been described as the first comprehensive liberal arts campus to be operated abroad by a major U.S. research university.

The decision about whether to offer a range of degrees abroad to local nationals is one that several universities had already made. Open deliberation among the faculty about how this decision might affect the character and resource map of the institution is usually minimal. The NYU case was no exception, reflecting a chronic lack of transparency on the administration's part and an eroded state of governance on the faculty's part. But, in practice, NYU, like its peers, had long ago informally crossed the threshold between onshore and offshore education, and in the larger world of higher education, the distinction—like that between private and public, or nonprofit and for-profit—had become very blurry indeed.

The distinction matters even less when viewed from the perspective of how the export trade in educational services is defined. The WTO, for example, recognizes four categories under this heading. Mode 1 involves arms-length or cross-border supply, such as distance learning. Mode 2 is consumption abroad, which is primarily covered by international students studying overseas. Mode 3 is commercial presence—basically foreign direct investment in the form of satellite branches of institutions. Mode 4 is movement of natural persons, such as academics teaching abroad.[2] The most rapid growth is in Mode 1 and Mode 3, and much of this is assumed to be linked to a perceived decline in Mode 2 growth.

Econometricians justify their own trade (as well as the core principles of free trade) by showing how these patterns of ebb and flow are interconnected. In response, and as a general fiscal principle, organizations will try to balance their budgets by pushing expansion in one area to compensate for shortfalls in another. This is how global firms have learned to operate, by assessing and equalizing the relative return on their investments in various parts of the world, both in the world of real revenue and in the more speculative realm of brand building for the future. University accounting departments have begun to juggle their budgets in a similar way. A deep revenue stream from a facility in the Middle East will be viewed as a way to subsidize unprofitable humanities programs at home (as is the case at one midwestern institution where I inquired), just as an onshore science center capable of capturing U.S. federal grant money may be incubated to help fund an Asian venture considered crucial to brand building in the region.

A Balance of Trade

In interviews I conducted with faculty and administrators at NYU and elsewhere, a clear pattern of talk about this kind of fiscal juggling emerged (though no hard numbers could be accessed with which to match the rhetoric). NYU's own global programs are an eclectic mix of ventures, spread across several schools and divisions, each of which has its own fiscal boat to float. When viewed in their entirety, it is clear that the programs do not hold to any overall rule about the demarcation of onshore from offshore education, let alone any systematic educational philosophy. Though they lack a coherent profile, they show a clear pattern of exponential growth and expansion to every continent—beginning, historically, with the Madrid and Paris study abroad programs in "old" Europe—and thereafter into each regional market as it was declared open to foreign direct investment.

While its ten study abroad sites are primarily for NYU students to spend a semester abroad, places are offered to non-NYU students when vacancies open up. In addition, as many as sixty summer study abroad programs are currently offered to non-NYU students in Brazil, Canada, China, Cuba, Czech Republic, England, France, Germany, Ghana, Greece, Ireland, Italy, Mexico, Netherlands, Russia, South Africa, Spain, Sweden, and Switzerland. With a quarter (and, very soon, half) of its students overseas at any one time, NYU has the option of increasing enrollment or reducing the costly expense of providing leased dorm space in downtown Manhattan. Either option has a huge impact on revenue and seems to be a primary motivation not only for university policy in this area, but also for other colleges to emulate NYU's successful fiscal example. By 1998, less than a decade after incoming president Jay Oliva pledged to shape a global university to match Ed Koch's global-city aspirations for New York itself, NYU had outstripped all other American universities in the volume of students it sent overseas. It also enrolled the highest number of international students. Oliva was known internationally as the founder and host of the League of World Universities, whose rectors met regularly in New

York to discuss how to respond to the challenge of globalization, and his successor, John Sexton, had made his name, in part, by pioneering a global law program as dean of the NYU School of Law.[3]

In the years since then, NYU has found itself in the forefront of online efforts to offer distance learning abroad (one of which, NYU Online, was a notorious twenty-million-dollar casualty of the dot-com bust, though its successor has thrived), while each of its schools has been encouraged to make global connections. The Stern School of Business entered into partnership with the London School of Economics and the École des Hautes Études Commerciales de Paris to offer an Executive MBA on a global basis, the law school set up a Master of Laws (LLM) program in Singapore for students from the Asia region, and the Tisch School of the Arts also chose Singapore as the location for a new master's program in film production. The scale of the university's planned joint venture with the AUP upped the ante. While it would not have involved more than a small minority of NYU students, its growth potential was tied to recruiting well beyond the eight hundred international students currently enrolled at the AUP. By the spring of 2008, the venture had fallen apart, reportedly because the NYU administration had balked at French labor laws that restrict the hiring, and firing, of contingent faculty.

Less conspicuously, perhaps, NYU's School of Continuing and Professional Studies (SCPS), which educates more than 50,000 adult learners annually in more than 125 fields, has become widely known for its provision of services abroad. This has even extended to graduate programs, which it has offered online since 1994, first through the Virtual College and now through NYU Online. SCPS was one of the first university institutions in the United States to register with the Department of Commerce's BUYUSA program, officially described as "an electronic marketplace that connects U.S. exporters with qualified agents, buyers, and partners overseas." In the words of one of the school's assistant deans, this program has helped SCPS to locate agents and partners in countries that they "never would have considered otherwise" (Moll 2008). Examples of the school's penetration in the China market include instructional seminars offered to executives in that country's publishing industry, and a program in real estate finance designed for brokers and developers active in the PRC's vast construction boom. SCPS is a hugely profitable arm of NYU, and its instruction is carried by an almost wholly adjunct workforce whose compensation in no way reflects the lucrative revenue harvested by course offerings in such nonorthodox disciplines as philanthropy and fundraising, life planning, food and wine, and real estate.

Not surprisingly, SCPS was one of the first educational institutions in the nation to receive the President's Export Award for its work in promoting U.S. educational services overseas. In the U.S. trade balance, education is the fifth-largest export service, bringing in twelve billion dollars in 2004, and arguably the one with the biggest growth potential. In New Zealand and Australia, among the other leaders in this field of trade, education is the third- and fourth-largest export service, respectively. Given the intensification of the global competition for high-skill jobs, educational services are increasingly a number-one commodity in rapidly developing countries. The Department of Commerce will help any U.S. university to develop this trade, here or abroad, in much the same way as it helps corporations. For relatively small fees, its Commercial Service will organize booths at international education fairs, find an international partner for one of a university's ventures, help with brand recognition in a new market, perform market research, and, through use of the premium Platinum Key Service, offer six months of expertise on setting up an overseas campus, and marketing said campus, in one of over eighty countries.

The Race to Deregulate

The Commerce Department's activities are fully aligned with the trade liberalization agenda of the WTO, where higher education falls under the General Agreement on Trade in Services (GATS). Dedicated, like all WTO agencies, to the principle that free trade is the best guarantee of best quality at lowest cost, GATS was formed in 1995, and higher education services were added to its jurisdiction largely as a result of pressure in 2000 from the U.S. representative to the WTO, backed by representatives from Australia, New Zealand, and Japan. This inclusion has been fiercely opposed by most higher education leaders in WTO member nations, most prominently by a 2001 joint declaration of four large academic organizations in North America and Europe (see http://www.aic.lv/bolona/GATS/jointdec.pdf), the 2002 Porto Alegre Declaration, signed by Iberian and Latin American associations (see http://www.gatswatch.org/educationoutofgats/PortoAlegre.doc), and resolutions adopted by Education International at its 2001 and 2004 World Congresses.

These resolutions and declarations recognize that trade liberalization risks weakening governments' commitment to and investment in public higher education, that education is not a commodity but a basic human right, and that its reliance on public mandates should make it distinct from other services. Yet the concerted opposition of these professional bodies has made little difference to the forty-five member states (the European Union counts as one) that had already made commitments to the education sector by January 2006 (Knight 2006). Indeed if the current (Doha) round of WTO negotiations had not been logjammed by acrimonious disagreements over agricultural trade, GATS would have concluded its work some time ago, imposing severe constraints on individual governments' rights to regulate education within their borders.

Such constraints are particularly debilitating to developing countries, who will lose valuable domestic regulatory protection from the predatory advances of service providers from rich nations. Indeed, a recent ministerial mandate at GATS allows demandeurs like the United States, New Zealand, and Australia to band together to put plurilateral pressure on the poorer target countries to accept their education exports (demandeur governments are those occupying the asking position under the WTO's request-offer process) (Robinson 2006). Officially, GATS is supposed to exclude services "supplied in the exercise of governmental authority"— that is, by nonprofit educational organizations—but most nations committed have chosen not to clarify the distinction between nonprofit and for-profit. With good reason, creeping, if not galloping, liberalization can be expected in all sectors if the GATS trade regime proceeds. After all, the free trade culture of WTO is one in which public services are automatically seen as unfair government monopolies and should be turned over to private, for-profit providers whenever possible, all in the name of full market access. From the standpoint of teaching labor, this tendency points in the direction of increasing precarity—an interim environment of job insecurity, deprofessionalization, and ever-eroding faculty governance in institutions stripped of their public service obligations and respect for academic freedom.

Even in the absence of any such formal trade regime, we have seen the clear impact of market liberalization at all levels of higher education; the voluntary introduction of revenue center management models where every departmental unit has to prove itself as a profit center; the centralization of power upward into managerial bureaucracies; the near abdication of peer review assessment in research units that are in bed with industry;

and the casualization of the majority of the academic workforce, for whom basic professional tenets like academic freedom are little more than a mirage in a desert, while the gap between the salaries of presidents and senior administrators and the pittance paid to contingent teachers is more and more in line with the spectrum of compensation observed in publicly listed corporations (Martin 1998; Slaughter and Rhoades 2004; Krause et al. 2008). None of this has occurred as a result of an imposition of formal requirements. Imagine then the consequences of a WTO trade regime that legally regards regulatory standards (affecting procedures of accreditation, licensing, and qualification) as potential barriers to free trade in services.

By the time that GATS negotiations over education were initiated in 2000, the range of educational organizations that had established themselves overseas was already voluminous. These included (1) corporate spinoffs that perform employee training and offer degrees, such as Motorola University, McDonald's Hamburger University, Microsoft's Certified Technical Education centers, GE's Crotonville colleges, Fordstar's programs, and Sun Microsystems' Educational centers; (2) private, for-profit education providers like the Apollo Group, Kaplan Inc., DeVry, and the mammoth Laureate Education group (which now owns higher education institutions all over South America and Europe, operates in over twenty countries, and teaches a quarter of a million students); (3) virtual universities, like Walden University and Western Governors Virtual University in the United States, the Learning Agency of Australia, India's Indira Gandhi National Open University, and the United Kingdom's Open University; (4) traditional universities that offer distance learning, especially in countries like Australia and New Zealand where governments mandated the marketization of higher educational services in the 1990s; and (5) for-profit arms of traditional universities, like NYU's SCPS, the University of Maryland's University College, and eCornell (Sauve 2002).

In the years since, the volume and scope of overseas ventures has expanded to almost every institution that has found itself in a revenue squeeze, whether from reduced state and federal support or skyrocketing expenses. As a result of market-oriented reforms in Australian higher education, every one of that country's public universities is aggressively involved in offshore education in Asia. A third of Australia's two hundred thousand international students are enrolled in offshore programs brokered by a class of educational entrepreneurs whose pursuit of monetary gain has inspired repeated calls for audits. Many of these programs carry large fiscal risks. For example, the University of New South Wales's much-vaunted stand-alone Singapore campus shut its doors in 2007 after two semesters of operations attracted only a trickle of enrollments. Because of these risks, the tendency increasingly is to favor conservative models like franchising or producing syllabi in Australia to be taught entirely by local instructors offshore (Rizvi 2004). There is not even a pretense of academic exchange involved in this arrangement in which education is little different from a manufacturing product designed at home, produced and assembled by cheaper labor abroad, and then sold to consumers in emerging markets.

Over the last decade, the U.S. for-profit sector has attracted the interest of private equity funds, and it was only a matter of time before this pattern of investments extended overseas. In October 2007, for example, the Apollo Group announced a joint venture with the Carlyle Group to invest one billion dollars in offshore educational programs in Latin America and Asia (Lederman 2007). Entrepreneurs with less pull among blue-chip investors have scrambled to meet overseas demand for degrees ("with no frills") that have an unambiguous market value. Many have also taken advantage of notoriously loose accrediting procedures to set up shop and pitch their product. Lax regulation in some southern and western states, offshore diploma-mill havens like St. Kitts and Liberia, or the infamous Sebroga, a small self-proclaimed principality in Italy that has granted accreditation to dozens of dubious degree-granting entities, all make it easy to license operators who open and close programs overnight to suit market demand.

Most recently, the widespread practice of outsourcing study abroad education to for-profit intermediaries has attracted investigative scrutiny. In August 2007, New York attorney general Andrew Cuomo's probe into the student loan kickback scandal was expanded to assess evidence that universities had received perks from companies that operated their study abroad programs. These included "free and subsidized travel overseas for officials, back-office services to defray operating expenses, stipends to market the programs to students, unpaid membership on advisory councils and boards, and even cash bonuses and commissions on student-paid fees" (Schemo 2007; Redden 2007a, 2007b). The investigations uncovered patterns of corruption endemic to the economy of subcontracting and offshore outsourcing.

With China's economy leapfrogging up the technology curve, the sharp demand for high-value, professional-managerial talent there has sparked a gold rush as foreign universities scramble to meet a need that the state (whose professed priority is to fund basic rural education) cannot. Legions of U.S. colleges have sent prospecting missions to China to scout out offshore opportunities in the last few years (Mooney 2006). As for their return on investment, many administrators come back from these trips pondering the lesson that foreign companies learned: it is not at all easy to make money in China, let alone break even, and least of all from a joint venture with a Chinese partner, which is the customary arrangement for most colleges (Redden 2008). Even in the absence of guaranteed revenue, many will set up shop for the same reason that corporations have persevered there—to build their brand in the China market or establish their name in the region in anticipation of a future windfall. Though there were over 1,300 joint-degree programs, as of August 2006, the record is littered with failed or hijacked ventures; those with experience in the China field have cautioned against any expectation of a smooth ride (Observatory on Borderless Higher Education 2006; Gow 2007). For universities dependent on state funding, the politics of operating in China amid a climate of domestic anxiety about outsourcing is especially fraught. As Ray Bromley, an administrator involved in a SUNY-Nanjing program, put it, "The net result is you're educating people who are taking our jobs" (Redden 2008).

The United Arab Emirates and neighboring Qatar have been especially successful in attracting foreign colleges with lavish offers, and they are engaged in a bidding war to outdo each other in adding cultural cachet to their portfolio of corporate brands (Lewin 2008). Before Abu Dhabi government representatives offered to build NYU a new branch campus, the Louvre, Sorbonne, and Guggenheim had all been approached and had signed on to similar deals for branches located in the cultural district of Saadiyat Island. Dubai, with less money than its neighbor, hosts a for-profit complex called Knowledge Village (see http://www.kv.ae/en) for offshore branch campuses from Pakistani, Russian, Canadian, and Indian, in addition to select British, Australian, and American, universities. In Qatar, six top-brand American universities, including Carnegie Mellon, Cornell, Georgetown, Texas A&M, Virginia Commonwealth, and Northwestern, are participants in Doha's 2,500-acre Education City (see http://www.qf.edu.qa). The royal family's Qatar Foundation covers all instructional expenses, as well as those incurred by its 1,000 students

Students in the Middle East have every reason to feel that they may not be welcome in the United States after 9/11, while the philosophical worldview associated with the War on Terror has provided administrators with an additional set of arguments to justify their newfound presence in the region. Many of their faculty are no doubt persuaded by Thomas Friedman–style reasoning that aspiring Middle Eastern students would be better served by a Western, liberal education than by the curriculum of a glorified madrassah. Never mind that the host countries in question are quasi-feudal monarchies that ruthlessly suppress Islamism, among other belief systems, and are in no small measure responsible, as a result, for the flourishing of terror in the Middle East and beyond. So the debate falls along familiar lines—is it better to try to influence the political climate in illiberal societies by fostering collegial zones of free speech, or is the instinct to engage student elites in such societies a naive or, at worst, a colonial instinct? Either way, the result has not been especially conducive to the cornerstones of academic employment. These campuses tend to be tenure-free zones, with workforces drawn from a floating international pool of instructors.

Notwithstanding the rhetoric of any university's overseas mission, it is not at all easy to distinguish some of the new offshore academic centers from free trade industrial zones where outsourcing corporations are welcomed with a lavish package of tax holidays, virtually free land, and duty-free privileges. Indeed, in many locations, Western universities are physically setting up shop in free trade zones. In Dubai, the foreign universities are basically there to train knowledge-worker recruits in the Free Zone Authority's other complexes—Dubai Internet City, Dubai Media City, Dubai Studio City, DubaiTech, and the Dubai Outsource Zone. In Qatar, the colleges share facilities with the global high-tech companies that enjoy tax- and duty-free investments under that country's free zone law. Some of China's largest free trade locations have begun to attract brand-name colleges to relieve the skilled labor shortage hampering the rate of offshore transfer of jobs and technology. In September, the University of Liverpool, in partnership with Xi'an Jiaotong and the American for-profit education company Laureate Education, opened a branch campus in Suzhou Industrial Park (which attracts more FDI than any other zone in the PRC). Its ads for entry-level teaching positions listed salaries beginning at $750 per month. The equivalent in Liverpool itself was eight times higher.

Corporate Universities?

Some readers might justifiably say that as long as the quality of education and integrity of research can be maintained, and the lure of excess monetary gain kept at bay, the push toward internationalization is something of a moral obligation for educators in affluent countries. Surely it is a way of sharing or redistributing the wealth that the reproduction of knowledge capital bestows on the most advanced nations. Surely the domestic hoarding of all this largesse only serves to perpetuate the privileges (not to mention the parochialism) of American students, while propping up the overdeveloped domestic economy supplied by our universities. At a time when our multinational corporations are plundering the resources of the developing world in the scramble to patent genetic material and copyright indigenous folk tales, surely educators are obliged to set a better example.

In response, I would ask whether the overseas spread of Anglophone colleges is really the best way of achieving such goals, especially when the main impetus for expansion to date has clearly been less philanthropic than revenue-driven, and when the crisis of domestic student debt is more likely to be exported in the form of a new "debt trap" for students in developing countries to bear. Isn't there a more direct way for universities to make globally available the knowledge and research they generate?

One obvious alternative is to give it away for free, with no intellectual property strings attached. In the Massachusetts Institute of Technology's pioneer OpenCourseWare project, the university makes its courses accessible online for self-learning and non–degree-granting purposes. Other colleges, like Tufts, Utah State, and Carnegie Mellon have followed suit. To date, MIT's courses are being translated into China and other Asian countries. While laudable in inspiration, the content being imported has a clear cultural standpoint, rooted as it is in Western knowledge traditions. If it is not absorbed alongside teachings from a local standpoint, it remains to be seen how this export model will differ, in the long run, from the tradition of colonial educations. All over the developing world, governments (desperate to attract foreign investment), global firms, and, now, global universities are channeling scarce public resources into education tailored to the skill sets of a "knowledge society" at the expense of all other definitions of knowledge, including indigenous traditions. Under these conditions, higher education is increasingly regarded as an instrumental training for knowledge workers in tune with capitalist rationality as it is lived within one of the urban footprints of corporate globalization.

If universities were to closely follow the corporate offshoring model, what would we expect to see next? In this labor-intensive industry (the majority of education costs go to teaching labor), the instructional budget is where an employer will seek to minimize costs first, usually by introducing distance learning or by hiring offshore instructors at large salary discounts. Expatriate employees—assigned to set up an offshore facility, train locals, and provide credibility for the brand—will be a fiscal liability to be offloaded at the first opportunity. If the satellite campus is located in the same industrial park as *Fortune* 500 firms, then it will almost certainly be invited to produce customized research for these companies, again at discount prices. It will only be a matter of time before an administrator decides that it will be cost-effective to move some domestic research operations to the overseas branch to save money. And once the local instructors have proved themselves over there, they may be the ones asked to produce the syllabi, and, ultimately, even teach remote programs for onshore students in the United States.

Inevitably, in a university with global operations, administrators who have to make decisions about where to allocate their budgets will favor locations where the return on investment is relatively higher. Why build expensive additions at home when a foreign government or free trade zone authority is offering you free land and infrastructure? Why bother recruiting overseas students when they can be taught more profitably in their countries of origin? If a costly program can only be saved by outsourcing the teaching of it, then surely that is what will be done.

Along the way, there will be much high-minded talk about meeting the educational needs of developing countries, and some pragmatic talk about reducing the cost of education for domestic students. Substandard academic conditions will be blamed on foreign intermediaries or partners, or else on "unfair" competition. Legislators and top administrators will grandstand in public and play along in private. Clerical functions and data-dense research will be the first to go offshore. As for teaching instructors, those in the weakest positions or the most vulnerable disciplines will feel the impact first, and faculty with the most clout—tenured full-timers in elite universities—will be the last and the least affected.

As far as the domestic record goes, higher education institutions have followed much the same trail as subcontracting in industry—first, the outsourcing of all nonacademic campus personnel, then the casualization of routine instruction, followed by the creation of a permatemps class on short-term contracts, and the preservation of an ever-smaller core of tenure-track full-timers, crucial to the brand prestige of the collegiate name. Downward salary pressure and eroded job security are the inevitable upshot. How can offshore education be expected to produce a different result?

From the perspective of academic labor, I don't believe that we should expect an altogether dissimilar outcome. But the offshoring of higher education, if and when it occurs to any substantial degree, will not resemble the hollowing out of manufacturing economies, with full-scale employer flight to cheaper locations. Nor will it exactly resemble the more recent select outsourcing of white-collar services, where knowledge transfer involves the uploading and downloading of skills and know-how from and to human brains on different sides of the planet. The scenario for education will be significantly different, given the nature and traditions of the services being delivered, the vested commitment of national governments to the goals of public education, and the complexity of relationships among various stakeholders.

Moreover, for all the zealous efforts to steer higher education into the rapids of enterprise culture, it would not be hard to demonstrate that, with the exception of the burgeoning for-profit sector, most universities do not and cannot function fiscally like a traditional marketplace. Indeed, the principles of collaboration and sharing that sustain teaching, learning, and research are not reducible, in the long run, to financialization after the model of the global corporation. Yet one could say much the same about the organizational culture of the knowledge industries. High-tech firms depend increasingly on internationally available knowledge in specialized fields. They collaborate with each other on research that is either too expensive or too multisided to undertake individually; and they depend, through high turnover, on a pool of top engineers to circulate brainpower throughout the industry. So, too, the management of knowledge workers has diverged appreciably from the traditions of Taylorism and is increasingly modeled after the work mentality of the modern academic, whose job is not bounded by the physical workplace or by a set period of hours clocked there. Modern knowledge workers no longer know when they are on or off the job, and their ideas—the stock-in-trade of their industrial livelihoods—come to them at any waking moment of their day, often in their most free moments. From this perspective, talk about the "corporate university" is a lazy shorthand. The migration of our own academic customs and work mentalities onto corporate campuses and into knowledge-industry workplaces is just as important a part of the story of the rise of knowledge capitalism as the importation of business rationality into the academy. But the traffic in the other direction is all too often neglected because of our own siege mentality.

In all likelihood, we are living through the formative stages of a mode of production marked by a quasi-convergence of the academy and the knowledge corporation. Neither is what it used to be; both are mutating into new species that share and trade many characteristics. These changes are part and parcel of the economic environment in which they function: where, on the one side, a public commons unobtrusively segues into a marketplace of ideas, and careers secured by stable professional norms morph into contract-driven livelihoods hedged by entrepreneurial risks; and, on the other side, the busy hustle for a lucrative patent or a copyright gets dressed up as a protection for creative workers, and the restless hunt for emerging markets masquerades as a quest to further international exchange or democratization.

It may be all too easy to conclude that the global university, as it takes shape, will emulate some of the conduct of multinational corporations. It is much more of a challenge to grasp the consequences of the *coevolution* of knowledge-based firms and academic institutions. Yet understanding the latter may be more important if we are to imagine practical educational alternatives in a civilization that relies on mental labor to enrich its economic lifeblood.

Conclusion

Maps and Charters

THANKS TO THE bestselling reach of journalist Thomas Friedman's book *The World Is Flat*, the concept of the flat world is now established in the public mind as a spatial picture of the new global landscape of work. In that book and elsewhere, Friedman has depicted globalization as a free-for-all where advanced technologies and trade liberalization are leveling all the competitive advantages once attached to geographic location. No one, he concludes, can depend on their address to guarantee anything like a secure livelihood (Friedman 2005). An alternative view—which insists that location is still all-important—is offered by Richard Florida, the influential academic consultant for regional policymakers, in a series of books, the most recent of which is subtitled "How the Creative Economy Is Making Where to Live the Most Important Decision of Your Life" (2002, 2004, 2008). His claim for the growth potential of talent clusters in creative cities argues the case for place-based development as an anchor for high-wage jobs and a formula for wealth creation. According to Florida's model, today's recipe for success in competing for employment and riches depends increasingly on being in the right place and having the right skills.

Both models have had a considerable impact on the public mind, and so they are influencing the ways in which people take stock of their own skills, loyalties, and opportunities. Just as significant, they are shaping how policymakers respond to new pressures imposed on their resources at hand. Individuals who are persuaded by Friedman see themselves competing directly with counterparts who may be thousands of miles away. Whoever wins the contest takes all the spoils. Those more partial to Florida's model try to imagine how they fit into his contest between regional clusters, where the decisive competitive factor lies in a combination of talent, resources, and local identity. The spoils in Florida's version are somewhat less tangible, and they are not divvied up in a zero-sum manner, but some locations do emerge as winners just as others fall short.

Though they appear to be categorically opposing views, both are aimed at capturing the attention of elites and their investment resources, each pits some populations against others, and neither is an antidote to the curse of uneven development, which rewards the few and denies the majority. In truth, there is no need to choose between Friedman's "flat world" and Florida's "spiky world," and every reason to reject both if paradigms of development that are more fair and equitable are to be favored. The case studies presented in these pages suggest that policies pursued in the name of both Friedman and Florida have generally led to more sharply uneven development, magnifying inequalities in all locations rather than mitigating them in some. Speculative investors—whether in production operations, skilled services, capital equities, or land valuation—tend to emerge with disproportionate gains, and those fortunate workers who experience upward mobility generally do so at the expense of a downgraded majority. This is the case whether the disadvantaged reside in some proximity (close to the spike) to the favored, or whether they eke out a living on the other side of the globe.

But, in response to Friedman and Florida, this book does not propose an alternative, and equally snappy, image—the corrugated world?— as a more accurate depiction of how globalization tends to rearrange and redistribute resources. For one thing, such glib metaphors accept, from the outset, that we should view the world in a fundamentally competitive light. They assume that the playing field is already set up as a game between contestants and all that remains is to figure out how to be among the winners. This model of gamesmanship is the preferred framework for free marketeers, and it is usually far from fair. In practice, the ground rules are heavily weighted toward delivering corporate welfare and investor benefits. In most developing countries, the managers of a typical free trade zone will be offering investors a long list of handouts: tax holidays, free land, discounted overheads, wage controls, substandard labor and environmental regulations, lax inspection regimes, and other policies shaped to guarantee lavish returns on their investments, no matter what. Indeed, the only thing that is free about this kind of trade are the freebies offered to investors. On this field, employees are almost always facing uphill.

Aside from its built-in neoliberal bias, there are other reasons for putting to rest the iconography of the playing field, whether in its flat or uneven version. It cannot do justice to environmental factors that will increasingly affect how livelihoods are shaped in the twenty-first century.

The public is more and more cognizant that prevailing consumption patterns are ecologically destructive, but there is much less awareness of what needs to change on the production side. Labor advocates have not generally prioritized this need, but it is self-evident that our pursuit and protection of jobs should be approached with an environmental audit in mind. Many jobs (churning out gas-guzzling vehicles, earth-poisoning armaments, and land-gobbling subdivisions) are simply not worth fighting to save in the long run if their expense of labor power contributes to the degradation of land and life. The future lies, most obviously, in green-collar employment, whether in renewable energy development, appropriate technologies, or other forms of carbon-free work. More promising results can be expected from cooperation of the sort pioneered by the Blue Green Alliance, a working relationship between the United Steel Workers and the Sierra Club (see http://www.bluegreenalliance.org); or the Apollo Alliance, a broader coalition of labor, environmental, and business leaders (http://apolloalliance.org). But the goal has to be much greater than mere job creation. A mode of production that sustains planetary life is one that generates livelihoods, in the fullest sense of the term.

The substance and outcome of environmental audits is much too complex to reduce to a two-dimensional field supposed to represent an open, or regulated, competition for jobs. Quantitative efforts to estimate the carbon emissions embedded in consumer products are already being pioneered; for example, Tesco, the leading British supermarket chain, has begun to put carbon labels on each of the seventy thousand products it sells. But there has been no comparable pressure on employers to assess the carbon footprints of each of the jobs on their payrolls, or those of their suppliers. Ecological costs—pollution, contamination, species loss, climate change—are still customarily regarded as "externalities," or hidden costs that are too composite or variable to break down and factor into a quantitative picture of labor markets.

Nor is it easy to graphically capture the march of contingency into so many of the occupational sectors scrutinized in this book, whether in the creative economy, in the knowledge industries, or in the low-wage immigrant or offshore labor markets. The impact of this insecurity has set in motion people and money on an unprecedented scale, defying any effort at inventory, let alone adequate depiction. Factor in the ever-present element of market instability (exacerbated by deregulation), the impact of new technologies that have facilitated the diffusion of work around the world, and the particularly volatile outcome of economic crises that periodically visit capitalist systems, and the accumulative result is a fluid landscape that resists any all-purpose, snapshot-friendly explanation of change.

The final reason for rejecting competition scenarios is because we reserve hope for a more equitable climate of development. This would be a world where speculative capital is disciplined and directed into socially minded investment, fair trade, and more sustainable pathways for populations to subsist on. "Another world is possible" has been the slogan favored in the alternative globalization movement for framing these hopes and initiatives. The cartography of justice it evokes is a largely imaginative exercise, but it is more of a work in progress than a utopian will-o'-the-wisp. After all, the heyday of predatory neoliberalism may soon be behind us, and the rollback in some regions could be as rapid as the rollout was. While large parts of the social landscape left behind will be scorched earth, the reconstruction of trust, cooperation, and fairness will no doubt inspire new iconographies on the part of those looking to supplant the neoliberal ones.

Revisionist maps have shown just how transformative these geographic pictures can be. The most well-known case, of course, is the 1974 atlas drawn according to the Peters projection, which challenged the picture of the world by scale and proportion offered by the Mercator projection, in universal use since 1569. Africa is fourteen times bigger than Greenland, yet, in the Mercator projection, they had been the same size. Though the Peters map had its own distortions, the political impact of the debate it generated revolved around the general principle that disadvantaged nations had somehow been restored to their rightful proportions. Other examples aimed at transforming conventional perceptions include South-Up maps, where the affluent North is the pictorial underbelly. Equally mind-bending are maps that depict the world by criteria other than area—for example, by Internet connectivity, by traffic fatalities, by fruit exports, or by often-preventable deaths (http://www.worldmapper.org).

Maps are indispensable to changing our view of the world, but they need to be accompanied by effective action to realize change. In this respect, it is important to acknowledge that while geography continues to affect the organization of labor, labor itself is not a passive force, to be amassed, marshaled, weakened, and dispersed at will: it can also play an active role in shaping the landscape (Herod 2001; Castree et al. 2004). Corporate-driven globalization has depleted the power of workers everywhere to secure their livelihoods, but it has also clarified the need for international cooperation and action on a global scale. Employers and investors communicate with ease, make deals, and act in concerted ways that protect and further their interests. There are relatively few obstacles in the path of their efforts to operate globally. By comparison, workers, and labor unions who want to do so are faced with formidable legal, informational, and civil hurdles. The alliances and strategies they need to function within the new environment are hampered at every turn by structures of ownership and power erected explicitly for the purpose of suppressing these efforts.

The task of building cross-border campaigns against global firms is well under way and, over time, may become a gold standard in industries where organized labor has a traditional foothold (Bronfenbrenner 2007; Harrod and O'Brien 2002; Gordon and Turner 2000; Youngdhal 2008). But the experience of New Economy workplaces has shown that this blueprint for globalizing the national, Fordist labor organizations cannot be the only one to follow. The organizing template of long-term stability and security in a single workplace is not well-suited to industries where a majority of workers shift their employers on a regular basis, whether voluntarily or involuntarily. More resilient forms of employee protection are clearly needed, such as the flexicurity system pioneered in EU countries, or even the new Chinese labor legislation aimed at building in a measure of security for longstanding employees.

Such efforts can appeal to social charters that offer a broad range of protection, from civil rights and welfare entitlements to guarantees of basic labor rights. The most prominent is the European Social Charter (adopted by the Council of Europe in 1961, and revised in 1996), and the most recent is the Social Charter of the Americas (adopted by the Organization of American States at its 2006 General Assembly). Yet the ultimate test of these charters lies in the treatment of the most precarious members of a society. Usually, that has meant undocumented migrants, whose habitual exclusion from protections, or criminalization under immigration law, is flagrantly at odds with their widespread recruitment for crucial labor roles. An estimated global population of two hundred million, and a rapidly rising workforce segment in all developed countries, migrants' status as outsiders who are nevertheless indispensable in so many service and manufacturing sectors makes them especially vulnerable and valued at one and the same time (Jayaraman and Ness 2005). Often considered to be "unorganizable," their labor power has become the strategic linchpin of the global economy—from the mass industrial army that sustains "Made in China" to the undocumented workforce that staffs heartland agribusinesses, construction sites, and urban nursery rooms in North America and Europe. When they withdraw their labor, as has happened chronically in areas of South China's export platform economy, or in strategic actions like the May Day U.S. work boycott of 2006, the uncredited potential of that power becomes visible.

It is not just migrants, of course, but also formal employees in select high-wage and low-wage sectors who increasingly find themselves in a precarious work-life environment. If cross-class alliances are to flourish in anything but name, organizers have to understand, and build on, the experience of precarity as a central element of people's lives, rather than as a temporary state of misfortune that can be remedied by a halfway decent contract. It may be that precarity is too diffuse a rubric around which to establish the kind of formative allegiances required of traditional political pressure and action. But too many people now share the experience of seeing their future as fundamentally uncertain for this experience to be regarded as an exception to the way things ought to be (Butler 2004). Any new social charter aimed at balancing protections with freedoms has to acknowledge that security tied to the lifeline of a fully loaded job contract is neither the opposite of precarity nor the only solution to flexploitation.

Those who clearly see a linear career track for themselves, hedged by expectations of security, are an increasingly small minority. The indefinite life may soon be the new standard: warily embraced by "free agents" and high-wage professionals at the jackpot end of the New Economy, and wearily endured by the multitude of contingent, migrant, or low-wage workers at the discount end. Taken together, they are the two sides of what is increasingly the coin of the realm, minted by neoliberal treasuries during the era of financialization. Advocates of sustainable livelihoods need to engage directly the experience of precarity that accompanies this currency because it is the mental stuff from which more authentic freedoms will be forged. Ultimately, the security that people need in order to seek out these freedoms does not have to be tied to job contracts. In the long run, it may best be delivered by a social charter, through a guaranteed income, or social wage, decoupled from the circumstances of employment.

Far from a world where such guarantees are imaginable, neoliberal financialization is little more than a high-stakes gamble, and the collapse of Wall Street players in the course of 2008 confirmed how far even the winners can fall. Nonetheless, one of its most resilient manifestations may prove to be in the field of intellectual property (IP). As the gains of industrial ownership increasingly revolve around IP claims, the legal and moral framework of this form of property needs to be redefined to deconcentrate the monopoly of benefits now in corporate hands. The spectrum of rewards has never been so closely tied to the division of labor that now exists between creative workers and those judged "noncreative" because they have no IP claims to make. Proximity to IP claims is more and more a defining feature of work compensation all across the burgeoning knowledge industries. In the twenty-first century, the treatment of copyrights and patents do not equate adequately with a labor theory of value, if they ever did. Antimonopolists will not succeed in delivering justice if they neglect the needs of those who fall outside of the golden orbit of IP claims.

The race to acquire IP has taken its toll on the distribution of resources within the research university. Moreover, there are few knowledge-based workplaces where the shrinkage of secure core employees is as transparent as in the academy. In the American sector, especially, contingency is now the norm, with only a third of all faculty still in the tenure stream—a number that is dropping fast. But it is not just the numbers but the allocation of benefits, privileges, and rewards that starkly reveal the gulf between the tenured core, some of whom are paid million-dollar salaries and hold shares in IP licenses on their research, and the part-timer majority, some of whom qualify for food stamps and have no access to an office. Not surprisingly, adjunct faculty and graduate teachers have taken the lead in organizing and bargaining over conditions and rights. As the moral center of the academic labor movement, they have also been the most active practitioners in forming bargaining units. On some campuses, they have been able to extract support and commitment from full-time faculty on the basis of their predicament, principles, and ideas for organizing, but it has not been easy going. The apathy of tenured faculty, tethered, as they are, to the individualized reward system, is not only a formidable obstacle, but it is also a shameful reflection on a profession that holds the privilege of academic freedom but will not use it to protect those who are excluded on a daily basis.

The exercise of academic freedom—the cornerstone of the profession—is a mirage to this adjunct workforce. But it has also been severely curtailed by the adoption, by so many research institutions, of IP capture as a desired source of revenue. Commercial ties with industry funders are more of a threat to academic freedom than Pentagon funding was in the heyday of the Cold War research institution (Washburn 2005; Lewontin 1997). When your salary is effectively being paid by an external funder, and when you stand to acquire an investment stake in the commercial gain from the funded research, there is little chance you will speak openly about that research. In this way, knowledge gets privatized further and further upstream, rather than flowing into the public domain downstream, according to the traditional academic model. Universities drawn toward this profile of knowledge capitalism devote more of their resources to technology transfer in the applied or entrepreneurial sciences, or else they invest directly in start-ups, real estate holdings, and other opportunities that will boost their IP portfolios. In the meantime, the administrations of colleges are more and more responsive to the corporate culture of marketization in their workforce policies.

The last chapter in this book debates whether the recent flourishing of the global university is an extension of these trends, and indeed whether the global university will increasingly resemble the global corporation in its offshore operations. While there is ready evidence to support the hypothesis that it will, I recommend a broader view that sees the coevolution of knowledge-based firms and research universities as key to the development of global capitalism. Both sectors display similar kinds of organization when it comes to stratification of the workforce, capitalization around IP ownership, and workplace mentality. Wal-Mart has been described as the "template of 21st century capitalism" in production, distribution, and consumption of goods (Lichtenstein 2006). The equivalent, in the knowledge field, lies somewhere in the physiognomy of the hybrid species evolving under the baggy rubric of the knowledge worker. These Schumpeterian creative entrepreneurs who feel just as much at home on the high-tech corporate campus as on the academic campus are as emblematic of our times as the migrant worker for whom "home" is more of a mentality than a lived arrangement.

Most academic readers of this book, and of others that focus on the restructuring of higher education (Slaughter and Rhoades 2004; Washburn 2005; McSherry 2001), may still find it difficult to accept that their workplaces are somehow on the advance edge of knowledge capitalism. The legacy of the "ivory tower" has only just begun to dissolve, and it is a quantum leap to supplant that cloistered mentality with one that is so worldly and of the moment. Yet readers who are persuaded are well placed to lend their attention and energy to any new kind of charter that embodies the concerns outlined in this book. As much as any I have discussed in these pages, the academic workplace is a timely gateway for introducing guarantees of every employee's right to choose their own balance of freedom and security. The task of building livelihoods that can last out the twenty-first century starts in our own backyard.

Notes

Chapter 1

1. The DCMS boosted employment by 500,000 and income by £36.4 billion by adding in the United Kingdom's software sector. Even so, influential DCMS consultant John Howkins, author of *The Creative Economy* (2001), regrets that the majority of science-based industries were left out of the DCMS definition, seeing no justification for excluding them from the rubric of creativity other than the administrative claim of another government department, Trade and Industry (Howkins 2002).

2. The movement has drawn on debates in select journals, such as *Mute, Transversal, Greenpepper, Multitudes, republicart, ephemera,* and *Variant*; Listservs such as *nettime and Fibreculture*; and has influenced the work of institutions like the European Institute for Progressive Cultural Policies and Institute for Network Cultures. For a map of active groups, see http://www.precarity-map.net.

Chapter 2

1. In his influential essay, "Turning Point in China," from the early 1970s, William Hinton argues that whereas the U.S. left was often bamboozled by these shifts in direction, the mainstream press was not. The editorial line in leading newspapers followed these very closely, and in his view, quite accurately. His chief example is the shift in bias that occurred when ultraleft groups, in his view rightist in essence, emerged to extend the process of overthrowing cadres in power. The U.S. press correctly interpreted these tendencies as counterrevolutionary in nature; smelling the imminent overthrow of Maoism, the press gave favorable coverage to their efforts. Practically speaking, the editorial line went from denouncing Red Guards as "hooligans" who were "attacking all that was good and civilized in China" to praising them as "idealistic young people whose democratic dreams and aspirations had been betrayed by Mao." Hinton concludes that "this about-face illustrates how class-conscious and politically sensitive the American ruling class really is. American radicals and revolutionaries were, in the main, bewildered by the cross currents of the Cultural Revolution, they were unable to distinguish revolution from counter-revolution when the latter marched under a red flag. Not so the American ruling class. Its well-trained experts and journalists sensed very quickly which flags to support and which flags to attack and they carried a number of naive radicals with them" (Hinton 2002: 52).

{

}

2. Here, the influence of Hinton's bestselling *Fanshen* (1966) was paramount in popularizing the practice. The Maoist model was not the only origin of consciousness-raising—the Freedom Summer experiences of the civil rights movement were a more immediate inspiration—but stories about women's liberation in China helped to magnetize its attraction to Western feminists.

3. Strictly speaking, economism was the term given to "opportunistic" demands that arose among marginalized workers during the first flush of worker rebellion in the Cultural Revolution. These were based on the grievances of contract, temporary, or nonunion laborers demanding back pay, the right to equal benefits, and changes in household registration, among others things. Redressing these grievances would have taken a heavy toll on state resources. See Elizabeth Perry and Li Xun's account of the emergence of economism and the campaign against it. Perry and Xun conclude that the grievances were, in many ways, a more fundamental criticism of socialist command economy than that offered by Cultural Revolution's ideological rebels. (1997: 117).

Chapter 3

1. NYLON was the name adopted by a study group of urbanists, based in London and New York, who met periodically between 2004 and 2007 to discuss the history and currency of transatlantic exchange between the two cites. The research for this chapter was initially undertaken for these meetings.

2. For an analysis of the horse-trading that invigorated (and cheapened) the voting process, see Campbell (2005).

3. The 2006 documentary *A Stadium Story: The Battle for New York's Last Frontier*, directed by Benjamin Rosen and Jevon Roush, offers a lively account of the standoff between the two coalitions.

Chapter 4

1. A discussion about whether the anti-sweatshop movement fits this description came up in the course of a workshop I attended at a conference called Global Companies-Global Unions-Global Research-Global Campaigns, held in New York City, in February 2006 (see http://www.ilr.cornell.edu/globalunionsconference). In part, this chapter is a response to that debate.

Chapter 5

1. The most comprehensive account can be found in Robert Bruegmann's *Sprawl: A Compact History* (2005). With the aid of density gradient charts, Bruegmann argues that the rate of urban decentralization peaked in the late 1960s and

early 1970s and has been slowing ever since. See my review of Bruegmann's book (Ross 2006b), along with those of other reviewers.

2. Acting in conjunction with the ACLU, the Mexican American Legal Defense and Educational Fund (MALDEF), a leading Latino legal organization, has been especially active, and successful, in pressuring cities to drop anti-immigrant ordinances that will not stand up to legal scrutiny. By contrast, a growing number of cities—including San Francisco, Los Angeles, and Cambridge, Massachusetts—have all declared themselves to be "immigrant sanctuaries," where new arrivals are assured safety, health, and dignity, regardless of their immigration status. A New Sanctuary Movement has formed, with an eclectic and ecumenical membership (see http://www.newsanctuarymovement.org).

3. A pioneer model was the series of studios set up under the University of Washington's BASIC initiative (Global Community Studio, Housing Solutions Studio, and the Local Neighborhood Studio). See Palleroni (2004).

4. Community gardens are not just symbolic links. Under forceful circumstances, this model can be turned into economy of scale. In the early 1990s during Cuba's Special Period, for example, when the collapse of Soviet support resulted in a drastic loss of cheap fuel supplies, the authorities initiated an extensive urban farming program in fallow lots all over Havana. By 2002, these small gardens were supplying 90 percent of the city's fresh produce. See Barclay (2004).

Chapter 6

1. James Kraft estimates that by 1934, twenty thousand theater musicians—"perhaps a quarter of the nation's professional instrumentalists and half of those who were fully employed"—lost their jobs as a result of the talkies. Exhibitors "saved as much as $3,000 a week by displacing musicians and vaudeville actors" (1996: 33, 49).

2. Fueling the movement for an information commons, a bevy of legal blogs provide daily input on the rapidly changing IP landscape: Copyfight, Importance Of (both on Corante), Berkman, Furdlog, GrepLaw, Law Meme, Tech Law Advisor, CopyFutures, bIPlog, CIS Blog, Academic Copyright, the Trademark Blog, Lessig Blog, Copyright Readings, and others. Public interest organizations have formed to lobby around IP disputes: Public Knowledge, Future of Music Coalition, Digital Future Coalition, Electronic Frontier Foundation, Center for the Public Domain, and Union for the Public Domain. The most high-profile cases in recent years in the IP wars have been *A&M v. Napster* (2001), *Eldred v. Ashcroft* (2003), *Tasini v. New York Times* (2001), and *MGM v. Grokster* (2004).

3. William Landes and Richard Posner note that the increasing regulation of IP from 1976 was out of sync with the general movement toward economic deregulation (Landes and Posner 2003).

4. *Workplace: A Journal of Academic Labor* (see http://www.cust.educ.ubc.ca/workplace) is an indispensable source of commentary.

5. According to a Department of Labor summary in 2003, only 26 percent of laid-off manufacturing workers find jobs that pay as well or better than their old jobs. Cited in Anderson and Cavanagh (2004: 43).

6. For example, it was a group of AOL employees who created Gnutella, the widely used file-sharing program. The program "escaped" into the public domain in the course of the few hours that it was posted on the AOL Web site before managers took it down.

Chapter 7

1. OECD figures, which only covered students studying abroad, were $30 billion for 1999 (Fuller 2003). Estimates of the global market for educational services vary wildly. For example, Richard T. Hezel, president of Hezel Associates, a research company focused on e-learning, valued the 2005 market at around $2.5 trillion (Redden 2006)

2. These basic GATS definitions can be found at http://www.wto.int/english/tratop_e/serv_e/cbt_course_e/c1s3p1_e.htm.
Mode 3, in particular, has seen intense plurilateral pressure on developing countries from OECD states to open up their services sectors.

3. The philosophical drive beyond NYU's global aspirations in the Oliva years is summarized in *NYU: The Global Vision* (Rice 1995). In that document, Duncan C. Rice, vice chancellor at the time, argued that NYU had a "unique obligation among colleges to become internationalized" because "it serves the greatest international entrepot in the world." The university's history of fulfilling the educational aspirations of the "sons and daughters of working Americans and waves of succeeding immigrants" made it an especially appropriate mission to undertake.

References

Abrahamson, Mark (2004) *Global Cities*. New York: Oxford University Press.

Abrams, Charles (1955) *Forbidden Neighbors: A Study in Prejudice in Housing*. New York: Harper.

Adbusters (1998) "Editorial" (Spring).

Adorno, Theodor, and Max Horkheimer (1972) "The Culture Industry," in *Dialectic of Enlightenment*. New York. Herder and Herder.

Alford, William (1995) *To Steal a Book Is an Elegant Offense: Intellectual Property Law in Chinese Civilization*. Stanford, Calif.: Stanford University Press.

Americans for the Arts (2004) *Creative Industries: Business and Employment in the Arts*, http://www.artsusa.org/information_services/research/services/creative_industries/default.asp.

American Community Survey (2006) U.S. Census Bureau, http://www.artsusa.org/information_services/research/services/creative_industries/default.asp.

Anderson, Sarah, and John Cavanagh, with Thea Lee (2004) *Field Guide to the Global Economy*. New York: New Press.

Armbruster-Sandoval, Ralph (2004) *Globalization and Cross-border Solidarity in the Americas: The Anti-sweatshop Movement and the Struggle for Justice*. New York: Routledge.

Architecture for Humanity (2006) *Design Like You Give a Damn: Architectural Responses to Humanitarian Crises*. New York: Metropolis.

Aronowitz, Stanley (2000) *The Knowledge Factory: Dismantling the Corporate University and Creating True Higher Learning*. Boston: Beacon.

(2001) *The Last Good Job in America: Work and Education in the New Global Technoculture*. Lanham, Colo.: Rowman and Littlefield.

Arpaio, Joe, and Len Sherman (1996) *America's Toughest Sheriff: How We Can Win the War against Crime*. Arlington, Tex.: Summit.

Arrighi, Giovanni (1994) *The Long Twentieth Century: Money, Power, and the Origins of Our Times*. London: Verso.

(2005) "Hegemony Unravelling," *New Left Review* 32, 33.

Baade, Robert Allen (1994) *Stadiums, Professional Sports, and Economic Development: Assessing the Reality*. Detroit: Heartland Institute.

Bacon, David (2006) *Communities without Borders: Images and Voices from the World of Migration*. Ithaca, N.Y.: Cornell University Press.

——— (2007) "The Political Economy of International Migration," *New Labor Forum* 16, 3–4.

——— (2008) *Illegal People: How Globalization Creates Migration and Criminalizes Immigrants*. Boston: Beacon.

Bagli, Charles, and Mike McIntire (2005) "Taxpayer Expense Is Less in Deal for New Stadium," *New York Times* (June 14).

Ballinger, Jeff (2008) "No Sweat? Corporate Social Responsibility and the Dilemma of Anti-sweatshop Activism," *New Labor Forum* 17, 2 (Summer).

Ballinger, Jeff, and Jean Ziegler (2007) "Just Don't Do It!" *New Internationalist* (December).

Barboza, David (2005) "Ogre to Slay? Outsource It to Chinese," *New York Times* (December 9).

Barclay, Eliza (2004) "Gardens Renew Cuba's Urban Core," *Metropolis* (March).

Baringer, Sandra (2005) "Repositioning the Ladder: A Cautionary Tale about Outsourcing," *Minnesota Review* 63–64 (Spring–Summer).

Barrientos, Stephanie, and Sally Smith (2007) "Mainstreaming Fair Trade in Global Value Chains: Own Brand Sourcing of Fruit and Cocoa in UK Supermarkets," in Raynolds, Murray, and Wilkinson.

Bassett, Roberta Malee (2006) *The WTO and the University: Globalization, GATS, and American Higher Education*. New York: Routledge.

Beck, Ulrich (1992) *Risk Society: Towards a New Modernity*, trans. Mark Ritter. London: Sage.

——— (2000) *The Brave New World of Work*, trans. Patrick Camiller. Cambridge: Polity.

Belasco, Warren (2006) *Appetite for Change: How the Counterculture Took on the Food Industry*. Ithaca, N.Y.: Cornell University Press.

Bell, Brian, ed. (2003) *Good Deeds, Good Design: Community Service Through Architecture*. Princeton, N.J.: Princeton Architectural Press.

Bell, Daniel (1956) *Work and Its Discontents: The Cult of Efficiency in America*. Boston: Beacon.

Belsky, Eric (2006) "Why We Need Immigrants," *Big Builder* (August 1).

Bender, Daniel, and Richard Greenwald, eds. (2003) *Sweatshop U.S.A: The American Sweatshop in Historical and Global Perspective*. New York: Routledge.

Berry, David, and Giles Moss (2005) "On the 'Creative Commons': A Critique of the Commons without Commonalty," *Free Software Magazine* 5, http://www.freesoftwaremagazine.com/free_issues/issue_05/commons_without_commonality.

Berry, Joe (2005) *Reclaiming the Ivory Tower: Organizing Adjuncts to Change Higher Education*. New York: Monthly Review.

Bérubé, Michael (1994) *Public Access: Literary Theory and American Cultural Politics*. New York: Verso.

Bettig, Ronald (1996) *Copyrighting Culture: The Political Economy of Intellectual Property*. Boulder, Colo.: Westview.

Blackburn, Robin (2007a) *Age Shock: How Finance Is Failing Us*. London: Verso.

(2007b) "A Global Pension Plan," *New Left Review* 47 (September–October).

Blake, Adam (2005) *The Economic Impact of the London 2012 Olympics*. Nottingham: Nottingham University.

Bollier, David (2002) *Silent Theft: The Private Plunder of Our Common Wealth*. New York: Routledge.

(2004) *Brand Name Bullies: The Quest to Own and Control Culture*. New York: Wiley.

Boltanski, Luc, and Eve Chiapello (2006) *The New Spirit of Capitalism*, trans. Gregory Elliott. London: Verso.

Bonacich, Edna, and Richard Appelbaum (2000) *Behind the Label: Inequality in the Los Angeles Apparel Industry*. Berkeley and Los Angeles: University of California Press.

Bousquet, Marc (2008) *How the University Works: Higher Education and the Low-wage Nation*. New York: NYU Press.

Bowe, John, Marisa Bowe, and Sabin Streeter, eds. (2000) *Gigs: Americans Talk about Their Jobs at the End of the New Economy*. New York: Crown.

Boyle, James (1996) *Shamans, Software, and Spleens: Law and the Construction of the Information Society*. Cambridge, Mass.: Harvard University Press.

Brecher, Jeremy, Tim Costello, and Brendan Smith (2006) "International Labor Solidarity: The New Frontier," *New Labor Forum* (Spring).

(2008) "Labor's War on Global Warming," *The Nation* (March 10).

Brenner, Neil (2005) *New State Spaces: Urban Governance and the Rescaling of Statehood*. New York: Oxford University Press.

Brenner, Neil, and Nicholas Theodore, eds. (2002) *Spaces of Neoliberalism: Urban Restructuring in Western Europe and North America*. Oxford: Blackwell.

Breyer, Stephen (1970) "The Uneasy Case for Copyright: A Study of Copyright in Books, Photocopies, and Computer Programs," *Harvard Law Review* 84.

Brooks, Ethel (2003) "The Ideal Sweatshop," in Bender and Greenwald, eds.

Bronfenbrenner, Kate, ed. (2007) *Global Unions: Challenging Transnational Capital Through Cross-border Campaigns*. Ithaca, N.Y.: Cornell University Press.

Brown, Michael (2004) *Who Owns Native Culture?* Cambridge, Mass.: Harvard University Press.

Bruegmann, Robert (2005) *Sprawl: A Compact History*. Chicago: University of Chicago Press.

Buck, N. H., I. R. Gordon, P. G. Hall, M. Harloe, and M. Kleinman (2002) *Working Capital: Life and Labour in Contemporary London*. London: Routledge.

Bullert, B. J. (2000) "Strategic Public Relations, Sweatshops, and the Making of a Global Movement," Working Paper, Joan Shorenstein Center on Press, Politics, and Public Policy, Harvard University.

Burbank, Matthew, Gregory Andranovich, and Charles Heying, eds. (2001) *Olympic Dreams: The Impact of Mega-events on Local Politics.* Boulder, Colo.: Lynne Rienner.

Burchell, Robert, Anthony Downs, Barbara McCann, and Sahan Mukherji (2005) *Sprawl Costs: Economic Impact of Unchecked Development.* Washington, D.C.: Island.

Butler, Judith (2004) *Precarious Life: The Power of Mourning and Violence.* New York: Verso.

Cagan, Joanna, and Neil deMause (1998) *Field of Schemes: How the Great Stadium Swindle Turns Public Money into Private Profit.* Monroe, Maine: Common Courage.

Campbell, Dennis (2005) "The Day Coe Won Gold," *The Observer* (July 10).

Carr, James (1998) "The Right to 'Poverty with a Roof,'" *Housing Policy Debate* 9, 2.

Cashman, Richard, and Anthony Hughes (1999) *Staging the Olympics: The Event and Its Impact.* Sydney: University of New South Wales Press.

Castel, Robert (2002) *From Manual Workers to Wage Laborers: Transformation of the Social Question,* trans. Richard Boyd. New Brunswick, N.J.: Transaction.

Castells, Manuel, and Pekka Himanen (2002) *The Information Society and the Welfare State: The Finnish Model.* New York: Oxford University Press.

Castree, Noel, Neil Coe, Noel Kevin Ward, and Mike Samers (2004) *Spaces of Work: Global Capitalism and Geographies of Labour.* London: Sage.

Cazes, Sandrine, and Alena Nespova (2007) *Flexicurity: A Relevant Approach in Central and Eastern Europe.* Washington, D.C.: Brookings Institution Press.

Center for Housing Rights and Evictions (2007) *Mega-events and Olympics,* http://www.cohre.org/mega-events.

Chase, Stuart, and F. J. Schlink (1927) *Your Money's Worth: A Study in the Waste of the Consumer's Dollar.* New York: Macmillan.

Chavez, Roberto, Julie Viloria, and Melanie Zipperer (2000) "Interview with John F. C. Turner," World Bank, Washington D.C., http://www.worldbank.org/urban/forum2002/docs/turner-tacit.pdf.

Chow, Rey (1993) *Writing Diaspora: Tactics of Intervention in Contemporary Cultural Studies.* Bloomington: Indiana University Press.

Claydon Gescher Associates (2004) *Changing China—The Creative Industry Perspective: A Market Perspective,* http://www.uktradeinvest.gov.uk.

Cochrane, Allan, Jamie Peck, and Adam Tickell (1996) "Manchester Plays Games: Exploring the Local Politics of Globalization," *Urban Studies* 33, 8.

Cohen, Phil (2005) "The Olympics Story," *Rising East* 1 (January).

Cohen, Tom (2001) "Toronto Bid Hit by Mayor's Gaffe," *The Independent* (June 23).

Colectivo Precarias a la Deriva (2004) *A la deriva, por los circuitos de la precariedad femenina.* Madrid: Traficantes de Sueños.

Comaroff, Jean, and John Comaroff, eds. (2001) *Millennial Capitalism and the Culture of Neoliberalism*. Durham, N.C.: Duke University Press.

Commoner, Barry (1971) *The Closing Circle: Nature, Man and Technology*. New York: Knopf.

"Corcoran Group Releases Third Quarter Harlem Report" (2000) *Real Estate Weekly* (November 29).

Correa, Carlos (2000) *Intellectual Property Rights, the WTO, and Developing Countries: The TRIPS Agreement and Policy Options*. London: Zed.

Creative 100 (2003) *The Memphis Manifesto*. Memphis: Memphis Tomorrow and Mpact.

Crittenden, Ann (1988) *Sanctuary: A Story of American Conscience and the Law in Collision*. New York: Weidenfeld and Nicholson.

Cronon, William (1983) *Changes in the Land: Indians, Colonialists, and the Ecology of New England*. New York: Hill and Wang.

Cruz, Teddy (2005) "Urban Acupuncture," *Residential Architect* (January).

——— (2007a) Personal Interview, New York (May).

——— (2007b) "Trans-border Flows: Urbanism Below the Poverty Line," *Temporary Urbanism—Between the Permanent and Transitory*, Holcim Forum, http://www.holcimfoundation.org/Portals/1/docs/F07/WK-Temp/F07-WK-Temp-allpapers01.pdf.

Culf, Andrew (2007) "MPs Demand Tighter Rein on Olympics Spending," *The Guardian* (July 10).

Cunningham, Stuart, Michael Keane, and Mark David Ryan (2005). "World's Apart? Finance and Investment in Creative Industries in the People's Republic of China and Latin America," *Telematics and Informatics* 22, 4.

Damiani, Bettina, Eileen Markey, and Dan Steinberg (2007) *Insider Baseball: How Current and Former Public Officials Pitched a Community Shutout for the New York Yankees*, Good Jobs New York, http://goodjobsny.org/Master_0717_mac_pdf4.pdf.

Davila, Arlene (2004) *Barrio Dreams: Puerto Ricans, Latinos, and the Neoliberal City*. Berkeley and Los Angeles: University of California Press.

Davis, Mike (2000) *Magic Urbanism: Latinos Reinvent the U.S. City*. New York: Verso.

——— (2006) *Planet of Slums*. New York: Verso.

DCMS (UK Department of Culture, Media, and Sport) (1998) *Creative Industries Mapping Document*, http://www.culture.gov.uk/reference_library/publications/4740.aspx.

Dean, Andrea Oppenheimer, and Timothy Hursley (2002) *Rural Studio: Samuel Mockbee and an Architecture of Decency*. Princeton, N.J.: Princeton Architectural Press.

——— (2005) *Proceed and Be Bold: Rural Studio After Samuel Mockbee*. Princeton, N.J.: Princeton Architectural Press.

de Graff, John, David Wann, and Thomas H. Naylor (2001) *Affluenza: The All-consuming Epidemic*. Barrett-Koehler: San Francisco.

Del Olmo, Carolina (2004) *The Role of Mega Events in Urban Competitiveness and Its Consequences on People*. Madrid: Universidad Complutense.

Delaney, Kevin, and Rick Eckstein (2003) *Public Dollars, Private Stadiums: The Battle over Building Sports Stadiums*. New Brunswick, N.J.: Rutgers University Press.

deMause, Neil (1999) "Dome to Nowhere," *This Magazine* (March).

——— (2006) "Yankee Lobbyists on Taxpayers' Tab" *Village Voice* (July 25).

——— (2007) "Yanks Reach First Place . . . In Stadium Subsidies." *Village Voice* (July 20).

Denning, Michael (1998) *The Cultural Front: The Laboring of American Culture in the Twentieth Century*. New York: Verso.

Devereux, Julien (2004) "Design Corps's Humane Housing for Migrant Workers," *Metropolis* (March 1).

Diaz, David (2005) *Barrio Urbanism: Chicano, Planning, and American Cities*. New York: Routledge.

Dibbell, Julian (2007) "The Life of the Chinese Gold Farmer," *New York Times Magazine* (June 17).

DiBona, Chris, Mark Stone, and Sam Ockman, eds. (1999) *Open Sources: Voices from the Open Source Revolution*. Sebastopol, Calif.: O'Reilly.

DiMento, Joseph, and LeRoy Graymer, eds. (1987) *Rental Housing in California*. Boston: Lincoln Institute of Land Policy.

Dougherty, John (2003) "Jerry's World," *Phoenix New Times* (October 16).

Downs, Jim, and Jennifer Manion, eds. (2004) *Taking Back the Academy: History of Activism, History as Activism*. New York: Routledge.

Drahos, Peter, with John Braithwaite (2002) *Information Feudalism: Who Owns the Knowledge Economy?* London: Earthscan.

Drahos, Peter, with Ruth Mayne (2002) *Global Intellectual Property Rights: Knowledge, Access, and Development*. New York: Palgrave Macmillan.

Dreier, Peter, and Richard Appelbaum (2004) "SweatX Closes Up Shop," *The Nation* (July 19).

Duany, Andres, Elizabeth Plater-Zyberk, and Jeff Speck (2001) *Suburban Nation: The Rise of Sprawl and the Decline of the American Dream*. Berkeley: North Point.

Duggan, Lisa (2003) *The Twilight of Equality: Neoliberalism, Cultural Politics, and the Attack on Democracy*. Boston: Beacon.

Dyer-Witheford, Nick (1999) *Cyber-Marx: Cycles and Circuits of Struggle in High-technology Capitalism*. Urbana: University of Illinois Press.

Economist, The (2004) "The Geography of Cool" (April 13).

Ehrenreich, Barbara, and Arlie Hochschild (2002) *Global Woman: Nannies, Maids, and Sex Workers in the New Economy*. Ithaca, N.Y.: Cornell University Press.

Ehrenstein, Amanda (2006) *Social Relationality and Affective Experience in Precarious Labour Conditions: A Study of Young Immaterial Workers in the Arts Industries in Cardiff.* School of Social Sciences, Cardiff University (Ph.D. dissertation).

Ehrlich, Cyril (1990) *The Piano: A History.* New York: Oxford University Press.

Esbenshade, Jill (2004) *Monitoring Sweatshops: Workers, Consumers, and the Global Apparel Industry.* Philadelphia: Temple University Press.

European Council (2000) *Lisbon Strategy,* http://europa.eu/scadplus/glossary/lisbon_strategy_en.htm.

European Commission (2007) *Culture Programme,* http://ec.europa.eu/culture/our-programmes-and-actions/doc411_en.htm.

European Expert Group on Flexicurity (2007) *Flexicurity Pathways: Turning Hurdles into Stepping Stones,* http://ec.europa.eu/employment_social/employment_strategy/pdf/flexi_pathways_en.pdf.

Fainstein, Susan, Ian Gordon, and Michael Harloe, eds. (1992) *Divided Cities: New York and London in the Contemporary World.* Oxford: Blackwell.

Fairfield, Roy, ed. (1974) *Humanizing the Workplace.* Buffalo: Prometheus.

Fantone, Laura (2007) "Precarious Changes: Gender and Generational Conflicts in Contemporary Italy," *Feminist Review* 87.

Fathy, Hassan (1972) *Architecture for the Poor: An Experiment in Rural Egypt.* Chicago: University of Chicago Press.

Featherstone, Lisa, and United Students Against Sweatshops (2002) *Students Against Sweatshops.* New York: Verso.

Fields, Belden (1988) *Trotskyism and Maoism: Theory and Practice in France and the United States.* Brooklyn: Autonomedia.

Fine, Janice (2006) *Worker Centers: Organizing Communities at the Edge of the Dream.* Ithaca, N.Y.: Cornell University Press.

(2007) "Why Labor Needs a Plan B: Alternatives to Conventional Trade Unionism," *New Labor Forum* 16, 2 (Spring).

Fisher, William (2004) *Promises to Keep: Technology, Law, and the Future of Entertainment.* Stanford, Calif.: Stanford University Press.

Flores, Juan (2000) "Salvacion Casita," and "Postscript: None of the Above," in *From Bomba to Hip-Hop: Puerto Rican Culture and Latino Identity.* New York: Columbia University Press.

Florida, Richard (2002) *The Rise of the Creative Class and How It's Transforming Work, Leisure, Community, and Everyday Life.* New York: Basic.

(2005) *The Flight of the Creative Class.* New York: Harper Business.

(2008) *Who's Your City? How the Creative Economy is Making Where to Live the Most Important Decision of Your Life.* New York: Basic.

Forsook, Paula (2000) *Cyberselfish: A Critical Romp through the Terribly Libertarian Culture of High Tech.* New York: Public Affairs.

Foti, Alex (2004) "Precarity and N/european Identity: An Interview by Merjin Oudenampsen and Gavin Sullivan," *Greenpepper* (October), http://www.metamute.org/en/Precarity-european-Identity-Alex-Foti-ChainWorkers.

(2006) Interview with Chris Carlsson, *The Nowtopian* (June 7), http://www.lipmagazine.org/ccarlsson/archives/2006/06/alex_foti_inter.html.

Frank, Andre Gunder (1998) *ReOrient: Global Economy in the Asian Age*. Berkeley and Los Angeles: University of California Press.

Frank, Dana (1999) *Buy American: The Untold Story of Economic Nationalism*. Boston: Beacon.

Fraser, Jill Andresky (2002) *White Collar Sweatshop: The Deterioration of Work and Its Reward in Corporate America*. New York: Norton.

Friedman, Thomas (2005) *The World Is Flat a Brief History of the Twenty-first Century*. New York: Farrar, Strauss and Giroux.

Frumkin, Howard, Lawrence Frank, and Richard Jackson (2004) *Urban Sprawl and Public Health, Designing, Planning, and Building for Healthy Communities*. Washington, D.C.: Island.

Fuller, Thomas (2003) "Education Exporters Take Case to WTO," *International Herald Tribune* (February 18).

Gaddis, William (2002a) *Agape Agape*. New York: Viking Penguin.

(2002b) "Stop Player: Joke No. 4," in *The Rush for Second Place: Essays and Occasional Writings*. New York: Viking Penguin.

Galvez, Martha, and Frank Braconi (2003) "New York's Underground Housing," *The Urban Prospect* 9, 2 (Citizens Housing and Planning Council).

García, Beatriz (2005) "De-constructing the City of Culture: The Long Term Cultural Legacies of Glasgow 1990," *Urban Studies* 42, 5–6.

Garcia, Maria Cristina (2006) *Seeking Refuge: Central American Migration to Mexico, the United States, and Canada*. Berkeley and Los Angeles: University of California Press.

Garcia, Yolanda, Eddie Bautista, and Barbara Olshansky (1996) "Melrose Commons: A Case Study for Sustainable Community Design," Planners Network Conference, http://www.plannersnetwork.org/publications/melrose.htm.

Garnham, Nicholas (2005) "From Cultural to Creative Industries: An Analysis of the Implications of the 'Creative Industries' Approach to Arts and Media Policy Making in the UK," *International Journal of Cultural Policy* 10, 1.

Garson, Barbara (1975) *All the Livelong Day: The Meaning and Demeaning of Routine Work*. Garden City, N.Y.: Doubleday.

Gelinas, Nicole (2006) "Believe It or Not, New York Was Too Capitalist to Win," *City Journal* 16, 1 (July 7).

Gill, Rosalind (2002) "Cool, Creative, and Egalitarian? Exploring Gender in Project-based New Media Work," *Information, Communication, and Society* 5, 1.

(2007) *Technobohemians or the New Cybertariat: New Media Work in Amsterdam a Decade After the Web*. Amsterdam: Institute of Network Cultures.

Gillham, Oliver (2002) *The Limitless City: A Primer on the Urban Sprawl Debate.* Washington, D.C.: Island.

Gitlin, Todd (1995) *The Twilight of Common Dreams: Why America Is Wracked by Culture Wars.* New York: Henry Holt.

Glickstein, Jonathan (1991) *Concepts of Free Labor in Antebellum America.* New Haven, Conn.: Yale University Press.

Golden, Renny, and Michael McConnell (1986) *Sanctuary: The New Underground Railroad.* Maryknoll, N.Y.: Orbis.

Goldstein, Paul (2003) *Copyright's Highway: From Gutenberg to the Celestial Jukebox.* Stanford, Calif.: Stanford University Press.

Gordon, David (1978) "Capitalist Development and the History of American Cities," in William Tabb and Larry Sawers, eds., *Marxism and the Metropolis.* New York: Oxford University Press.

Gordon, Jennifer (2005) *Suburban Sweatshops: The Fight for Immigrant Rights.* Cambridge, Mass.: Harvard University Press.

Gordon, Michael, and Lowell Turner, eds. (2000) *Transnational Cooperation among Labor Unions.* Ithaca, N.Y.: Cornell University Press.

Gorman, Robert (1998) "Intellectual Property: The Rights of Faculty as Creators and Users," *Academe* 3, 14 (May–June).

Gow, Ian (2007) "British Universities in China: The Reality beyond the Rhetoric," *Agora: A Forum for Culture and Education,* http://www.agora-education. org/pubs/index.php.

Graff, Gerald (1992) *Beyond the Culture Wars: How Teaching the Conflicts Can Revitalize American Education.* New York: Norton.

Gray, Lois, and Ronald Seeber (1996) *Under the Stars: Essays on Labor Relations in Arts and Entertainment.* Ithaca, N.Y.: Cornell University Press.

Greenpepper, along with P2P Fightsharing and Candida TV (2004) *Precarity* (DVD). Amsterdam, http://process.greenpeppermagazine.org//tiki-index. php?page=Precarity+DVD+Insert.

Grossberg, Lawrence (1992) *We Gotta Get Out of This Place: Popular Conservatism and Postmodern Culture.* New York: Routledge.

Hardt, Michael, and Antonio Negri (2000) *Empire.* Cambridge, Mass.: Harvard University Press.

Harrod, Jeffrey, and Robert O'Brien (2002) *Global Unions: Theories and Strategies of Organized Labour in the Global Political Economy.* London: Routledge.

Hartley, John, ed. (2004) *Creative Industries.* Oxford: Blackwell.

Hartman, Chester (1988) "The Case for a Right to Housing," *Housing Policy Debate* 9, 2.

Harvey, David (2001) "The Art of Rent: Globalization and the Commodification of Culture," in *Spaces of Capital: Towards a Critical Geography.* New York: Routledge.

(2005) *A Brief History of Neoliberalism.* New York: Oxford University Press.

Hassan, Gerry, Melissa Mean, and Charlie Tims (2007) *The Dreaming City: Glasgow 2020 and the Power of Mass Imagination*. London: Demos.

Heath, Joseph, and Andrew Potter (2004) *Rebel Sell: Why the Culture Can't Be Jammed*. New York: HarperCollins.

Heim, Carol (2001) "Leapfrogging, Urban Sprawl, and Growth Management: Phoenix, 1950–2000," *American Journal of Economics and Sociology* 60, 1.

Henwood, Doug (2003) *After the New Economy*. New York: New Press.

Herbert, Bob (1998) "In America: Ball Pork" *New York Times* (April 19).

Herod, Andrew (1997) "Labor as an Agent of Globalization and as a Global Agent," in Kevin Cox, ed., *Spaces of Globalization: Reasserting the Power of the Local*. New York: Guilford.

(2001) *Labor Geographies: Workers and the Landscapes of Capitalism*. New York: Guilford.

Hesmondhalgh, David (2007) *The Cultural Industries* (rev. ed.). London: Sage.

Hesmondhalgh, David, and Andy Pratt, eds. (2005) "The Cultural Industries and Cultural Policy," special issue of *International Journal of Cultural Policy* 11, 1.

Hess, Sabine (2005) *Globalisierte Arbeite: Au-Pair als Migrationsstrategie von Frauen aus Osteuropa*. Wiesbaden: Verlag fur Socialwissenschaften.

Hinton, William (1966) *Fanshen: A Documentary of Revolution in a Chinese Village*. New York: Monthly Review.

(2002) "Turning Point in China," in *China: An Unfinished Battle: Essays on Cultural Revolution and the Further Developments in China*. Kharagpur, India: Cornerstone.

Holmes, Brian (2008) "One World, One Dream," *Continental Drift* (January 8), http://brianholmes.wordpress.com/2008/01/08/one-world-one-dream/#more-262.

Hong Kong Christian Industrial Committee (2001) *How Hasbro, Mattel, McDonald's, and Disney Manufacture Their Toys in China*. Hong Kong: HKCIC.

Housing First! (2005) "A Home For All New Yorkers: Housing First! 2005 Policy Update" (August), New York.

(2006) "Housing New York's Future: Community Development and Homes for All New Yorkers" (July), New York.

Howard, Alan (2007) "The Future of Global Unions: Is Solidarity Still Forever?" *Dissent* (Fall).

Howkins, John (2001) *The Creative Economy: How People Make Money from Ideas*. London: Allen Lane.

(2002) "The Mayor's Commission on the Creative Industries" in Hartley, ed.

Hu, Jintao (2007) Keynote Speech to Seventeenth National Congress, Chinese Communist Party, http://english.people.com.cn/90002/92169/92187/6283148.html.

Hunter, James Davison (1992) *Culture Wars: The Struggle to Define America*. New York: Basic.

Huws, Ursula (2003) *The Making of a Cybertariat: Virtual Work in a Real World.* New York: Monthly Review.

ed. (2007) "The Creative Spark in the Engine," inaugural issue of *Work, Organization, Labour, and Globalization* 1, 1.

Iles, Anthony (2007) "Of Lammas Land and Olympic Dreams," *Mute* (January), http://www.metamute.org/en/Of-Lammas-Land-and-Olympic-Dreams.

Institute for Policy Studies Working Group on Housing (1989) *The Right to Housing: A Blueprint for Housing the Nation.* Washington, D.C.: IPS.

Jackson, Kenneth (1985) *Crabgrass Frontier: The Suburbanization of the United States.* New York: Oxford University Press.

Jacobs, Jane (1961) *The Death and Life of Great American Cities.* New York: Random House.

Jaschik, Scott (2006) "Codes Don't Work," *Inside Higher Ed* (September 28), http://www.insidehighered.com/news/2006/09/28/wrc.

Jaszi, Peter, and Martha Woodmansee, eds. (1994) *The Construction of Authorship: Textual Appropriation in Law and Literature.* Durham, N.C.: Duke University Press.

Jayaraman, Sarumathi, and Immanuel Ness, eds. (2005) *New Urban Immigrant Workforce: Innovative Models for Labor Organizing.* Armonk, N.Y.: M. E. Sharpe.

Jennings, Andrew, and Vyv Simson (1992) *The Lords of the Rings: Power, Money, and Drugs in the Modern Olympics.* London: Simon and Schuster.

Johnson, Benjamin, Patrick Kavanagh, and Kevin Mattson, eds. (2003) *Steal This University: The Rise of the Corporate University and the Academic Labor Movement.* New York: Routledge.

Jonas, Andrew, and David Wilson, eds. (1999) *The Urban Growth Machine: Critical Perspectives Twenty Years Later.* Albany, N.Y.: SUNY Press.

Jones, Charles, ed. (1998) *The Black Panther Party (Reconsidered).* Baltimore: Black Classic.

Jonnes, Jill (2002) *South Bronx Rising: The Rise, Fall, and Resurrection of an American City.* New York: Fordham University Press.

Jonsson, Patrik (2006) "To Curb Illegal Immigration, South Cracks Down on Housing Codes," *Christian Science Monitor* (January 18).

Jørgensen, Henning, and Per Kohnshoj Madsen (2007) *Flexicurity and Beyond: Finding a New Agenda for the European Social Model.* Copenhagen: DJØF.

Jowell, Tessa (2004) "Government and the Value of Culture," Department of Media, Culture, Media, and Sports, UK, http://www.culture.gov.uk/reference_library/publications/4581.aspx.

(2007) "Foreword" to Will Hutton et al., eds., *Staying Ahead: The Economic Performance of the UK's Creative Industries.* London: Work Foundation.

Kabeer, Naila (2000) *The Power to Choose: Bangladeshi Women and Labour Market Decisions in London and Dakha.* London: Verso.

Kallet, Arthur, and F. J. Schlink (1933) *100,000,000 Guinea Pigs: Dangers in Everyday Foods, Drugs, and Cosmetics*. New York, Vanguard.

KEA European Affairs (2006) *The Economy of Culture in Europe*, http://ec.europa.eu/culture/key-documents/doc873_en.htm.

Keane, Michael (2004) "Brave New World: Understanding China's Creative Vision," *International Journal of Cultural Policy* 10, 3.

(2007) *Created in China: The Great New Leap Forward*. London: Routledge Curzon.

Kelber, Harry (2004) "AFL-CIO's Dark Past," *The Labor Educator*, http://www.laboreducator.org/darkpast.htm.

Keller, George (2003) *Higher Ed, Inc.: The Rise of the For-profit University*. Baltimore: Johns Hopkins University Press.

Kelley, Robin D. G. (1994) *Race Rebels: Culture, Politics, and the Black Working Class*. New York: Free Press.

(1998) *Yo' Mama's Dysfunktional: Fighting Culture Wars in Urban America*. Boston: Beacon.

(2001) "Without a Song: New York Musicians Strike Out against a Technology," in Howard Zinn, Dana Frank, and Robin D. G. Kelley, eds., *Three Strikes: Miners, Musicians, Salesgirls, and the Fighting Spirit of Labor's Last Century*. Boston: Beacon.

(2002) *Freedom Dreams: The Black Radical Imagination*. Boston: Beacon.

Kelly, Owen, and Charles Landry (1994) *Helsinki: A Living Work of Art—Towards a Cultural Strategy for Helsinki*. City of Helsinki Information Management Centre.

Keynes, Maynard (1945) "The Arts Council; Its Policy and Hopes," in Wallinger and Warnock, eds.

Kirp, David (2004) *Shakespeare, Einstein, and the Bottom Line: The Marketing of Higher Education*. Cambridge, Mass.: Harvard University Press.

Klein, Naomi (2000) *No Logo: Taking Aim at the Brand Bullies*. New York: Picador.

Knight, Jane (2006) "GATS: The Way Forward after Hong Kong," *International Higher Education* 43 (Spring).

Kornblatt, Tracy (2006) *Setting the Bar: Preparing for London's Olympic Legacy*. London: Institute for Public Policy Research.

Kornblatt, Tracy, and Max Nathan (2007) *Paying for 2012: The Olympics Budget and Legacy*. London: Institute for Public Policy Research.

Kotkin, Joel (2005) "On Uncool Cities," *Prospect* (October), http://www.prospect-magazine.co.uk/article_details.php?id=7072.

Kotkin, Joel, and Fred Siegel (2004) "Too Much Froth," *Blueprint* 6.

kpD (2005) "The Precarization of Cultural Producers and the Missing 'Good Life,'" *Transversal*, trans. Aileen Derieg (June), http://transform.eipcp.net/transversal/0406/kpd/en.

Kraft, James (1996) *Stage to Studio: Musicians and the Sound Revolution, 1890–1950*. Baltimore: Johns Hopkins University Press.

Krause, Monika, Mary Nolan, Michael Palm, and Andrew Ross, eds. (2008) *The University against Itself: The NYU Strike and the Future of the Academic Workplace*. Philadelphia: Temple University Press.

Krimsky, Sheldon (2003) *Science in the Private Interest: Has the Lure of Profits Corrupted Biomedical Research?* New York: Rowman and Littlefield.

Krupat, Kitty (1997) "From War Zone to Free Trade Zone," in Ross, ed.

Kwong, Peter (2007) "Chinese Migration Goes Global," *YaleGlobal Online* (17 July), http://yaleglobal.yale.edu/display.article?id=9437.

Lafargue, Jules (1883) *The Right to Be Lazy*. New York: Charles Kerr.

Landes, William, and Richard Posner (2003) *The Economic Structure of Intellectual Property Law*. Cambridge, Mass.: Harvard University Press.

Landry, Charles (1990) *Glasgow: The Creative City and its Cultural Economy*. Glasgow: Development Agency.

(1998) *Helsinki: Towards a Creative City*. Helsinki: City of Helsinki Urban Facts.

(2000) *The Creative City: A Toolkit for Urban Innovators*. London: Earthscan.

(2002) *Helsinki's Cultural Futures*. London: Comedia.

Lange, David (1981) "Recognizing the Public Domain," *Law and Contemporary Problems* 44.

Larson, Gary (1997) *American Canvas: An Arts Legacy for Our Communities*. Washington, D.C.: National Endowment for the Arts.

Lasn, Kalle (1999) *Culture Jam: The Uncooling of America*. New York: Morrow.

Lazzarato, Maurizio (1996) "Immaterial Labor," in Paolo Virno and Michael Hardt, eds., *Radical Thought in Italy*. Minneapolis: University of Minnesota Press.

Lederman, Doug (2007) "Apollo Goes Global," *Inside Higher Ed* (October 23), http://insidehighered.com/news/2007/10/23/apollo.

Lee, Ching Kwan (2007) *Against the Law: Labor Protests in China's Rustbelt and Sunbelt*. Berkeley and Los Angeles: University of California Press.

Leitner, Helga, and Eric Sheppard (1998) "Economic Uncertainty, Inter-urban Competition, and the Efficacy Of Entrepreneurialism," in Tim Hall and Phil Hubbard, eds., *The Entrepreneurial City*. Chichester: Wiley.

(1999) "Transcending Interurban Competition: Conceptual Issues and Policy Alternatives in the European Union," in Jonas and Wilson, eds.

Lemons, Stephen (2007) "Who's the Bigger (Media) Whore: Joe Arpaio or Paris Hilton?" *Phoenix New Times* (June 11).

Lessig, Lawrence (2001) *The Future of Ideas: The Fate of the Commons in a Connected World*. New York: Random House.

(2004) *Free Culture: How Big Media Uses Technology and the Law to Lock Down Culture and Control Creativity*. New York: Penguin.

Levitt, Peggy (2001) *The Transnational Villagers*. Berkeley and Los Angeles: University of California Press.

Lewin, Tamar (2008) "In Oil-rich Mideast, Shades of the Ivy League," *New York Times* (February 11).

Lewinski, Silke von (2004) *Indigenous Heritage and Intellectual Property: Genetic Resources, Traditional Knowledge, and Folklore*. The Hague: Kluwer Law International.

Lewontin, Richard (1997) "The Cold War and the Transformation of the Academy," in Noam Chomsky et al., eds., *The Cold War and the University*. New York: New Press.

Ley, David (1996) *The New Middle Class and the Remaking of the Central City*. New York: Oxford University Press.

Li, Wuwei (2006) Remarks of Chairperson of Shanghai's Creative Industry Association, at a session of the Shanghai People's Congress (SPC), http://www.designtaxi.com/news.jsp?id=1807&monthview=1&month=1&year=2006.

Lichtenstein, Nelson, ed. (2006) *Wal-Mart: The Face of Twenty-first-century Capitalism*. New York: New Press.

Lin, Chun (2006) *The Transformation of Chinese Socialism*. Durham, N.C.: Duke University Press.

Lipman, Barbara (2003) "America's Newest Working Families: Cost Crowding and Conditions for Immigrants," *New Century Housing* 4, 3 (July).

Litman, Jessica (2001) *Digital Copyright Protecting Intellectual Property on the Internet*. New York: Prometheus.

Locke, John (1980) *Second Treatise of Government*. Indianapolis: Hackett.

Loescher, Gil, and John Scanlon (1986) *A Calculated Kindness: Refugees and America's Half-open Door, 1945–Present*. New York: Free Press.

Logan, John, and Harvey Molotch (1987) *Urban Fortunes: The Political Economy of Place*. Berkeley and Los Angeles: University of California Press.

Lott, Eric (2006) *The Disappearing Liberal Intellectual*. New York: Basic.

Louie, Miriam Ching Yoon (2001) *Sweatshop Warriors: Immigrant Women Workers Take on the Global Factory*. Cambridge, Mass: South End.

Lovink, Geert, and Ned Rossiter, eds. (2007) *MyCreativity Reader: A Critique of Creative Industries*. Amsterdam: Institute of Network Cultures.

Lustig, Jeff (2004) "The Mixed Legacy of Clark Kerr: A Personal View," *Academe* (April).

Mabrouki, Abdel (2004) *Génération précaire*. Paris: Le Cherche Midi.

Macaulay, Thomas (1914) *Speeches on Copyright*. London: C. Gaston.

Malanga, Steven (2004) "The Curse of the Creative Class," *City Journal* (Winter).

Maliszewski, Paul (2004) "Flexibility and its Discontents," *The Baffler* 16.

Marcuse, Peter (2003) Review of *The Rise of the Creative Class* by Richard Florida, in *Urban Land* 62.

Maricopa Association of Governments (2001) *Report on "Demographics and Social Change,"* commissioned from BRW Inc. as part of the Regional Transportation Plan Update (June).

Martin, Randy, ed. (1998) *Chalk Lines: The Politics of Work in the Managed University.* Durham, N.C.: Duke University Press.

Marx, Karl (1861) *Grundrisse: Foundations of the Critique of Political Economy,* http://www.marxists.org/archive/marx/works/1857/grundrisse.

Mathiason, Nick (2005) "Olympic Costs Set to Double," *The Observer* (November 20).

Maurrasse, David (2006) *Listening to Harlem: Gentrification, Community, and Business.* New York: Routledge.

May, Christopher (2000) *Global Political Economy of Intellectual Property Rights.* New York: Routledge.

McChesney, Robert (2004) *The Problem of the Media: U.S. Communications Politics in the 21st Century.* New York: Monthly Review.

McLay, Farquar, ed. (1990) *Workers City: The Real Glasgow Stands Up.* Glasgow: Clydeside.

McLeod, Kembrew (2005) *Freedom of Expression (R): Overzealous Copyright Bozos and Other Enemies of Creativity.* New York: Doubleday.

McRobbie, Angela (2004) "'Everyone Is Creative': Artists as Pioneers of the New Economy?" in Tony Bennett and Elizabeth Silva, eds., *Contemporary Culture and Everyday Life.* London: Routledge.

(2007) "The Los Angelisation of London: Three Short-waves of Young People's Micro-economies of Culture and Creativity in the UK," *Transversal* (January), http://transform.eipcp.net/transversal/0207/mcrobbie/en.

McSherry, Corynne (2001) *Who Owns Academic Work? Battling for Control of Intellectual Property.* Cambridge, Mass.: Harvard University Press.

Mendez, Michael (2002) *Latino Lifestyle and the New Urbanism: Synergy against Sprawl.* Massachusetts Institute of Technology (master's thesis).

(2005) "Latino New Urbanism: Building on Cultural Preferences," *Opolis* 1, 1.

Menger, Pierre-Michel (2002) *Portrait de l'artiste en travailleur.* Paris: Seuil.

Messer-Davidow, Ellen (1993) "Manufacturing the Attack on Liberalized Higher Education," *Social Text* 36 (Fall).

Mezzadra, Sandro (2001) *Diritto di fuga: Migrazioni, cittadinanza, globalizzazione.* Verona: Ombre Corte.

Michigan, Department of Labor and Economic Growth (2004). *Cool Cities.* Lansing: State of Michigan.

Milkman, Ruth (2006) *LA Story: Immigrant Workers and the Future of the U.S. Labor Movement.* New York: Russell Sage Foundation.

Milkman, Ruth, and Kim Voss, eds. (2004) *Rebuilding Labor: Organizing and Organizers in the New Union Movement.* Ithaca, N.Y.: Cornell University Press.

Miller, Paul, ed. (2008) *Sound Unbound: Sampling Digital Music and Culture.* Cambridge, Mass.: MIT Press.

Miller, Toby, and George Yudice (2003) *Cultural Policy.* London: Sage.

Minichbauer, Raimund (2006) "Chanting the Creative Mantra: The Accelerating Economisation of EU Cultural Policy," *Transversal* (February), http://eipcp. net/policies/cci/minichbauer/en.

Mitropoulos, Angela (2005) "Precari-us" *Mute* 29, http://www.metamute.org/ en/Precari-us.

Moberg, David (2007) "What Vacation Days?" *In These Times* (June 18).

Moll, Jennifer (2008) "Trade in Education and Training Services: Excellent Opportunities for U.S. Providers," *Export America: The Federal Source for Your Global Business Needs*, http://www.ita.doc.gov/exportamerica/New Opportunities/no_edu_0902.html.

Molotch, Harvey (1976) "The City as a Growth Machine," *American Journal of Sociology* 82.

Mooney, Paul (2006) "The Wild, Wild East," *The Chronicle of Higher Education* (February 17).

Morris, William (1886) *Useful Work versus Useless Toil.* London: Socialist League Office.

Moses, Stanley (2005) "The Struggle for Decent Affordable Housing, Debates, Plans, and Policies," in *Affordable Housing in New York City: Definitions/Options.* New York: Steven Newman Real Estate Institute, Baruch University.

Moulier Boutang, Yann (1998) *De l'esclavage au salariat: Economie historique du salariat bridé.* Paris: Presses Universitaires de France.

Moulier Boutang, Yann, with Stany Grelet (2001) "The Art of Flight: An Interview with Yann Moulier," *Rethinking Marxism* 13, 3–4 (September).

Nabeshima, Kaoru, and Shahid Yusuf (2003) "Urban Development Needs Creativity: How Creative Industries Can Affect Urban Areas," *Development Outreach*, special issue on "Unknown Cities, World Bank" (November), http:// www1.worldbank.org/devoutreach/nov03/article.asp?id=221.

National Labor Committee (NLC) (1992) *Paying to Lose Our Jobs: Free Trade's Hidden Secrets: Why We Are Losing Our Shirts*, http://www.nlcnet.org/ campaigns/archive/payingtolose/paytolose92.pdf.

(2002) *Toys of Misery.* New York: NLC.

National Wildlife Federation (2005) *Endangered by Sprawl: How Runaway Development Threatens America's Wildlife*, http://www.nwf.org/nwfwebadmin/ binaryVault/EndangeredBySprawlFinal.pdf.

Needham, Joseph (1986). *Science and Civilization in China.* Cambridge: Cambridge University Press.

Neilson, Brett, and Ned Rossiter (2005) "From Precarity to Precariousness and Back Again: Labour, Life, and Unstable Networks," *Fibreculture* 5, http://journal.fibreculture.org/issue5/neilson_rossiter.html.

Nelkin, Dorothy (1984) *Science as Intellectual Property: Who Controls Research?* New York: Macmillan.

Nelson, Cary (1997) *Manifesto of a Tenured Radical*. New York: NYU Press.

Nelson, Cary, and Stephen Watt (1999) *Academic Keywords: A Devil's Dictionary for Higher Education*. New York: Routledge.

Nesbitt, Rebecca Gordon (2008) "The New Bohemia," *Variant* 32 (Summer), http://www.variant.randomstate.org/32texts/CSG.html.

Newfield, Christopher (2004) *Ivy and Industry: Business and the Making of the American University, 1880–1980*. Durham, N.C.: Duke University Press.

Newfield, Christopher, and Ronald Strickland, eds. (1995) *After Political Correctness: The Humanities and Society in the 1990s*. Boulder, Colo.: Westview.

Newman, Katherine (1988) *Falling from Grace: The Experience of Downward Mobility in the American Middle Class*. New York: Free Press.

Noble, David (2002) *Digital Diploma Mills: The Automation of Higher Education*. New York: Monthly Review.

Noll, Roger, and Andrew Zimbalist (1997) *Sports, Jobs, and Taxes: The Economic Impact of Sports Teams and Stadiums*. Washington, D.C.: Brookings Institution Press.

Oakley, Kate (2004) "Not So Cool Britannia: The Role of the Creative Industries in Economic Development," *International Journal of Cultural Studies* 7.

Observatory on Borderless Higher Education (2006) *Sino-foreign Joint Education Ventures: A National, Regional and Institutional Analysis*, http://www.une.edu.au/chemp/projects/monitor/resources/sino_foreign_observatory.pdf.

Onion, The (2005) "Chinese Factory Worker Can't Believe the Shit He Makes For Americans" 41, 24 (June 15), http://www.theonion.com/content/node/31049.

Oudenampsen, Merijn (2006) "Extreme Makeover," *Mute* (October), http://www.metamute.org/en/Extreme-Makeover.

——— (2007) "Back to the Future of the Creative City," in Lovink and Rossiter.

Palleroni, Sergio, in collaboration with Christina Eichbaum-Merkelbach (2004) *Studio at Large: Architecture in Service of Global Communities*. Seattle: University of Washington Press.

Palmer Rae Associates (2004) *European Capitals of Culture*. Brussels, http://ec.europa.eu/culture/pdf/doc654_en.pdf.

Panzieri, Raniero (1973) *La crisi del movimento operaio*. Milan: Lampugnani Nigri.

Papadopoulos, Dimitris, Niamh Stephenson, and Vassilis Tsianos (2008) *Escape Routes: Control and Subversion in the 21st Century*. London: Pluto.

Parrenas, Rachel (2001) *Servants of Globalization: Women, Migration, and Domestic Work*. Palo Alto, Calif.: Stanford University Press.

Peck, Jamie (2005) "Struggling with the Creative Class," *International Journal of Urban and Rural Research* 29, 4.

Pena, Devon (2005a) *Mexican Americans and Their Environment: Tierra y Vida.* Tucson: University of Arizona Press.

(2005b) "Autonomy, Equity, and Environmental Justice," in David N. Pellow and Robert J. Brulle, eds., *Power, Justice, and the Environment: A Critical Appraisal of the Environmental Justice Movement.* Cambridge, Mass.: MIT Press.

(2009) "Toward a Critical Political Ecology of Latino/a Urbanism," forthcoming in David R. Diaz, ed. *Latinos and Urbanism: Planning, Politics, and Social Movements.* New Brunswick, N.J.: Rutgers University Press.

People's Daily (2006a) "China World's Third Largest Exporter of Creative Products and Services" (November 24).

People's Daily (2006b) "Creative Industry: New Economic Engine in Beijing" (December 15).

Perelman, Michael (2002) *Steal This Idea: Intellectual Property Rights and the Corporate Confiscation of Creativity.* New York: Palgrave Macmillan.

Perrons, Diane (2003) "The New Economy and the Work Life Balance: A Case Study of the New Media Sector in Brighton and Hove," *Gender, Work and Organisation* 10, 1.

Perry, Elizabeth, and Li Xun (1997) *Proletarian Power: Shanghai in the Cultural Revolution.* Boulder, Colo.: Westview.

Pink, Daniel (2001) *Free Agent Nation: How America's New Independent Workers Are Transforming the Way We Live.* New York: Warner.

Pitman Hughes, Dorothy (2000) *Wake Up and Smell the Dollars! Whose Inner-city Is This Anyway! One Woman's Struggle against Sexism, Classism, Racism, Gentrification, and the Empowerment Zone.* New York: Amber.

Preuss, Holger (2004) *The Economics of Staging the Olympics: A Comparison of the Games, 1972–2008.* London: Edward Elgar.

Prowse, Michael (2006) "Creation Myths?" *The Quarter* 2 (Spring).

Pun, Ngai (2005) *Made in China: Women Factory Workers in a Global Workplace.* Durham, N.C.: Duke University Press.

Pyatok, Michael (1999) "Elegant, Empathetic, Affordable Housing," interview in *Whole Earth* (Summer).

Radosh, Ronald (1969) *American Labor and United States Foreign Policy.* New York: Random House.

Raunig, Gerald (2004) "Anti-precarious Activism and Mayday Parades," *Traversal* (June), http://eipcp.net/transversal/0704/raunig/en.

(2007) "The Monster Precariat," *Transversal* (October), http://translate.eipcp. net/strands/02/raunig-strands02en.

Raymond, Eric (2001) *The Cathedral and the Bazaar.* Sebastopol, Calif.: O'Reilly.

Raynolds, Lauren, Douglas Murray, and John Wilkinson, eds. (2007) *Whither Fair Trade? Negotiating a Global Movement.* London: Routledge.

Reagan, Ronald (1966). "The Creative Society," Speech at the University of Southern California (April 19).

Redden, Elizabeth (2006) "No Risk, No Reward," *Inside Higher Ed* (December 7), http://insidehighered.com/news/2006/12/07/for_profit.

(2007a) "The Middlemen of Study Abroad," *Inside Higher Ed* (August 20), http://insidehighered.com/layout/set/print/news/2007/08/20/abroad.

(2007b) "Study Abroad Under Scrutiny," *Inside Higher Ed* (August 14), http://insidehighered.com/layout/set/print/news/2007/08/14/abroad.

(2008) "The Phantom Campus in China" *Inside Higher Ed* (February 12), http://insidehighered.com/news/2008/02/12/china.

Reidl, Sybille, Helene Schiffbanker, and Hubert Eichmann (2006) "Creating a Sustainable Future: The Working Life of Creative Workers in Vienna," *Work, Organization, Labour, and Globalization* 1, 1.

Reyes, Oscar (2005) "The Olympics and the City," *Red Pepper* (April).

Rhoades, Gary (2001) "Whose Property Is It? Negotiating with the University," *Academe* (September–October).

Rice, Duncan (1995) *NYU: The Global Vision.* New York: New York University.

Rifkin, Jeremy (1998) *The Biotech Century: Harnessing the Gene and Remaking the World.* New York: Jeremy Tarcher.

Rizvi, Fazal (2004) "Offshore Australian Higher Education," *International Higher Education* 37.

Robbins, Tom (2005) "The Deputy Mayor for the Olympics," *Village Voice* (February 1).

Roberts, Russell (2003) "An Interview with Lawrence Lessig on Copyrights," *Library of Economics and Liberty* (April 7), http://www.econlib.org/library/Columns/y2003/Lessigcopyright.html.

Roberts, Sam (2006) "Immigrants Swell Numbers Near New York" *New York Times* (August 15).

Robinson, David (2006) "GATS and Education Services: The Fallout from Hong Kong," *International Higher Education* 43.

Robson, Garry (2002) *"No One Likes Us, We Don't Care": The Myth and Reality of Millwall Fandom.* London: Berg.

Roche, Maurice (2000) *Mega-events and Modernity: Olympics and Expos in the Growth of Global Culture.* London: Routledge.

Rodgers, Daniel (1978) *The Work Ethic in Industrial America, 1850–1920.* Chicago: University of Chicago Press.

Roediger, David (1991) *The Wages of Whiteness: Race and the Making of the American Working Class.* New York: Routledge.

Rorty, Richard (1999) *Achieving Our Country: Leftist Thought in Twentieth-century America.* Cambridge, Mass.: Harvard University Press.

Rose, Fred (2000) *Coalitions across the Class Divide: Lessons from the Labor, Peace, and Environmental Movements.* Ithaca, N.Y.: Cornell University Press.

Rose, Tricia (1994) *Black Noise: Rap Music and Black Culture in Contemporary America.* Middletown, Conn.: Wesleyan University Press.

Rosenberg, Harold (1975) "The Profession of Art: The WPA Art Project," in *Art on the Edge: Creators and Situations*. New York: MacMillan.

Rosentraub, Mark (1997) *Major League Losers: The Real Cost of Sports and Who's Paying For It*. New York: Basic.

Ross, Andrew, ed. (1997) *No Sweat: Fashion, Free Trade, and the Rights of Garment Workers*. New York: Verso.

——— (1998) *Real Love: In Pursuit of Cultural Justice*. New York: New York University Press.

——— (2002) *No-Collar: The Humane Workplace and Its Hidden Costs*. New York: Basic.

——— (2004) *Low Pay, High Profile: The Global Push for Fair Labor*. New York: New Press.

——— (2006a) *Fast Boat to China: Corporate Flight and the Consequences of Free Trade—Lessons from Shanghai*. New York: Pantheon.

——— (2006b) Review of *Sprawl* by Robert Bruegmann, in *Harvard Design Magazine* (Fall).

Ross, Kristin (2002) *May '68 and Its Afterlives*. Chicago: University of Chicago Press.

Ross, Robert (2006) "A Tale of Two Sweatshops: Successful Resistance to Sweatshops and the Limits of Firefighting," *Labor Studies Journal* 30, 4 (Winter).

Rossiter, Ned (2005) "Interview with Su Tong: Created in China," trans. Du Ping, *My Creativity* (Nettime) mailing list (May 26).

——— (2007) *Organized Networks: Media Theory, Creative Labour, New Institutions*. Amsterdam: NAI.

Ruitheiser, Charles (1996) *Imagineering Atlanta: The Politics of Place in the City of Dreams*. New York: Verso.

Ryan, Mark (2000) "Manipulation Without End," in Wallinger and Warnock, eds.

Saha, Debrata (2004) Statement at Geneva Declaration on the Future of the World Intellectual Property Organization (October 1), http://www.cptech.org/ip/wipo/genevadeclaration.html.

Sassen, Saskia (1991) *The Global City: New York London Tokyo*. Princeton, N.J.: Princeton University Press.

Saunders, Frances Stonor (2000) *The Cultural Cold War: The CIA and the World of Arts and Letters*. New York: New Press.

Sauve, Pierre (2002) "Trade, Education, and the GATS: What's In, What's Out, What's All the Fuss About?" *Higher Education Management and Policy* 14, 3.

Saxenian, Annalee (2006) *The New Argonauts: Regional Advantage in a Global Economy*. Cambridge, Mass.: Harvard University Press.

Schemo, Diana Jean (2007) "In Study Abroad, Gifts, and Money For Universities," *New York Times* (August 13).

Schijndel, Marieke van, and Joost Smiers (2005) "Imagining a World Without Copyright," *International Herald Tribune* (October 8).

Schor, Juliet (1998) *The Overspent American: Upscaling, Downshifting, and the New Consumer.* New York: Basic.

Schram, Stuart (2002) "Mao Tse-Tung's Thought from 1949–1976," in Merle Goldman and Leo Ou-Fan Lee, eds., *An Intellectual History of Modern China.* Cambridge: Cambridge University Press.

Schumpeter, Joseph (1942) *Capitalism, Socialism, and Democracy.* London: Unwin.

Scott, Allen, ed. (2001) *Global City-Regions: Trends, Theory, and Policy.* New York: Oxford University Press.

Scott, Tony, Leo Parascondola, and Marc Bousquet (2003) *Tenured Bosses and Disposable Teachers: Writing Instruction in the Managed University.* Carbondale: Southern Illinois University Press.

Seabrook, Jeremy (1996) *In the Cities of the South: Scenes from a Developing World.* New York: Verso.

Selwood, Sara (2003) *Valuing Culture.* London: Demos.

Sennett, Richard (1998) *The Corrosion of Character: The Personal Consequences of Work in the New Capitalism.* New York: Norton.

Shiva, Vandana (1997) *Biopiracy: The Plunder of Nature and Knowledge* Boston: South End.

(2001) *Protect or Plunder? Understanding Intellectual Property Rights.* London: Zed.

Shukaitis, Stevphen (2007) "Whose Precarity Is It Anyway? *Fifth Estate* 41, 3.

Shulman, Seth (1999) *Owning the Future: Inside the Battles to Control the New Assets That Make up the Lifeblood of the New Economy.* New York: Houghton Mifflin.

Silver, Beverly (2003) *Forces of Labor: Workers' Movements and Globalization since 1870.* Cambridge: Cambridge University Press.

Silverman, Amy (1995) "Outing Infill," *Phoenix New Times* (September 21).

Slaughter, Sheila, and Larry Leslie (1997) *Academic Capitalism: Politics, Policies, and the Entrepreneurial University.* Baltimore: Johns Hopkins University Press.

Slaughter, Sheila, and Gary Rhoades (2004) *Academic Capitalism and the New Economy: Markets, State, and Higher Education.* Baltimore: Johns Hopkins University Press.

Sleeper, Jim (1997) *Liberal Racism.* New York: Viking.

Smiers, Joost (2002) "The Abolition of Copyrights: Better for Artists, Third World Countries and the Public Domain," in Ruth Towse, ed., *Copyright in the Cultural Industries.* Cheltenham: Edward Elgar.

Smith, Chris (1998) *Creative Britain.* London: Faber and Faber.

(1999) "Government and the Arts," in Wallinger and Warnock, eds.

Smith, Neil (1996) *The New Urban Frontier: Gentrification and the Revanchist City.* New York: Routledge.

(2006) *Mexican New York: Transnational Lives of New Immigrants*. Berkeley and Los Angeles: University of California Press.

Soderberg, Johan (2002) "Copyleft vs. Copyright: A Marxist Critique," *First Monday* 7, 3 (March), http://www.firstmonday.org/issues/issue7_3/soderberg.

Solinger, Dorothy (1999) *Contesting Citizenship in Urban China: Peasant Migrants, the State, and the Logic of the Market*. Berkeley and Los Angeles: University of California Press.

Solnit, Rebecca (2007) *Storming the Gates of Paradise: Landscapes for Politics*. Berkeley and Los Angeles: University of California Press.

Stallman, Richard, Lawrence Lessig, and Joshua Gay, eds. (2002) *Free Software, Free Society: Selected Essays of Richard M. Stallman*. Boston: Free Software Foundation.

Stevens, Robert William, and Habitat for Humanity, eds. (1982) *Community Self-help Housing Manual: Partnership in Action*. Croton-on-Hudson, N.Y.: Intermediate Technology Development Group of North America.

Storrs, Landon (2000) *Civilizing Capitalism: The National Consumers' League, Women's Activism, and Labor Standards in the New Deal Era*. Chapel Hill: University of North Carolina Press.

Sugrue, Thomas (1996) *The Origins of the Urban Crisis*. Princeton, N.J.: Princeton University Press.

Sun, Mercy (2006) "Creative Industry, New Force in Beijing's Economy," *Beijing This Month* (June 14).

Tan, Kenneth Paul (2003) "Sexing Up Singapore," *International Journal of Cultural Studies* 6, 4.

Taylor, Monique (2002) *Harlem between Heaven and Hell*. Minnesota: University of Minnesota Press.

Teitelbaum, Michael (1985) *Labor Migration North: The Problem for U.S. Foreign Policy*. New York: Council on Foreign Relations.

Terkel, Studs (1974) *Working: People Talk About What They Do All Day and How They Feel About What They Do*. New York: Pantheon.

Terranova, Tiziana (2000) "Free Labor: Producing Culture for the Global Economy," *Social Text* 18, 2.

(2004) *Network Culture: Politics for the Information Age*. Ann Arbor: University of Michigan Press.

Thierer, Adam, ed. (2001) *Copy Fights: The Future of Intellectual Property in the Information Age*. Washington, D.C.: Cato Institute.

Tomasky, Michael (1996) *Left for Dead: The Life, Death, and Possible Resurrection of Progressive Politics in America*. New York: Free Press.

Tronti, Mario (1966) *Operai e Capitale*. Turin: Einaudi

(1980) "The Strategy of Refusal," in Sylvere Lotringer and Christian Marazzi, eds., *Italy: Autonomia: Post-political Politics*. New York: Semiotexte.

Turner, John (1972) "Housing as a Verb," and "Reeducation of a Professional," in *Freedom to Build: Dweller Control of the Housing Process*. New York: Mac-Millan.

(1991) *Housing by People: Towards Autonomy in Building Environments* (repr. ed.). London: Marion Boyars.

Tyler, Gus (1995) *Look for the Union Label: A History of the International Ladies' Garment Workers' Union*. Armonk, N.Y.: ME Sharpe.

UNCTAD (2008) Report of the Secretary-general's High-level Panel on the Creative Economy and Industries for Development, prepared for UNCTAD's Twelfth Session, Accra, Ghana (April), http://www.unctad.org/Templates/webflyer.asp?intItemID=4494.

U.S. Census Bureau News (2007) (March 22), http://www.census.gov/Press-Release/www/releases/archives/population/009756.html.

U.S. Department of Health, Education, and Welfare (Report of Special Task Force) (1973) *Work in America*. Cambridge, Mass.: MIT Press.

U.S. Conference of Mayors (2004) Adopted Resolution on the Creative Industries Index, Boston, Seventy-second Annual Meeting.

Vaidhyanathan, Siva (2002) *Copyrights and Copywrongs: The Rise of Intellectual Property and How It Threatens Creativity*. New York: NYU Press.

(2004) *The Anarchist in the Library: How the Clash between Freedom and Control Is Hacking the Real World and Crashing the System*. New York: Basic.

Veblen, Thorstein (1899) *The Theory of the Leisure Class*. New York: Macmillan.

Virno, Paolo (2004) *A Grammar of the Multitude*, trans. Isabella Bertoletti, James Cascaito, and Andrea Casson. New York: Semiotext[e].

Virno, Paolo, and Michael Hardt (1996) *Radical Thought in Italy: A Potential Politics*. Minneapolis: University of Minnesota Press.

Vishmidt, Marina (2005) "Precarious Straits" *Mute* 29, http://www.metamute.org/en/Precarious-Straits.

Vishmidt, Marina, and Melanie Gilligan, eds. (2003) *Immaterial Labour: Work, Research, and Art*. London: Black Dog.

Voas, Jeremy (2001) "House Hold," *Phoenix New Times* (May 24).

Von Eschen, Penny (2004) *Satchmo Blows up the World: Jazz, Race, and Empire in the Cold War*. Cambridge, Mass.: Harvard University Press.

Waddell, Helen (1989) *The Wandering Scholars*. Ann Arbor: University of Michigan Press.

Waldinger, R., C. Erickson, R. Milkman, D. Mitchell, A. Valenzuela, K. Wong, and M. Zeitlin (1998) "Helots No More: A Case Study of the Justice for Janitors Campaign in Los Angeles," in K. Bronfenbrenner, S. Friedman, R. W. Hurd, R. A. Oswald, and R. L. Seeber, eds., *Organizing to Win: New Research on Organizing Strategies*. Ithaca, N.Y.: Cornell University Press.

Wallinger, Mark, and Mary Warnock, eds. (2000) *Art for All? Their Policies and Our Culture*. London: Peer.

Wang, Jing (2004) "The Global Reach of a New Discourse: How Far Can 'Creative Industries' Travel?" *International Journal of Cultural Studies* 7, 1.

Ward, Peter (1982) *Self-help Housing: A Critique*. London: Mansell.

Wark, McKenzie (2003) *A Hacker Manifesto*. Cambridge, Mass.: Harvard University Press.

Warnock, Mary, eds. (2000) *Art for All? Their Policies and Our Culture*. London: Peer.

Washburn, Jennifer (2005) *University, Inc.: The Corporate Corruption of American Higher Education*. New York: Basic.

Washington Post (2005) "Manassas's War on Immigrants" (editorial) (December 30).

Weber, Steven (2004) *The Success of Open Source*. Cambridge, Mass.: Harvard University Press.

Wei, William (1993) *The Asian American Movement*. Philadelphia: Temple University Press.

Williams, Sam (2002) *Free as in Freedom: Richard Stallman's Crusade for Free Software*. Sebastopol, Calif.: O'Reilly.

Wilthagen, Tom, F. H. Tros, and Harm van Lieshout (2004) "Towards 'Flexicurity'? Balancing Flexibility and Security in EU Member States," *European Journal of Social Security* 6, 2.

Woodmansee, Martha (1984) "The Genius and the Copyright: Economic and Legal Conditions of the Emergence of the 'Author,'" *Eighteenth-century Studies* 425.

—— (1994) "On the Author Effect: Recovering Collectivity," in Jaszi and Woodmansee, eds.

Woolf, Virginia (1989) "Thunder at Wembley," in Andrew McNeillie, ed., *The Essays of Virginia Woolf, 1919–1924*. New York: Harcourt.

Xinhua (2004) "China Badly Needs 'Gray-collars' for Manufacturing," *China Daily* (March 21).

Yan, Hairong (2008) *New Masters, New Servants: Migration, Development and Women Workers in China*. Durham: Duke University Press.

Youngdhal, Jay (2008) "Mapping the Future: Cross-border Unionizing Strategies," *New Labor Forum* 17, 2 (Summer).

Yudice, George (2004) *The Expediency of Culture: Uses of Culture in the Global Era*. Durham, N.C.: Duke University Press.

Zaccai, Edwin, ed. (2007) *Sustainable Consumption: Ecology and Fair Trade*. London: Routledge.

Zerzan, John (1974) "Organized Labor versus 'The Revolt against Work': The Critical Contest," *Telos* (Fall).

Zhang, Jingcheng, ed. (2007) *The Development of the Creative Industries in China*. Beijing: China Economic Publishing House.

Zhang, Li (2001) *Strangers in the City: Reconfigurations of Space, Power, and Social Networks within China's Floating Population.* Palo Alto, Calif.: Stanford University Press.

Zimbalist, Andrew (2003) *May the Best Team Win: Baseball Economics and Public Policy.* Washington, D.C.: Brookings Institution Press.

Zinser, Lynn (2005) "London Is Chosen For Olympics as New York Bid Falls Short," *The Guardian* (July 6).

Zukin, Sharon (1989) *Loft Living: Culture and Capital in Urban Change.* New Brunswick, N.J.: Rutgers University Press.

(1994) *Cultures of Cities.* Oxford: Blackwell.

Index

Abu Dhabi, 200
academic professionals: contract-driven livelihoods, 205; deprofessionalization, 8, 172–173, 197; intellectual property (IP), 176; as "last good job in America," 12
"adbusters," 126
Adbusters (magazine), 128
Adidas, 120
Aeolian Music Company, 164–165
AFL, 51, 129
AFL-CIO, 111, 113, 118
Alfred the Great, 96
alienation, 5, 8, 127
Alliance of Motion Picture and Television Producers, 177
"Alone Again (Naturally)" (O'Sullivan), 181
Alternative Law Forum Bangalore, 185
"alternative" sites/institutions, power to, 52
Althusser, Louis, 68, 71–72
amateurism, 21–22
American Apparel, 116–117
American Canvas (National Endowment for the Arts), 36
American cultural criticism, 65–66, 72–74
American Federation of Musicians (AFM), 163–164, 178
American Federation of Television and Radio Artists, 177

American Guild of Variety Artists, 177
American Institute for Free Labor Development, 118
American Maoists, 70
American University of Paris (AUP), 193, 195
Americans for the Arts, 39
Amsterdam, culture-driven revitalization, 32
anti-capitalism, 125–126
anti-consumerist movement, 126–129; "adbusters," 126; alienation in the workplace, 127; anti-sweatshop movement, 108, 126–127, 128; Buy Nothing Day, 126; "culture jammers," 126; ethical consumption, 108; fair trade, 115; freeganism, 114; global justice activism, 126; gospel of growth, 127; immorality of consumption, 128; individual acts of moral volunteerism, 129; internationally observed social marketing campaigns, 126; middle-class nutritional habits, 114; "pure church" advocates, 126; scavenging, 114; TV Turnoff Week, 126; workers' livelihoods, 108, 128, 129; working less, appeal to, 113
anti-globalization movement, 108
anti-immigrant sentiments, 137, 146
anti-precarity movement, 34, 49

245

About the Author

ANDREW ROSS is Professor and Chair of the Department of Social and Cultural Analysis at New York University. He is the author and editor of numerous books, including *Fast Boat to China: Corporate Flight and the Consequences of Free Trade*, *No-Collar: The Humane Workplace and Its Hidden Costs*, *The Celebration Chronicles: Life, Liberty, and the Pursuit of Property Value in Disney's New Town*, *No Respect: Intellectuals and Popular Culture*, and *Strange Weather: Culture, Science, and Technology in the Age of Limits*, as well as *Anti-Americanism* (2005) and *Real Love: In Pursuit of Cultural Justice* (1998), both available from NYU Press.